*Acclaim for Michael Erard's*

# Um . . .

"Erard deftly picks his way through a junkyard of spoken debris to inform, enlighten and entertain in equal measure."
—*BookPage*

"Erard dives deep into the hows and whys of verbal blunders and the biological realities of language, letting us off the psychological hook." —*Minneapolis Star Tribune*

"You can feel when an author is enjoying himself, and Erard's survey of these most common of dysfunctions in our dysfunctional society is written with unexpected humor, grace and high spirits." —*Louisville Courier-Journal*

"An absorbing survey of the (mis)spoken word, from ancient Egyptian cases of speechlessness to television bloopers."
—*O, The Oprah Magazine*

"Erard blurs the lines between breezy, anecdotal storytelling and advanced scientific study. Erard sheds light on what we can and cannot learn from ancient Greek orators, TV bloopers, slip collectors, and even our current Blunderer in Chief. . . . A surprisingly entertaining, humorous read." —*The Onion*

*Michael Erard*

# Um . . .

Michael Erard, a graduate of Williams College, received an M.A. in linguistics and a Ph.D. in English from the University of Texas. His articles about language have appeared in *The Atlantic Monthly, The New York Times, Science, Seed, The Texas Observer,* and many other publications. His website is www.michaelerard.com. He lives in Austin, Texas, and Portland, Maine.

# Um . . .

Um . . . Um .

# Um . . .

## Slips, Stumbles, and Verbal Blunders, and What They Mean

# MICHAEL ERARD

*Anchor Books*
A Division of Random House, Inc.
New York

FIRST ANCHOR BOOKS EDITION, AUGUST 2008

The Library of Congress has cataloged the Pantheon edition as follows:
Erard, Michael.
Um—slips, stumbles, and verbal blunders, and what they mean / Michael Erard.—1st ed.
p.   cm.
Includes index.
1. Speech errors.   I. Title.   II. Title: Slips, stumbles, and verbal blunders, and what they mean.
P37.5.S67E73       2007
401'.9—dc22       2006103208

**Anchor ISBN: 978-1-4000-9543-8**

*Author photograph © Wyatt McSpadden*
*Book design by Virginia Tan*

www.anchorbooks.com

Printed in the United States of America
10   9   8   7   6   5   4   3   2   1

*for my parents,*
*who gave me the slip of gifts*

I want some hot poppered butt corn—I mean cot buttered bop corn—that is—corn buttered pop butt, or
rather cuttered pot born, I mean—oh well, gimme some
peanuts.

*Thesaurus of Humor, 1940*

If you are a young man, for instance, will it not be from
small pointers that you will conclude that you have won a
girl's favor? Would you wait for an express declaration of
love or a passionate embrace? Or would not a glance,
scarcely noticed by other people, be enough? A slight
movement, the lengthening by a second of the pressure
of a hand? . . .

So do not let us underestimate small indications; by
their help we may succeed in getting on the track of
something bigger.

*Sigmund Freud*

# Contents

# A Note to the Reader

As you read this book, you may find that you begin to notice how people actually speak. That reaction is perfectly normal. You may also become more aware of your own speaking. This, too, is normal.

Your heightened awareness may also make you want to point out to your friends, loved ones, colleagues, and even random talkers their every verbal blunder. This is not recommended. For the sake of harmony, point out only the most interesting ones.

What is an interesting verbal blunder? You'd be surprised.

# Um...

# *Introduction*

Transcribers at the Federal News Service in Washington, D.C., encounter bucketloads of verbal blunders every weekday morning. Their small office contains six desks with computers and dictaphones and a shelf filled with almanacs and dictionaries. On a wall hangs a whiteboard scrawled with the unfamiliar words, names, and· acronyms of this news cycle. Today it's "Tamiflu," "LIHEAP," and "III-MEF." Next to a government spokesman's name, someone's scribbled a heart—he sounds like he's good-looking, one of the transcribers teases. Across the hall in another small room, dozens of Marantz tape recorders on shelves are prepared to catch audio feeds from around the city and the country. At ten o'clock, the world of government and business begins to talk in earnest, and the words from White House briefings, federal agency press conferences, congressional hearings, and corporate speeches begin to flow to the recorders, now alive and humming, or through audio streamed through the Web. Once a cassette contains about four minutes of speaking, the news director carries it to the transcribers' office and lines it up on a low cabinet with other tapes. A transcriber will bring the tape to his or her cubicle, put it in the transcribing machine, and start typing the segment. There's no talking in the room, only the sounds of fingers on keyboards, feet on foot pedals, and tapes rewinding. For eight hours a day the transcribers turn speech into text, spinning these ordinary words, Rapunzel-like, into a commodity posted on Web sites and sold to hundreds of clients.

The transcripts have to be readable, so the transcribers generally clean up people's speaking, as instructed by an in-house style guide that cautions, "Don't type 'um,' 'ah,' 'er,' or partial words." The style guide also stipulates that transcribers should "clean up a false start or starts consisting of only one or two words if the omission of the words does not affect the meaning."*

There is one exception to those rules: "DO NOT clean up major policymakers, including the president," the style guide says, "since not only what they say but how they say it often makes the news." When George H. W. Bush was president he gave a speech commemorating Pearl Harbor Day but mistakenly gave the date as September 7, so the Federal News Service (FNS) transcribers kept September 7. (The White House corrected the error to December 7.) Alice Tate, a cherub-faced woman with red hair who is the supervisor of the news transcription team and has been an FNS employee for twenty years, mentioned that President George W. Bush had recently praised the efforts of a national counterism director.

Tate left "counterism" intact. "Sometimes he kind of stum-

---

*Thus, "I—we think it's important" would become "We think it's important," but "I think, I think—we think it's important" would stand.

bles," she says of Bush, "and we have to make a decision—since we don't type partial words—is a word a combination of words he's messed up?" Bush isn't the only contributor to a document circulated in the office, the "duh files," which contains many of the gaffes, flubs, solecisms, and bloopers that fall into transcribers' laps. There was Howard Dean trying to say "incentivize," which came out like this: "What that does is incense providers to do more than just park kids in front of the television." There was an Atlanta reporter asking Secretary of Defense Donald Rumsfeld, "Is our current situation such that the harder we work, the behinder we get?"

More common verbal blunders don't make the duh files—they're excised from transcripts, scrubbed out for the sake of readability. Another veteran transcriber, Cate Hagman, says that she's stopped hearing "uh" and "um" in people's speech. Because FNS cuts them from transcripts, she automatically wipes them from what she hears, too. Other verbal tics still irritate her, though. "Transcribing makes you very sensitive to verbal tics. 'Like,' 'you know,' 'I mean.' Our parents were right—we should drop them from our speech, but you'd be surprised to see how many responsible people put them in." Surely the politicians say them unconsciously—just as the ordinary listener unwittingly lets them pass by.


On the other side of the country, a team of robotics researchers at SRI International, a research institute in Menlo Park, California, paid attention to the fillers and interruptions of ordinary speaking with another purpose in mind. In the early 1990s, they developed a robot named Flakey, a three-foot-tall black box designed to roam around the SRI offices, like a large, mobile, single-minded filing cabinet that could move out of the way of walking humans and navigate obstacles. It could also understand spoken commands to retrieve objects from various places in the institute. The problem was, however, that if you ordered Flakey to go on a mission, you didn't know for several seconds if the robot had comprehended what you said. It would sit there, humming. So you might repeat yourself, giving Flakey two commands to process and perhaps confuse, making it stall.

This didn't make for the smoothest human-machine relationships. Liz Shriberg, a speech researcher who was studying how "uh" and "um" function in human communication, suggested that her colleagues program Flakey to say "uh." One could say, "Flakey, go to so and so's office and get me the folder," and the robot would say "uh," in order to signal that it had heard the command and was processing it. The pause filler was an effective signal to the human that the robot wasn't, in fact, broken down, and in so doing, eased the interaction between human and machine. (Even more effective would have been an "uh" with the proper intonation, Shriberg said. Otherwise, Flakey's monotone "uh" sounded like an oddly long beep.)

As nearly as anyone can estimate, humans have been using language more or less in the form that we know it for about one hundred thousand years. They've probably been making verbal blunders for about as long. When you speak, you hesitate, you. Stop. You also pereat, repeat—you repair, you fix, you repair your sentences, you utter the wrong words and confuse them in the most headbutted ways, you say "uh," you linger on "um." But this is normal. Our ordinary speech is notoriously fragmented, and all sorts of verbal blunders swim through our sentences like bubbles in champagne. They occur on average once every ten words, by some accounts. So if people say an average of 15,000 words each day, that's about 1,500 verbal blunders a day. Next time you say something, listen to yourself carefully. You st-st-stutter; you forget the words, you swotch the sounds (and when you type, you rverse the lttres—and prhps omt thm, too). The bulk of these go unnoticed or brushed aside, but they're all fascinating, as much as for why they're ignored as why they're noticed.

Some of these verbal blunders are "slips of the tongue" (as when Howard Dean said "incense" or George Bush said "counterism"); far more frequent are the unsmooth moments that the transcribers at the Federal News Service clean up. Called "speech disfluencies," these include fillers like "uh" and "um," repeated words, repeated sounds, or repaired (and restarted) sentences. If I'm speaking off the top of my head then I might, uh, alter the the syntax in the middle of my sentence, and that's not all, because interruptions—look, over there!—and rep rep repetitions and changes in vocal INTENSITY THEY HAPPEN A LOT along with streeeetched vowels and ratesofspeech-speedingup and. Getting. Slow. Er.

As unavoidable as they are ineradicable, verbal blunders are rich with meaning. Until recently, they've been treated as meaningless filler, played for laughs, or used to reinforce stereotypes of people who were already disliked or mistrusted. Which is to say, we've missed other ways of listening to them that could tell us more about each other, about our era, and about our individual selves.

Profuse and varied, verbal blunders exist in all the world's languages, spoken and signed. They permeate our daily speaking, even the speech of the most golden-tongued. Omnipresent, they have unique tales to tell about the inner workings of language and mind.

A verbal blunder is also an indelible mark of humanness. Difficult to predict, verbal blunders are one human behavior that cannot be simulated by computers. Flakey's "uh" had to be programmed into him. Other animals that have sophisticated means to communicate, too, often blurt and stumble. (Zebra finches, for example, are used in stuttering research because some birds repeat parts of their songs.) But verbal blunders are native only to humans; they separate us from animals, because we're the only ones with language. And to seal the connection, each individual human being blunders uniquely, in as many styles as there are of speaking, a fingerprint of the self that we leave floating in the air.

A verbal blunder can be either a momentary loss of control over speaking, called a "slip of the tongue," or one of the blurps and interruptions in what we think should be smoothly flowing talk, called a "speech disfluency."

A slip of the tongue is an inadvertent accident, as the time that Democratic presidential candidate Senator John Kerry, tired from campaigning, said "wasabi" instead of "Wahhabi." Kerry hadn't mistaken a Japanese spice for the fundamentalist Islamic sect. He'd planned to say "Wahhabi," had said it many times before. But his plan went awry—when he reached to retrieve "Wahhabi" from memory, "wasabi" jumped out in front of his brain. (That both are non-English words probably helped, too.) Such moments, which are also known as "speech errors" or often just "slips," appear when the mental machinery that turns ideas into spoken (or signed) words crashes into itself. Replacing "Wahhabi" with "wasabi" was a slip that involved a whole word. Similar accidents can also occur with individual sounds ("black bloxes"), parts of words ("groupment," "they sit there motionly"), phrases ("I have to smoke my coffee with a cigarette"), and even intonation ("on your look OUT—on your LOOK out—I mean—on your OUT look"). In these slips, pieces of language are swapped ("heft lemisphere," "fuwtmeeving"), dropped ("tubbled"), blended ("momentaneous," "slickery"), rushed ("telefathic fox") or slowed ("a phonological fool").*

Human behavior teems with what Bernard Baars, a cognitive scientist, calls "momentary control problems." A concert pianist may have rehearsed for months but still plunks the wrong notes on opening night. A skilled baker puts in a tablespoon, not a teaspoon, of salt. The psychology of error is full of insights into the causes of air disasters, medical mistakes, friendly-fire casualties in warfare, automobile accidents, even walking into the other room and forgetting why you're there. Because they represent the unpredictable human element in increasingly complex technical systems, errors have led to antilock brakes and robot surgeons and other designs that reduce the costs of human error. By contrast, humans already perceive slips of the tongue quite flexibly, and their costs are low—despite, of course, the brief mortification you feel when you ask the hostess for her delicious gahspetti recipe.†

---

*In a classic 1968 article on slips of the tongue, Donald Boomer and John Laver defined a slip as "an involuntary deviation in performance from the speaker's current phonological, grammatical, or lexical intention"—that is, the sounds, syntax, and words a person intended to say. For a complete taxonomy of slips of the tongue and the other verbal blunders, see Appendix B.

†Though if you're Bill O'Reilly, who mistakenly called a "loofah" a

Meanwhile, a speech disfluency is something that interrupts the continuity of speaking. Such smoothness is an ideal. Like glossy locks of hair or smooth, clear skin, this ideal is elusive, even unattainable, by most people. Listeners generally prefer when one word is followed promptly by another, and another. Speakers, too, generally intend to get their words in order in time. Yet they still say "uh" and "um." They repeat words. They forget words and repeat sounds and syllables. With all of these they've disrupted the flow of speaking. Elongating a vowel, pausing for too long, even speaking arhythmically can be considered interruptions. But the dimensions of human communication are so wide and subtle, such wild moments don't, in fact, impede communication when they crop up. At times they may even aid it. After all, successful communication doesn't solely depend on the unimpeded downloading of information into your head. It's not the information in the joke that makes you laugh, just as it's not the information in your lover's final phone call that makes you cry.

Speech disfluencies are a hallmark of spontaneous, unscripted speaking and conversation, as in this snippet from an interview: "Let's stop this for a minute and I'll, um, ask you some questions and then we can, uh, w-well, we can talk a little bit about your participation and, kinda roll in th— in these group meetings and then maybe we could just . . . look at it a little bit from that point of view." In truth, you can hear disfluent moments almost anywhere: newscasts, political debates, presentations at work, radio talk shows, town meetings, speeches, prayers, sermons, arguments. They happen because talking is

---

"falafel" in an infamous monologue of his captured on tape, you may feel no mortification whatsoever.

an activity that takes place in time, and disfluencies are signs of the inevitable friction between thinking and speaking. It's almost as if you can either think or speak—but rarely manage both simultaneously in a timely way. (It's the rare person who can, reliably and consistently.)

Laughing, crying, shouting, sighing, panting, yawning, coughing, throat clearing, spitting, belching, hiccuping, or sneezing aren't verbal blunders. The slurred words of the drunk or the person who's recently woken up aren't either. Neither are disorders of speaking and language: aphasia, vocal cord tremors, or chronic stuttering. It's worthwhile to read about how people experience these disorders, particularly stutterers, to put one's own occasional stumbles into perspective. Blundering isn't saying yes ("uh-huh") or no ("uh-uh") or keep going ("mm-hmm"). And while there's much to be learned from slang ("ain't"), nonstandard dialects (like Ebonics), and regionalisms ("I'm fixin' to go to the store"), they're social phenomena, not verbal blunders. Verbal blunders arise from organic flashes in the brain. Simply put, verbal blundering is something that normal speakers speaking normally do. For that reason alone, verbal blunders, so frequent yet so misunderstood, deserve a closer listen.

This book is a work of applied blunderology, and it began with my listening to speech in public and private. During the 2000 presidential campaign, I became fascinated with how George W. Bush's speech was portrayed, even fetishized, by the media and other observers, a fad that lasted into the early months of his presidency. Whether you sympathized with Bush's politics or not, you had to recognize that the critics of his verbal style took gleeful liberties in diagnosing what his speech patterns meant. They were also as inaccurate about how people normally speak as they were unreflective about the standards that govern speech. Why do we care how Bush talks? Did (and do) we care more with this president than any other? If so, why? These questions weren't discussed. Of course, Americans expect their political leaders to speak a particular way—though our leaders rarely do. This puzzling disparity has neither buried the ideal nor, apparently, hampered the reflexive talk of politicians when microphones are thrust in their faces. (In fact, it may have hampered the ambitions of many able politicians we've never heard of.)

To most observers' surprise, Bush's speaking, blunders and all, turned out to be more of a political asset than a liability. In 2000 and 2004, around half of the American electorate seemed willing to accept his verbal blunders as an authenticity that they found lacking in smoother-tongued politicians. Perhaps they liked it for the same reason that public radio listeners love the shuffling voice of Ira Glass: the quirky casual, whether it's intentional or spontaneous, can inspire more trust than the slick and polished. This seemed to be a remarkable moment in the public life of language in the United States. But no one stepped up with an explanation of what was going on and why. Eventually I decided to write the book myself. This is that book.

Around the same time, I was working as a journalist and listening to myself in interviews I had taped. Now, I speak slowly, in a way that some would call saturnine; I make my points, but I take my time getting there, as much out of habit as preference. As a writer, I struggle on a daily basis to make my own writing as good as it can be, a form of self-expression in which I feel most comfortable. Yet my own talking resists improvement, which can be frustrating. I became curious: How much of my verbal style belongs to me? How much to my family or my community? How much of my perceptions of that style are shared by my listeners?

As it turns out, our perceptions don't match. Where I heard my pauses and restarts and "um"s as deviations, others perceived them as a cool intelligence. We like how much time you spend choosing your words, people said, it makes you seem like you care about what you're saying. I admit, I was baffled by this compliment—it seemed akin to praising a quarterback with a sprained shoulder for the quirky skew of his incomplete passes. Still, the norms that govern daily life tolerate varying types of verbal performances, and I was curious about that flexibility. For one thing, why would we be flexible in our actual speaking and listening, yet so perfectionistic and demanding when we teach or reflect on them?

The questions asked by this book spring from both personal and political listening. Why do verbal blunders happen? What do they mean? And why do they matter?

# 1

## The Secrets of Reverend Spooner

I f the world of verbal blunders were the night sky, the Reverend William Archibald Spooner of Oxford University could play the role of the North Star. Spooner, who was born in 1844, was famous for verbal blundering so incorrigible that his exploits have been immortalized in poems and songs and, most enduringly, by lending his name to a type of slip of the tongue he was unusually prone to make. In the spoonerism, sounds from two words are exchanged or reversed, resulting in a phrase that is inappropriate for the setting. For Spooner, these embarrassments ranged from wild to mild. Toasting Queen Victoria at dinner, Spooner said, "Give three cheers for our queer old dean," and he greeted a group of farmers as "noble tons of soil." There was the time he cautioned young missionaries against having "a half-warmed fish in their hearts." He described Cambridge in the winter as "a bloody meek place." Once Spooner berated a student for "fighting a liar in the quadrangle." "You have hissed all my mystery lectures," he reportedly said. "In fact, you have tasted two whole worms and you must leave Oxford this afternoon by the next town drain." A spoonerism can also involve the reversal of two words, as in "Courage to blow the bears of life," or, when saying good-bye to someone, "Must you stay, can't you go?"

Undergraduates at Oxford University were playfully fond of Spooner, whom they nicknamed "the Spoo." They also coined the term "spoonerism" around 1885, after Spooner had been a fellow at New College for almost twenty years. By 1892, his reputation for absentmindedness was well known; students came to New College expecting to hear a spoonerism. "Well, I've been up here for four years, and never heard the Spoo make a spoonerism before, and now he makes a damned rotten one at the last minute," wrote one student. (Spooner had assured students that experience would teach them that "the weight of rages will press harder and harder upon the employer.") Spooner himself knew of his public image. Privately he referred to his "transpositions of thought." At the end of a speech he once gave to a group of alumni, he said, "And now I suppose I'd better sit down, or I might be saying—er—one of those things." The scientist Julian Huxley (a New College fellow under Spooner for six years), who was present at the scene, said that the audience reacted with "perhaps the greatest applause he ever got."

The British humor magazine *Punch* called Spooner "Oxford's great metaphasiarch."* Spooner's reputation was also carried beyond Oxford and even out of England by newspapers' joke columns, funny pages, and "quips and quirks" sections. One example of screwy language from around this time is

*From the Greek word *metaphasis,* literally "the transposition of sounds."

an 1871 collection by the American writer C. C. Bombaugh, titled *The Book of Blunders*. Though it didn't mention Spooner, Bombaugh's book promised a grab bag anthology of "Hibernicisms, bulls that are not Irish and typographic errors."* In addition to slips of the printing press, Bombaugh included slips of the telegraph. A French cleric was once greeted at the train station by a funeral bier—intended for him—because the telegraph operator had mistaken *Père Ligier et moi* (Father Ligier and I) for *Père Ligier est mort* (Father Ligier is dead). One New Yorker ordered flowers from a florist in Philadelphia, telegraphing a need for "two hand bouquets," which the telegraph clerk printed as "two hund. bouquets." When the New Yorker refused to pay for 198 unwanted bouquets, the florist sued him and lost. Then the florist sued the telegraph company and (according to Bombaugh) won. Such were the legal liabilities of a verbal blunder. On the face of it, slurs against the Irish and accidents of typography seem to have little in common. Yet the opportunity to mock and laugh about either one neutralized the perceived threats of immigrants and technological change.

The public's taste for outrageous jabberwocky may have predated Spooner, but his sayings appeared so frequently and widely that the spoonerism was known around the English-speaking world early in the twentieth century. On a visit to South Africa in 1912, Spooner said in a letter to his wife that "the Johannesburg paper had an article on my visit to Johannesburg, but of course they thought me most famous for my Spoonerisms, so I was not greatly puffed up." In the 1920s,

---

*"An Irish Bull may very well be defined as any remark which appears rotund and meaningful enough, until our apprehension actually arrives upon it, when there is simply nothing there," as Max Eastman put it. Example: "May you never live to see your wife a widow."

Spooner encountered an American woman at a concert who asked if he was Dr. Spooner. As Spooner wrote in his diary, "She replied I was the best known name in America except Mr. Hudson Shaw [*sic*] . . . to have known a celebrity, even the author of 'Spoonerisms' means a good deal, tho' I explained to her that I was better known for my defects than for any merits."*

In all, Spooner spent almost sixty years as a member of New College, starting as a student in 1862, then as a fellow in 1867. To get the position, he had to take an oral exam, which he not only passed but excelled at. He ascended the ranks until he became warden, a sort of chaplain, from 1903 to 1924. He was married, had seven children, and lived in a sixteen-bedroom mansion staffed with eleven servants. When he was fifty-two years old, he tried to learn to ride a bicycle. (Or "a well-boiled icicle," as he put it.) He was also a revered classics scholar and a respected school leader. He had a rare gift, said Huxley, "of making people feel that he was deeply interested in their own particular affairs." As an albino ("not a full albino with pink eyes," Huxley remembered, "but one with very pale blue eyes and white hair just tinged with straw color"), Spooner had horrifically poor eyesight and could read only with his eyes several inches from the page. He also spoke with a squeaky, high-pitched voice and said "uh" a lot—perhaps because he was trying to avoid making the slips he'd become famous for.

"He looked like a rabbit, but he was brave as a lion," said the historian Arnold Toynbee. Spooner himself was more modest. "I am, I hope, to some extent a useful kind of drudge," he wrote in a letter, "but not a ruler of men."

---

*She may have meant George Bernard Shaw.

. . .

Spoonerisms are the comfortable shoes of slips of the tongue: when it comes time to illustrate the universality of speech errors, they're so familiar and broken in, they always get a laugh. Far from the funny pages, though, they exhibit properties that have been observed in Latin, Croatian, German, English, Greek, and French (among other languages). Spoonerisms all work the same way: the reversed sounds come from the beginnings of the words, rarely at the ends, and very often from the syllable that carries the stress.* Spooner wouldn't likely have accused a student of "righting a file in the quadrangle" or announced the hymn in chapel as "conkingering kwers their titles take."

The scientific name for a spoonerism is an exchange, or in the Greek, *metaphasis.* Just as the word "Kleenex" now refers to all paper tissues, "spoonerism" serves as the blanket term for all exchanges of sounds. In general, consonants are more often transposed than vowels. As the psychologist Donald MacKay has observed, the sounds reverse across a distance no greater than a phrase, evidence that a person planning what to say next does so at about a phrase's span in advance. Cognitively it would be nearly impossible for Spooner (or anyone else) to say something like, "For womework tonight you will read and translate the first page of Caesar's *Gallic Whores.*"

---

*Word stress can also determine whether or not slips occur. Manjari Ohala, a linguist at San José State University, has claimed that Hindi speakers (of which she's one) do not make exchange slips because, she speculates, Hindi words don't have a syllable with stronger stress. She's asked linguists in India to listen for slips, but they've reported nothing. This makes Hindi a language that lacks verbal blunders, at least of some types.

We might want to distinguish the spoonerism from the more generic exchange—certainly there's a difference between one that results in two actual words (as in, "May I sew you into a sheet?") and one that results in nonsense (as in praying that the congregation would be filled with "fresh veal and new zigor"). The distinction is necessary because it raises a legitimate linguistic question: do slips of the tongue like these result in real words more frequently than they result in nonwords? The implication is that if real words ("sew you into a sheet") are more frequent, then how our minds produce words becomes a bit clearer. Specifically, it suggests that in the rapid processes involved in thinking and speaking, a speaker inspects a word as a whole, not as a sequence of specific sounds. Thus, a word that "looks right" to the speaker—or, more precisely, to a sort of internal editor or blunder checker—will be cleared for pronouncing, like planes are cleared for takeoff. In fact, studies have shown that people tend to make more speech errors that involve individual sounds and produce legitimate words.*

This bias for spoonerizing to make real, not invented, words is one way that slips of the tongue, though they intrude unexpectedly, are less random than one might think. When one looks at a large group of slips, the patterns and tendencies that emerge share a strong resemblance to the language itself. For instance, in English, slips with sounds tend to appear as sequences of sounds that are possible in English. Thus, while Spooner might have said that he gave someone a "poppy of his caper," he wouldn't have said the un-English "a ocppy of his

---

*Among adult native speakers, slips of sounds are more frequent than slips of words. According to Kay Bock, 40 percent of exchange errors involve sounds; slightly more than 35 percent involve words.

cper." Likewise, spoonerisms in Choctaw probably won't sound much like those in French.

What hasn't been determined, however, is whether the exchange that produces a spoonerism is more or less frequent than two other types of speech errors. Some scientists with an interest in slips of the tongue argue that a type of slip, an "anticipation" (as in "the American worth ethic," a phrase not actually uttered by Spooner, though he could have) occurs more often. What we plan to say (albeit only a few seconds in the future) contaminates what we say in the present. Others disagree and report that another type of slip, a "perseveration," (such as "the Battle in the Belgium Belch," also not Spooner's) happen just as often. These open questions point to a central issue in the scientific study of verbal blunders: do we more readily perceive some types of slips in our own talking or others' while other slips wriggle by? And if so, why do we hear the ones we do? Or do we hear them all?

All of these distinctions color how we understand Reverend Spooner—and other famous verbal blunderers. The facts of Spooner's life very strongly suggest that he didn't make as many verbal blunders as are attributed to him. Of the blunders he did make, very few were "true" spoonerisms. The myths about the man, which were spun out of fancy and admiration, say more about our fascination with verbal blunders than about the blunders or the man.


Since the 1960s, in a search for the historical Spooner, linguists and historians have been sifting the evidence for attested examples of his errors. In an essay, "The Warden's Wordplay," the historian R. H. Robbins claimed Spooner made no more than three "true" spoonerisms during his life.* A student at New College from 1894 to 1898, taking notes during a Spooner lecture, noted that Spooner said, "So you will be abily easle to chase the train of thought." As a guest at someone's house, Spooner said that he'd "lately tasted a most delicious madeira when he was in Banana." And at a meeting of the Kensington Poetry Lovers' Circle in 1888 or 1889, he began a reading from Tennyson: "Come into the garden, Maud/for the black gnat-bite has flown."†

Some of Spooner's colleagues also reported a dearth of spoonerisms. "I was almost daily meeting Dr. Spooner for some forty years from 1882 onwards," remembered one, "and I can remember hearing hardly any of the transpositions attributed to him." His daughter, Rosemary, claims she never heard him spoonerize at all.

According to Robbins, Spooner made far more slips of the tongue that were generic exchanges (in the sense that real words weren't the result). He recounted several that had been observed by more than one person or verified. In chapel, Spooner once announced the hymn as "Kinkering Congs Their Titles Take"; in a sermon he announced that "but now we see

---

*Robbins noted that the first transposition isn't a "true" spoonerism, though the second one is. Robbins hews to a strict definition of the "true" spoonerism, which requires "(1) transposition of individual letters (generally initial) between words, or transposition of complete syllables or words. (2) The consequent formation by such metathesis of legitimate words, including slang, but not including jabberwocky. (3) The achievement of a humorous effect by the unexpected incongruity."

†The actual first stanza of Tennyson's poem is:

Come into the garden, Maud,
For the black bat, night, has flown . . .

through a dark glassly," and he once told a stranger, "Excuse me, but I think you are occupewing my pie." Spooner also asked a Japanese dinner guest, "Do you practice ju-jusit?" And during a classics lecture, he referred to the figures of Irenaeus and Collypark. (He meant Polycarp.)

If the Spoo didn't make as many true spoonerisms as were attributed to him, he did utter a slew of slips of the tongue. "He was rather a small man with a strange, rather butterfly sort of quality in his voice." Huxley wrote, "And finally, he did say, and write, and do some very odd things." Someone reported hearing him say that the story of Noah's great flood was "barrowed from Bobylon." When he officiated at a wedding he announced the bride and groom as "loifully jawned in holy matrimony." (This has also been written as "jawfully loined," which may be evidence of its apocryphal status.)

Robbins and other biographers do consider reliable many other instances of the Spoo's absentminded eccentricities. Sir Charles Symonds told of the time he was instructed to visit the warden's office urgently. When he arrived, Spooner couldn't remember why he had summoned Symonds, so he dismissed him just as abruptly. "Well, you may go," Spooner said.

When Spooner was interviewed in 1930, the year he died, he remembered making only the "Kinkering Congs" blunder. Robbins quoted a witness as saying, "There was a hush and the Doctor calmly repeated his slip. I am afraid that we all burst into laughter. I think the Doctor then saw his mistake."

If Spooner was a garden-variety blunderer, why did the legend of his profuse, extravagant blundering grow so quickly? Spoonerisms are funny, of course. That Spooner was a clergyman must have contributed: the seriousness of the pulpit throws into relief the preacher who lectures on the "synospel Goptics," or praises God as a "shoving leopard," or describes St. John the Baptist's "tearful chidings." But the easy, immediate humor of the spoonerism also begs the question, Why didn't they take some other blunderer's name? William Hayter supposed the reason was that Spooner was affiliated with New College during a dynamic period in its history, when school leaders took a closed, stagnant place and transformed it into a more open, intellectually vibrant community. As warden, Spooner held a moderate course—not introducing any more change than his predecessors, but not returning to more traditional ways. So he may have been associated with free-floating anxieties that sought a comfortable mark. Hayter called it "ironical" that a man who was remembered, admired, and mentioned in memoirs by Arnold Toynbee, Julian Huxley, and many others is known most for "trivial absurdities, most of them apocryphal."

Spoonerisms were also invented by students—one of them, Charles W. Baty, admitted inventing "a camel passing through the knee of an idol." The bulk of errors attributed to Spooner were actually this kind of creative invention. But why were the verbal inventions attributed to Spooner circulated outside the university community as well? Perhaps an answer can be found by looking at what spoonerisms were called before Spooner. An early alternative was "marrowskying," defined by the *Oxford English Dictionary* (*OED*) as "a variety of slang, or a slip in speaking, characterized by transposition of initial letters, syllables, or parts of two words." There are suggestions that "Marrowsky" was somehow related to Joseph Boruwlaski, a famous dwarf who toured the courts of Europe in the eighteenth century, but no attested connection has been found.* Scholars of

English slang have also pointed to the terms "medical Greek" or "hospital Greek," a verbal game created by medical students in London in order to disguise ordinary English, a sort of pig Latin that involved reversing the sounds of pairs of words.

Spooner came along at a time when the archetype of the blunderer was changing from someone who blundered deliberately to someone who did so accidentally. "Marrowskying" named a deformation of language by a person who wanted to get laughs. An utterance out of the mouth of Spooner? It was accidental, a moment in which self-control not only failed but whose very existence came into question. There was an aspect of social class to the spoonerism as well; until the late nineteenth century, the famous blunderers of literature (think Sancho Panza of *Don Quixote* or Dogberry of *Much Ado About Nothing*) had been either peasants, incompetents, or fools. Reverend Spooner embodies an emerging figure of modernity as much as an icon of verbal blundering: the educated, upstanding citizen who suffered inexplicable accidents in public.

In its earliest days the science of psychology tried to understand the nature of self-control and its relationship to consciousness. The human self had once been conceived as autonomous and the center of its world. The individual's challenge was to know one's self and the divine power that granted free will. But experiments in perception and consciousness demonstrated that the bulk of mental life occurred without our awareness. Self-knowledge would not always lead to self-control. One could be fully self-knowing and still make

---

*Boruwlaski was famous for sitting on the laps of royal women and falling in love with their ladies-in-waiting. That, and the fact that he was twenty-eight inches tall.

speech errors; one could also be highly educated and fall prey to accidents.

Around the time that spoonerisms became popular, technological systems, such as railroads, were becoming larger and more complex and hence harder to coordinate. In these circumstances, small human errors had larger consequences. In 1889, an article in *Scribner's* on railway management mentioned the term "heterophemy," which American writer Richard Grant White had given to moments when someone thinks one thing yet says, thinks, or does another. The writer described one incident in which a dozen lives were lost when a train operator became heterophemous.

Meanwhile, slips of the tongue of all types were being folded into larger attempts to understand human cognition, its robustness, and its frailties. In 1881 James Sully, a British psychologist, wrote the first general survey of human error. In 1900, H. Heath Bawden, an American psychologist, published *A Study of Lapses,* which noted a variety of speech errors, such as the man who asked the druggist for "Phosford's Acid Horsephate" and a "portar and mestle," or the professor who referred to the "tropic of Cancercorn," or the father who told his son to put the "barn in the cart." (Bawden doesn't mention Reverend Spooner by name, though he quotes some classic spoonerisms.)

In Bawden's time, slips were taken as signs that consciousness was partly made of automatic mechanisms that weren't voluntary and partly made of voluntary mechanisms that couldn't be controlled. Slips were considered "fringes" of consciousness, the leftovers of attention. They were, Bawden said, the kin of absentmindedness, as when a man puts a sock on over his shoe or a woman smells her watch to see if it's stopped. He noted that "instances are not infrequent in which the word 'glad' is written in place of the word 'sorry' in letters of condolence," which happened for a range of reasons, often because someone was embarrassed, in a hurry, preoccupied, tired, stupid, or nervous.

One of the most prominent figures who helped shape our view of the modern self, Sigmund Freud, was also the first to understand speech errors as something more fundamental to human consciousness. His view of slips departed from that of Bawden and others. As Freud would posit, the slip of the tongue was a sign of a true self seeking the light, a seeping of the unconscious out from under its loosening lid.

# 2

# *The Life and Times of the Freudian Slip*

With its broad boulevards and monumental buildings, Vienna did not seem to be a city where small events like slips of the tongue would be noticed. But at the close of the nineteenth century and the dawn of the twentieth, slips, gaffes, and lapses found a special home in the city's collective mind. Sophisticated, decadent, and vibrant, Vienna, a city of 1.6 million people, was the capital of the sprawling Austro-Hungarian Empire, which struggled to consolidate its power. The vastness of the empire, its mix of ethnicities and languages, and the absence of a single national identity put many people who spoke distinct languages in contact and made the Viennese highly attuned to subtle spoken cues. They noted the various German dialects, whether the nasal language of the high nobility, the slightly idiomatic German spoken by the emperor, army officers, civil servants, and the intelligentsia, or the street slang of salesgirls. They listened for the fractured German of assimilated immigrants. Vienna was also home to an emotionally restrained, socially disciplined middle class.

Despite the public propriety, the city's intellectuals (such as Sigmund Freud and Richard Freiherr von Krafft-Ebing, who studied sexual deviance) pioneered the study of sexuality, and Vienna was proud of its cabarets and prostitutes. Other contradictions, both intellectual and political, gave the place an atmosphere of secrecy and amorality. In 1990, Bruno Bettelheim argued that only in Vienna could psychoanalysis have been born. It was "one of the major intellectual developments of a time when a pervasive awareness of political decline led Vienna's cultural elites to abandon politics as a subject to take seriously, to withdraw their attention from the wider world and turn inward," Bettelheim wrote.

Sigmund Freud began his career in Vienna in the 1880s, treating female patients suffering from hysteria. He worked with Josef Breuer, an older doctor, who taught Freud how to treat psychological problems by getting patients to talk about early memories and experiences and the emotions connected to them. Breuer called this the "cathartic method." Breuer's patient, Bertha Pappenheim, who was twenty-one years old when Breuer was first called to see her, named it the "talking cure" and "chimney sweeping." Working with Bertha and other patients, Freud and Breuer became aware of the importance of symbolism in dreams. Freud started to write down his own. By 1896, he was writing down dreams and his interpretations of them as well as slips of the tongue, forgotten names, and misrememberings. All of these he took to be eruptions of the unconscious self's desires.

In 1901, Freud published *The Psychopathology of Everyday Life*, placing his stamp on verbal blunders forever. *Psychopathology* (which was first an article, then a book, published in 1904) turned the marginalia of people's lives, including their speech errors, into spotlights on the unconscious self. With its mundane examples of conscious intentions gone awry, it became one of Freud's most popular books. In its early editions, it makes the Viennese look like an awkward people, prone to faltering and gaffing and as equally embarrassed by their lapses and faults. In later editions of the book, Freud added some of his encounters with strangers who approached him to talk about their slips, a more frequent situation once he and psychoanalysis became better known. Sometimes his fellow Viennese submitted their slips to his scrutiny, as if he were a fortune-teller or an astrologer, not a doctor.

Freud never enjoyed the convenience of using the term "Freudian slip," and it's unlikely he ever met someone at a costume party dressed in a negligee, a goatee, and a wink. Instead he wrote of *Fehlleistung,* or "faulty performance." For Freud, a verbal blunder was like a thread strung through a labyrinth. By following such threads, the psychoanalyst could uncover the lair where the monstrous intentions of the neurotic patient were imprisoned. Deep conflicts existed in the unconscious self, deeper than a person could know or reflect upon. The unconscious conveyed its own desires via verbal blunders.

The famous example of a Freudian slip, perhaps the textbook example, was the case of the forgotten *aliquis.* In *Psychopathology,* Freud recounted a conversation with a young man about the anti-Semitic prejudice they both faced. The young man tries to quote a line from Virgil in Latin: *"Exoriare aliquis nostris ex ossibus ultor,"* which means, "May someone rise, an avenger, from my bones." In Virgil, the lines are spoken by Dido, the Queen of Carthage, enraged that the wandering adventurer Aeneas is about to leave her. But to Freud, the young man is expressing his hope for someone to punish people who discriminate against Jews.

But the young man misquotes the line. *"Exoriare ex nostris ossibus ultor,"* he says. Freud noted the changes. He ignored the two words that the young man reversed *(ex nostris* for *nostris ex),* and focused instead on the dropped *aliquis,* eventually building a complicated interpretation to explain it.

Why did I do that? the young man asks Freud.

"We can get to the root of it at once," Freud tells him, "if you'll tell me everything that occurs to you when you concentrate on the word you forgot." To Freud, the forgotten name, the omitted word, or the transposed sound all had the same source: they'd been cut off, intruded upon, rerouted, diverted, or blocked by a deeper, secret intention of the unconscious, a desire that the speaker was repressing. Freud called uncovering the desires of the unconscious "psychoanalysis," and he would try to make it a science. Others would call it overinterpretation, even charlatanism. Still others would call it an art, a sort of modern poetry of the soul.

The young man recognizes Freud, whom he knows as the founder of psychoanalysis, and he submits to an analysis on the fly. From *aliquis,* the young man thinks and says the word "liquid," then recalls a Catholic relic in a church, a vial of blood that belonged to St. Januarius, which liquefies only once a year, and how horrified the people of the parish feel when the liquefaction occurs too late.

Aha, says Freud. You're worried that your lover is pregnant.

"How on earth did you guess that?" asks the astonished young man. (The assessment was accurate.)

"It's not so difficult," the older man replies, then walks the young man backward through the chain of associations he'd interpreted.

Now we use the term "Freudian slip" to label lapses that are salacious, obscene, or hostile—and whose impropriety is immediately evident. When you read in *Psychopathology* about the anatomy professor who replaced the word *Versuche* with the word *Versuchungen* and said to his class that "The study of the female genitals, despite many temptations, I beg your pardon, experiments," you almost expect him to tack on, "Well, I guess that's a Freudian slip there." He doesn't, of course. That's because he hadn't lived with Freudian slips as long as we have. By contrast, the case of the forgotten *aliquis* seems too subtle to be a Freudian slip. It is, however, a good illustration of how deeply Freud dug to get to personal truths. To him, any slip or gaffe, however seemingly innocuous, hid a secret intention that could be unburied through investigation.

Sigmund Freud's methods for relating the trivial edges of life to its central dramas came from a source that, at first glance, seems unlikely: an Italian art historian and physician named Giovanni Morelli who, between 1874 and 1876, published a series of essays about Italian paintings. In the essays, Morelli offered to solve a problem that plagued the world of art until the days of Fourier transform spectroscopy and polarized light microscopy: how do you determine the authenticity of a painting? The historian Carlo Ginzburg has argued that Morelli, who put his finger on a new method of reading evidence, helped Freud develop his ideas and methods. The powerfully inferential method that Morelli laid out was a knowledge tool that professionals could hone, which they did. His ideas were reflected in the detective methods that Sir Arthur Conan Doyle attributed to Sherlock Holmes, in the biological measurements by Francis Galton that led to the science of fingerprinting, and later to

Andrew Ellicott Douglass's discovery that counting tree rings could help date archaeological sites. They also shaped Freud's psychoanalysis.

As Morelli pointed out, the traces and clues on paintings that were imperceptible to most people were, in fact, valuable evidence about the person who painted them. If you try to authenticate a painting by matching its major attributes to the representative ones of a painter's style—such as how he used colors, how he represented light, even his subject matter—you will easily be deceived. After all, such techniques are widely taught and copied. They're signatures. And like signatures, they can be forged.

But an artist always left a unique mark in the details that were casually, perhaps carelessly, tossed off: earlobes, finger-nails, the shapes of fingers and toes, and other flourishes, trills, and decorations all captured an artist's unintentional signature. An authenticator should learn to examine these details, even trust them, Morelli argued. In such details an artist would not be so intent on working in his or her style; artists tend to pro-duce this kind of visual marginalia without much thinking or planning. Yet an artistic sensibility—and identity—left its unique traces behind.

Freud read Morelli's essays sometime between 1883 and 1896. By 1898, he had purchased a copy of Morelli's collected essays, *Della Pittura Italiana*. Ginzburg argues forcefully that Freud's psychoanalytic method originated with Morelli. "It was the idea of a method of interpretation," Ginzburg writes, "based on discarded information, on marginal data, considered in some way significant." Connoisseurs of Freud will note that Morelli did not share Freud's conception of the unconscious as a matrix of desire. But Freud himself compared his method to Morelli's.

"It seems to me that [Morelli's] method of inquiry is closely related to the technique of psychoanalysis," he wrote in an essay about Michelangelo's marble sculpture of Moses.

For Freud, slips of the tongue that had once been marginalized by laughter, embarrassment, or sheer ignorance were, in fact, valuable data. Where a person's conscious control falters, a true intention shines out. An unconscious motivation takes the disguise of a dream, a slip, or a neurotic symptom. In *Psychopathology* he mentions various types: forgetting proper names, foreign words, phrases, childhood memories; slips of the tongue; slips of writing, hearing, and reading; and other inadvertent actions. Some of the slips were embarrassing gaffes. Freud once asked a patient how her uncle was; she replied, "I don't know, these days I see him only *in flagranti*." (She had meant to say *en passant*.) Other slips are more pointed. A woman was asked what regiment her soldier son was in. "The Forty-second murderers," she replied. (In the German she'd said *Mörder* instead of *Mörser*, or "mortars.")

Freud took speech errors as something more than the "fringes of consciousness." Unlike H. Heath Bawden, Freud wasn't willing to say they were accidental or unintentional. They were products of will—willed by the dynamics of the unconscious. Neither were such intentions marginal or unimportant. In Freud's view, the repressing of unconscious desires was the main mechanism by which the conscious self, or the ego, was created. They were central, not marginal. The slip of the tongue took the temperature of this process, pointing to places where psychic pressure needed release.

It has been widely acknowledged that Freud cherry-picked slips for *Psychopathology* that were particularly juicy or easy to interpret. Everyday life was bursting with slips of the tongue. But his method simply had no way of accounting for them all. Instead he focused on the ones that suited his theory of a repressed unconscious.

Methods of Freudian interpretation unpacked the drama of an ego inherent in a slip of the tongue. They also illuminated the relationships among ordinary but disparate phenomena like jokes and dreams. By 1910, Freudian memes had migrated to America, where they drew much attention in literary and artistic circles. Translated into.English, Freud's *Fehlleistung* was rendered as "parapraxis." The American modernist writer Sherwood Anderson described meeting the bohemian guru Floyd Dell in 1913 in Chicago. Dell and his friends set about "psyching" people—reading the details of their behavior, noting their slips and gestures. What we now take as a central plot point in the pulpiest detective novel, Dell and his gang did for fun. "Freud had been discovered at the time and all the young intellectuals were busy analyzing each other and everyone they met," Anderson wrote in his memoir. "And now [Dell] had begun psyching us. Not Floyd alone but others in the group did it. They psyched me. They psyched men passing in the street. It was a time when it was well for a man to be somewhat guarded in the remarks he made, what he did with his hands."

The Freudian slip (the term would not be coined until the 1950s) eventually took on a pop icon status, acquiring a forbidden, often sexual, flavor that Freud had not intended. It also lost its depth and stopped serving as a window into inscrutability. People who had never read Freud called any mere slip a Freudian slip to mitigate their embarrassment; saying the term becomes a magic incantation, socially useful in the way that an apology clears the air without replacing the shattered window or mending the broken heart. Announcing that "I must have made a Freudian slip" works as a social salve. It's a way of demonstrating that you're aware that you've spoken an infelicity while also giving you a way to ignore what you accidentally revealed about yourself. To Freud, all slips were Freudian. Not so for the rest of us.

Among the other roles that it has played in the culture, the Freudian slip has invited attacks on psychoanalysis itself. Sebastiano Timpanaro, an Italian philologist, carried a personal grudge against psychoanalysis: it had never cured him of his fear of public speaking (which kept him from getting a job as a professor), and he lived much of the last part of his life indoors, stricken by an agoraphobia that he felt psychoanalysis could not dent. A committed Marxist, he skewered the Freudian slip in a 1976 book, *The Freudian Slip*, attempting to take down the edifice of psychoanalysis with it. In Timpanaro's view, if the theory of repression were valid, and given how sexually uptight people in Vienna were and how high tensions ran in the politically repressive Austro-Hungarian empire, Freud should have detected more slips about sex and revolution. But he didn't. So, concluded the Marxist, Freud must have been coddling the bourgeoisie with his talking cure.

Timpanaro proposed unextraordinary reasons for slips of the tongue. An expert in the changes that occur in medieval texts as they're copied by successive generations of monks, Timpanaro knew how easily a scribe could introduce an error by substituting a simple word for a hard one, leaving out letters, or reversing words. He called these mundane errors "banalization." This explained even the famous *aliquis* example. Timpanaro argued that *exoriare aliquis nostris ex ossibus ultor* has an unusual word order in Latin, which the young man regularized according to the word order in German, his native language.* Thus, it was not surprising that he'd stumbled over it. Consequently, he forgot *aliquis* as well—while deciding whether or not to fix his stumble, he left *aliquis* out. This might be explained by a simple look at the work of medieval monks, who tended to leave out words that were less important to the meaning of the whole sentence. *Aliquis,* or "someone," was one such word.

Timpanaro pointed out that many of Freud's examples of slips, forgotten words, or forgotten names were words in languages the speakers didn't speak natively. Surely a slip in an unfamiliar language counted differently than a slip in one's native tongue. The point is minor but effective—for all the mysterious powers of the unconscious, is it supposed to be multilingual, too?

Timpanaro makes another move so playful and inspired, it's worth relating. Recall that the young man in the *aliquis* example turns out to be waiting for news from his lover that she's not pregnant. He forgets *aliquis,* thereby implicating himself. But Freud's method of deciphering the meaning of the slip suggests that *aliquis* is the only word that could launch the discovery of the anxiety about an unintended pregnancy. That particular slip, not any other, was the only entrance into the young man's unconscious. Is this genuinely the case? Does *aliquis* uniquely lead to fears of a pregnant lover?

What if the young man had slipped up on, say, *exoriare,* which means "arise"? Timpanaro wonders. You could get from "arise" to "birth" easily. What if he forgot *nostris*? Then he

---

*Timpanaro argues the young man opts for the more typical word order in Latin, preposition-adjective-noun *(ex nostris ossibus),* which differs from the adjective-preposition-noun order of the quote *(nostris ex ossibus).* Also intruding is German word order, which would also put the preposition first.

might have thought of the Catholic "Our Father" (the *pater nos-ter*), then slid down the chain of associations to saints, their relics, and the liquid blood (though remember that the young man is Jewish). Freud's analysis had no monopoly on the conclusion; the interpretation seemed arbitrary, up to the whims of the analyst.

Since Vienna was a fertile place for the birth of psychoanalysis, it was also a natural place to find more than one way to dissect a speech error. Around 1889, another Viennese professor, a middle-class Catholic named Rudolf Meringer, began collecting slips of the tongue. With the help of a colleague, the neurologist Carl Mayer, Meringer eventually amassed eighty-eight hundred slips. Meringer and Mayer published them in a book titled *Misspeaking and Misreading* (or *Versprechen und Verlesen*) in 1895, six years before the first appearance of "Psychopathology" as an article in 1901, and long before Freud's stature as a cornerstore of twentieth-century intellectual culture became a reality.

Meringer's main interests as a philologist ("a lover of words," in the ancient Greek, but basically a historian of written language) had nothing at all to do with slips. He embarked on his speech error project as a tangent from his other project on the histories of words. Other philologists looked for invariant phonetic laws that explained how, over centuries, one sound in a language became another. The prevailing view was exemplified by the linguist Jacob Grimm (who with his brother, Wilhelm, collected the famous fairy tales), who devised an explanation for how certain consonants changed in languages over thousands of years. Now called "Grimm's Law," it asserts, in part, that starting with the oldest Indo-European languages, the sound "p" became an "f," the "b" became a "p," and the "bh" (an aspirated consonant) became "b." This is how we know (for instance) that the Latin *labium* is related to the English "lip." (How the vowel changed is another story.)

Though Grimm's Law said *how* those changes occurred, it was silent on *why*. Meringer thought he had an answer. Unlike many of his contemporaries, he believed that language was more like a living organism than a machine. Following the suggestions of another philologist, Hermann Paul, Meringer went digging among slips. His reasoning was this: if the sound changes of a language described by Grimm's Law were likened to an avalanche, then a single slip of the tongue might be the pebble that triggers a falling mountain. As a living system, language was prone to such catastrophic changes. If enough individuals made the same type of speech error, Meringer reckoned, they might eventually think of it as the correct form.

Meringer's approach to the histories of words showed a similar sensitivity. Rather than show how sounds in words had changed, Meringer examined how the objects those words referred to had evolved. One of his famous examples was that the German word for the "wall of a room," or *Wand,* had originally referred to walls made of mud-daubed branches twisted around each other. Hence *Wand* was similar to *winden,* the German verb for "to wind." Another Meringer-style analysis is the history of the English word "hose," the Dutch *hoos,* and the German *Hose.* All refer to pants (not stockings). The ancestors of modern pants were a three-piece operation involving the breeches, worn around the waist, and two stockings, or hose, one on each leg. When a single article of clothing was invented out of the three pieces, it retained the name of two of them: hose. Meringer appreciated ordinary objects like pants—he specialized in household objects and architecture, especially barns, stables, and houses, as well as bathtubs, furniture, kitchens, bedrooms, and living rooms. At the heart of his research lay a celebration of everything pan-German, all things of "the people."

This was also the way Meringer and Mayer collected their slips of the tongue. They regularly sat down for lunch with a group of other men, most of them professors at the University of Vienna. Across Vienna, middle-class families were eating in their ornate dining rooms, but these professors were unmarried; it was their standing date, a lunch group for academic bachelors, but also a scene of ongoing scientific investigation. Nothing's known about where they ate, perhaps a restaurant somewhere near their faculty offices, which weren't located on campus but were clustered throughout the city. Wealthy Vienna had attracted talented cooks from all over Europe, and the cuisine they developed is now thought of as opulent and voluptuous. Whether or not the professors ate schnitzel or goulash or boiled beef, their meal would have unfolded, course after course, over an hour or two, giving them ample time to talk about the issues of the day. They conversed like divers bouncing off a diving board, each one waiting until the previous man was finished speaking before talking himself. Once in a while, one of the men would make a slip of the tongue. When he did, Meringer, then in his early thirties, scribbled it down.

Meringer and Mayer also collected slips from students, family members, and colleagues. Most of what they wrote down were only those that had been heard by two people, for scientific verification. Yet for all this slip collecting, Meringer's evidence couldn't support his hypothesis that speech errors caused language change—they were too diverse to produce changes as specific as those mapped by Jacob Grimm.

Yet the eighty-eight hundred slips, as well as his subsequent writing about them, made Meringer the first blunderologist of the modern world. He was one of the first scientists to show that speech errors are worth collecting and classifying. Whereas Freud used slips to get a handle on the self, Meringer used them to get a handle on language. He was the first person to do this. No one before Meringer had noticed that slips aren't random, or that they are patterned according to the structure of the language, or that you could explain why they sound as they do by looking at sounds or words in the environment of the error itself. It seems obvious to us now. Even Heath Bawden believed that errors originated in the speaker, not in the act of speaking; in the self, not the event. To Meringer, a slip didn't have a mysterious, individual cause. It didn't take the shape it did because an individual had a pregnant lover or an absent father or an overbearing mother.

This made it easier to classify slips, which was another contribution of Meringer's. He gave them names, such as the "anticipation" *(Anticipationen)* and the "perseveration" *(Postpositionen),* two terms that are still used today. The anticipation is sometimes called a "forward error," since the slip substitutes a sound appearing later in the sentence. Meringer used the example of *Sappelschlepper,* an incorrect version of *Sattelschlepper.*

Conversely, the perseveration is a backward error, in which a sound stays around longer than it should. Meringer gave the example of *die größte Börse der Wölt,* where the vowel "o" invaded the phrase *der Welt* (the whole phrase should have been "the largest stock exchange in the world"). Both the anticipation and the perseveration could be explained by pointing to another sound in the same utterance. Meringer concluded that the source of most speech errors was the utterance contaminating itself.

Of course, some slips of the tongue resulted from interference by sounds or words that weren't in the utterance at all. (They were "noncontextual.") Meringer acknowledged these, which might come from another way the speaker might have said the same thing (for instance, colliding the synonyms "lesson" and "lecture" into "leksun"). They might also come from objects or names in the speaker's physical environment. "My wife has called the dog with my name, Rudolf; I've called my dog Johannes, which is my boy's name," Meringer wrote. "My wife has called it Gretel as well, the name of our daughter." His next comment gives a taste of how vehemently he would disagree with Freud about noncontextual errors. "What shocking light psychoanalysis would no doubt throw on our household!" he wrote.

Meringer's contemporaries weren't unified in their praise for *Misspeaking and Misreading;* some called it "hairsplitting." A few complimented him, but many more were academic rivals who criticized him for publishing the names of the blunderers he quoted—what sensible Viennese person would want his indignities to be publicized? Meringer explained that he'd collected the names to be scientifically thorough and published them to make the point that everyone blunders. If slips were printed with the names of the people who said them, it was proof that his collection hadn't been filled by a few particularly prodigious blunderers.

His insistence on identifying the blunderer anchored his observations that errors weren't random and that everyone turbing element is either a single thought that has remained unconscious, which manifests itself in the slip of the tongue . . . or it is a more general psychical motive force which is directed against the entire utterance." That that single thought could only be uncovered by "searching analysis"—psychoanalysis.

The philologist reacted with disgust to Freud's rebuff. He called Freud's book "a scientific bluff" and a "hoax." He bristled at Freud's suggestion that *Misspeaking and Misreading* was "preliminary work." Despite his joke about calling on psychoanalysis to explain why he called the dog his wife's name, he was incensed that Freud had used his examples—and then only a few choice examples of the many that he'd worked so hard to collect. He also disagreed with Freud's analysis of the origin of slips, because he disputed the fundamentals of psychoanalysis and the repressive unconscious.

Meringer's pitched battle against Freud took place in journal articles, letters, and newspaper articles. In 1908, he published another treatise on slips, *Scenes from Out of the Life of Language*, in which he ranted against Freud. At first, Freud didn't acknowledge that attack—he was too famous to have to. In November 1908, Freud wrote to Carl Jung, then his disciple: "Professor Mehringer in Graz (slips of the tongue) is outdoing himself in vicious polemics." (His misspelling of Meringer's name is a cutting inside joke: a *mehr-inger* was an overdoer, someone who went over the top.) Jung replied that he was "delighted" with the controversy. In 1910, Freud riposted in the third edition of *Psychopathology*, rebutting Meringer and admitting that he'd been mistaken to give the philologist any credit in the first place. This didn't dissuade Meringer, who'd thickened his hide in other arguments, notably with Vienna's architectural community. In a 1912 article, Meringer responded sharply that he wasn't merely a scientific opponent of Freud's— he also hated any supporter or believer of Freud's.

But by 1923, the academic catfight was coming to a close, mostly because it had become a one-sided affair. Meringer published an article in his journal, *Wörter und Sachen*, that rebutted Freud's explanation for every example in *Psychopathology*'s sixth edition in 1919.

One last time, Meringer argued that most slips could be explained through simple phonetics. He also noted that Freud must contort himself intellectually—recall the example of the forgotten *aliquis*—to explain slips even though a simple phonetic explanation was sufficient. Meringer criticized Freud for not having a method of explaining all slips, selecting only ones that fit his theory. For instance, when a slip of the tongue results in an obscenity, Meringer wrote, Freud believed that the speaker must be repressing an obscene wish. "With what right does Freud make his suppositions when in countless other cases of transposition and substitution, nothing offensive is manifested?" Meringer argued. He had a point—most everyday slips are so banal we overlook them.

Even in the case of noncontextual errors, Meringer claimed, the error still comes from speech, not the unconscious. "If a slip seems obscure to me," Meringer wrote, "I immediately ask 'What other thoughts were you thinking?' From this method I've discovered regular 'word vagrants'—the word image that swims through the mind." For instance, when Meringer first went to school as a child, his father introduced him as "Karl," his older brother, who wasn't around. This type of slip was less important to Meringer's analysis, but Freud (as Meringer pointed out) elevated it so it was the most important source of slips. Indeed, remembered best (when he's remembered at all) for *Misspeaking and Misreading,* a book that became a founding document and a guiding light for the linguists and psychologists of the next century who really put slips of the tongue under the microscope.


As I was preparing this chapter, President George W. Bush made a slip of the tongue in a press conference that perfectly illustrates how Freud's approach differs from Meringer's. Though the tradition of slip science inaugurated by Meringer offers a more thorough way of listening to slips, drawing on both approaches makes the slip that much more interesting.

Bush, who was defending his decision to go to war in Iraq by pointing to the signs of an emerging democracy there, said, "Who could have possibly envisioned an erectsh—an election in Iraq at this point in history?" A scientist explaining this slip in linguistic terms would, à la Meringer, say it's obvious that the context of sounds resulted in a slip. Technically, Bush committed an anticipation—he anticipated the "r" in Iraq—though it might also be considered an exchange, with the "r" in Iraq and "l" in "election" switching places. We'll never know for sure, because Bush caught his error and fixed it—a moment called a "repair."

Such an analysis is probably accurate, but it's perfectly unexciting, not to mention a wasted opportunity for political critique, if you're so inclined. For color, we look to a Freudian interpretation, which, à la Morelli, might analyze the unexpected appearance of a word about sexual function in a political speech, then note the full (and more embarrassing) phrase that Bush narrowly avoided: "erection in I lack." To a Freudianminded critic, a man who feels sexually inadequate might be motivated to go to war to prove his masculinity. At that unconscious level the slip was intended, intentions that can be attributed to the individual. Freud might have added that it would be necessary to hear Bush talk about his slip—the work of analysis was for both doctor and patient.

The Freudian slip is a sort of poetry that tells the dreams of speech and illuminates the passages of a person's thoughts and feelings. But speakers produce many more slips that are banal, a profusion that has yet to be proven meaningful in consistent Freudian terms. Meanwhile, from Meringer's point of view, you can more easily sort accidents, pathologies, and evil intentions if you pay more attention to language and the circumstances of speaking than you give to the self. These ideas would eventually influence a whole generation of linguists and psychologists who set out to understand slips more thoroughly.

The first real attempt by a linguist whose ideas we would recognize as closest to our own occurred in 1951, when Rulon Wells, a linguist at Yale University, embarked on a study of blends. A blend is a type of speech error that combines two or more words, such as "lettitor" for "letter to the editor," or "cumbersable" for "cumbersome" and "practicable," or even two phrases, such as "he knows nothing at ever," which blends "nothing at all" and "nothing whatever." Wells predicted several ways that blends would behave—not when they'd occur, but how, when they occurred, they'd sound.

His first "law" stated that "a slip of the tongue is practically always a phonetically possible noise"—the blend would favor "scrin," "scring," and "scrill" over "ktin," "pmpik," or "ksob." According to Wells's second law, if two words have the same stress patterns, then their blend will, too. Thus a blend of "beHAvior" and "dePORTment" would have three syllables and a stress on the second syllable. Indeed, Wells had observed someone saying "beHORTment."

His third law said that if two words have one sound in the same place, the blend will also have that sound. A blend of "maneuverable" and "removable" would contain the sound of "v" in the middle of the word. It would also end with "able." Hence, "removerable."

The next linguist to take up slips (apparently independently of Wells) was R. J. Simonini Jr., a linguist who, in 1956, exploited the cache of slips he found, not among his friends and colleagues, but in a popular set of records filled with "bloopers"—speech errors that had been broadcast on live radio or television. Ignoring the "malapropisms, illiteracies, indiscreet remarks, off-the-air remarks, innuendoes, double meanings, inebriated discourse, and uncontrollable laughter" on the records, Simonini focused on the slips for which Rudolf Meringer had first provided a terminology.

Simonini noted the familiar types of anticipations: the exchanges of sounds ("Here is the weather report: tomorrow, roudy followed by clain") and of words ("And now, we present our homely friendmaker"), the substitutions ("When you try Phillips Dental Magnesia, you will find it makes an excellent mouse wash"), and the additions ("Ask to see the Ford Ferguson with the crow crap cultivator"). He also noted the perseverations, what he called "lags" ("a battle in the Belgian Belch"), those with substitutions ("You now hear the chimes of hysterical New York"), and those with additions ("the Russian freighter that crapsized in Portland's harbor").

These early studies of slips had to wrangle with Freud and the Freudian slip. No other theory existed to make slips more than trinkets and slip collectors more than hobbyists. That theory would emerge in the 1960s, when a paradigm shift in the study of language opened an opportunity for slips of the tongue to become crucial evidence for the hidden workings of the mind.

Neither Freud nor Meringer knew that in the one hundred years after the publication of *The Psychopathology of Everyday Life* and *Misspeaking and Misreading*, psychologists, psychiatrists, linguists, writing teachers, speech pathologists, computer scientists, and technology designers would turn to slips and speech disfluencies, counting, measuring, correlating, interpreting, collecting them in the wild and even provoking them in the laboratory, finding them in conference discussions, therapy sessions, radio and television broadcasts, telephone conversations, interviews with psychiatric patients, family gatherings, newspaper and magazine stories, town meetings, bars, role plays, lectures, and undergraduate seminars. This science has no name. But it has attracted people from a variety of disciplines, including linguistics, psychology, cognitive science, rhetoric, English, computer science, psychiatry, engineering, communications, and political science. All these efforts share one goal: rather than ignoring verbal blunders, the researchers made them tell their tales.

# 3

## *Some Facts About Verbal Blunders*

L istening to verbal blunders more closely, one is immediately struck by the fact that they are about as ubiquitous as ants at a picnic. In 1930, three scientists from Bell Laboratories analyzed recordings of 1,900 phone calls to figure out how, exactly, business people were communicating with each other on the phone. They amassed eighty thousand words, a surprising 25 percent of which consisted of half-completed words and sentences, as well as nonwords like "uh," "ah," and "yeah." They noted that exclamations ("yes," "no," "well," "yeah," "uh-huh," "oh," "all right," "hello," and "good-bye," as well as laughter and profanity) amounted to about 10 percent of speech. "Uh" alone amounted to 4 percent.

Nearly twenty-five years later, when psychologist George Mahl began counting the slips and blurps of patients at his clinic at Yale University, he counted eight types of interruptions. He called them "speech disturbances": filled pauses like "uh" and "um"*; restarted sentences; repeated words; stutters; the omission of a word or part of a word; incomplete sentences; slips of the tongue; and something he called an "intruding incoherent sound."† His tally? During spontaneous talk, one disturbance every 4.4 seconds.

The most common blunders? "Uh" and "um." These pause fillers amounted to 40 percent of all the speech disturbances in Mahl's sample. Another 45 percent were restarted sentences and repeated words. By contrast, the least common were slips of the tongue, which occurred a measly 1 percent of the time or less.* Since Mahl's day, scientists have estimated that an average person says a slip of the tongue (saying "counterism" for "counterterrorism," for example) no more on average than twice every one thousand words (in English, anyway).** One irony is that the slip of the tongue, the rarest of the verbal blunders, has had the richest career—speech errors have long appeared to humorous effect in literature and drama before spoonerisms circled the globe (in *Don Quixote,* for instance, Sancho Panza's capacity for beatings and other slapstick is outstripped by his propensity to say the wrong word), and Freud and Meringer built their intellectual careers around them. Until fleeting disfluencies could be frozen in recordings, however, we hardly noticed them.

*I refer to these instead as "pause fillers."

†Such as the "dh" in the sentence that Mahl transcribed, "If I see a girl now I'd like to take out I just . . . dh . . . ask her."

*More recent accounting has come up with similar numbers. In 2004, Robert Eklund estimated that about 6 percent of all words counted as disfluent. That is, they contained filled pauses, silent pauses, prolongations of individual sounds, some explicit editing terms, truncations, mispronunciations, and repairs, but not counting silent pauses or slips of the tongue.

**Verbal blundering in English is well studied for the simple fact that most of the early researchers spoke English.

As surprising as these numbers may be, they also make clear that verbal blundering is integral to language, not something that intrudes upon it. Because human language has ways to deal with accidents and interruptions, they must have evolved alongside language itself. To take an architectural metaphor, one can say that a window is merely a hole in a wall—a lack of wall. Or one might say that a window is part of the wall that includes it. Verbal blunders more resemble the second instance. Just as houses don't come without windows, languages don't come without moments we can call verbal blunders.

People around the world fill pauses in their own languages as naturally as watermelons have seeds. In Britain they say "uh" but spell it "er," just as they pronounce the "er" of "butter" ("buttah").* The French say something that sounds like *euh,* and Hebrew speakers say *ehhh.* Serbs and Croats say *ovay,* and the Turks say *mmmm.* In Dutch you can say *uh* and *um,* in German *äh* and *ähm.* In Swedish it's *eh, ah, aaah, m, mm, hmm, ooh, a,* and *oh;* in Norwegian, *e, eh, m,* and *hm.* According to Willem Levelt, a Dutch speech scientist, "uh" is the only word that's universal across languages.

The ancient Vedic tradition defines the sound "om" as the primordial sound of the universe. Intriguingly, "um" might be the more accurate manifestation of the universe's indecision.

While some languages fill pauses with a low vowel, other languages do so with actual words. An English speaker can say

---

*If you actually pronounce "er," you're saying it incorrectly—there's no pause filler with an "r" sound. People who do say it have been influenced by the British spelling of the word, in which the final "r" is silent.

"well," "so," and "you know," while speakers of Turkish say *shey, shey, shey,* which literally means "thing." The Japanese say *eto* and *ano,* the Spanish *este* and *eh.* A Hebrew speaker says *uv-xen,* or "therefore." In Mandarin Chinese, people say *neige,* which means "that," and in Yue Chinese, they say *ku,* which can also mean "this." Cantonese speakers in Hong Kong say *tsik hai,* or "equal," and in the Wichita language, people say *kaakiri,* which means "something."

Sign languages also have ways to indicate pauses. Signers usually look their listeners or interlocutors in the eye; to pause, they break this gaze. They can also freeze a sign. Wiggling the fingers is another option. A signer of American Sign Language is more apt to have the palms of his or her hands facing the body as the fingers wiggle; signers of Nicaraguan Sign Language, which erupted spontaneously among the children at a deaf school in the late 1970s, say "um" by wiggling their fingers with the hand they were using most recently for a sign.

The pause filler is so universal that even invented languages, created by hobbyists for fun, possess them. One such constructed language is Loglan (for "logical language"), invented in the 1950s by James Cooke Brown, a linguist and science fiction writer. Another version called Lojban followed. Lojban grammarian John Cowan says that a Lojban speaker fills a pause with a sound that's called a glottal stop that's tacked on either side of "uh." (To make a glottal stop, say "I bet ya" several times quickly until your tongue stops hitting the top of your mouth to make the "t" sound. The resulting consonant, which comes from the back of your throat, is a glottal stop.) Lojban also has words to help a speaker fix an erroneous statement: like backspacing the cursor on a computer screen, the word *si* erases the last word; the word *su* erases everything a person said in a conversation. According to Cowan, the earlier language, Loglan, also used *si* and *su* until the "uh" sound was introduced to the language, as well as a simple "rrr" sound. Cowan jokingly says "rrr" invokes an imaginary god named "R," who is the patron deity of hesitation.

This profusion of verbal blunders maps our life spans, which is a journey dotted with linguistic mile markers. It's a blunderful beginning. Children produce many times more speech errors and speak at least twice as disfluently as adults. Ehud Yairi and Noel Clifton concluded that normal preschool children made an average of seven disfluencies every one hundred words. High school seniors, with an average of four disfluencies per one hundred words, were the least disfluent of all. In general, as children get older, they become more fluent. They also talk faster, not because they articulate their words more quickly, but because their pauses shrink in size and number.

But fluency doesn't increase throughout life unchecked. Children's speaking may become less interrupted and fragmented as they mature, but as adults enter later life, they begin to sound more like children again. The seniors studied by Yairi and Clifton (ranging from sixty-nine to eighty-seven) uttered almost as many disfluencies as the children, more than six per one hundred words. They say "uh" and "um" more frequently, linger on pauses longer, restart more sentences, and repeat more words than younger adults. How fluent you are at the end of your life depends on how long you live. The basic picture is that we learn language only to blunder with it, then the growing flocks of those same blunders augur the changes to come.

A different kind of research into another type of verbal blunder—forgetting a word that you know, what is called a "tip of the tongue" experience, or TOT—has also shown age-related changes. The average young adult reports about one tip of the tongue experience a week. As people enter their sixties, they begin to report two to four per week. (Yet you have probably done this all your life—children younger than three years old reportedly have tip of the tongue experiences, too.)

Forgetting a word certainly interrupts the flow of a sentence; it can also be embarrassing (especially if it's the name of a person you know) and sometimes leads to social isolation. All adults forget names and proper nouns more often than other words, but older adults forget nouns for abstract things more frequently. (Psychologists who study the TOT state are stumped about why this occurs—they suggest that the young adults in their experiments, many of them college students, encounter more abstract nouns in their classes.) Men and women have the same number of TOT experiences. The question of whether they occur as equally to the highly educated as to the relatively uneducated is controversial. Donna Dahlgren, a psychologist at Indiana University Southeast, found that the larger someone's vocabulary, the more TOTs they experienced. She believes that increased age isn't enough to explain why more TOTs occur. Rather, older people have more knowledge about and experience of the world, which intrude upon their word selections. Meanwhile, Deborah Burke, a psychologist at Pomona College, has stated that TOTs happen as equally to the highly educated as to the relatively uneducated. This suggests that age, and age-related changes in the speed of finding something in memory, are major factors in TOTs.* Both explanations seem

---

*About the term "tip of the tongue": Psychologist Bennett Schwartz found that speakers of forty-five out of fifty-one languages have an idiomatic expression that refers to the tongue to name this experience, such as Korean ("sparkling at the end of my tongue"). In Cantonese, Mandarin, Hindi, Hausa, and Ibo, the idiom is some version of "in the mouth."

plausible, but it's easy to see which one an aging population might prefer.

During the 1984 presidential campaign, the second debate between President Ronald Reagan and Minnesota senator Walter Mondale, on October 28, 1984, may be best remembered as the time Reagan wittily defended his age. He was seventy-three years old, already the oldest U.S. president. A debate with Mondale three weeks earlier had exhausted him, aides reported. So *Baltimore Sun* reporter Henry Trewhitt asked the president, "I recall, yes, that President Kennedy, who had to go for days on end with very little sleep during the Cuba missile crisis. Is there any doubt in your mind that you would be able to function in such circumstances?"

Perhaps the question angered Reagan. Perhaps he recognized the slow pitch floating in the strike zone. His face flared. He swung. Hard. "Not at all, Mr. Trewhitt, and I want you to know," Reagan replied, "that I will not make age an issue of this campaign. I am not going to exploit for political purposes my opponent's youth and inexperience." The audience laughed. (Mondale was fifty-six.) "If I still have time," Reagan added, "I might add that it was Seneca or it was Cicero, I don't know which, that said if it was not for the elders correcting the mistakes of the young, there would be no state."

His wit? Sharp as a tack. His ability to deliver a scripted line? As good as ever. But his language showed his age—even as he blunted the criticism with words. In 1984, Reagan spoke more slowly, had longer pauses, and made more grammatical mistakes than four years earlier, according to Brian Butterworth, a British neuropsychologist who'd tracked Reagan's spoken language in his debates in 1980 with Jimmy Carter and with Mondale in 1984. At seventy-three years old, Reagan spoke in more fragments of sentences without correcting or repairing them.

Butterworth also counted Reagan's slips of the tongue: 2.2 per one thousand words in 1980, perhaps normal for a person under pressure. In 1984, they had risen to 2.6. A more significant increase was in Reagan's pausing. In 1984, Reagan had five times more pauses that lasted longer than a second than in 1980. He paused this way about five times every one thousand words. He also spoke more slowly, uttering about fifteen fewer words per minute. Butterworth also noted "confusional errors," or places where Reagan appeared confused by the question. To Butterworth, who's not a medical doctor, these were signs of mental decline—well before Reagan was diagnosed with the Alzheimer's that darkened his final years.

Not everyone agrees with Butterworth. To Susan Kemper, a psycholinguist at the University of Kansas who studies language across the life span (including a group of nuns, some of whom developed Alzheimer's late in life), Reagan's performance looked like the effect of normal aging, not the onset of disease. For instance, she's found a sharp decline in the size of a person's active vocabulary after seventy years old, and between seventy-four and seventy-eight years old, people rapidly lose their ability to produce complex sentences. The result? They tell more complex stories with simpler sentences, though often they're embarrassed by communicating with such difficulty, so they talk less. However, this didn't necessarily mean that they're experiencing Alzheimer's or some other chronic mental condition.

Intriguingly, people who are lucky enough to live one hundred years are no more disfluent than they are at seventy. Jeffrey Searl, a speech pathologist, listened to oral history recordings of seven centenarians who had no speech disorders and hadn't suffered strokes. As the centenarians answered questions about their lives, Searl counted their disfluencies and found them well within the normal range of 6.2 per hundred words. They spoke more slowly than younger adults but weren't remarkably more disfluent.

We may grudgingly admit that, like it or not, verbal blunders have the inevitability of gravity. The next question is why? It's because speaking is one of the most complicated human activities that we do, at any age. The average adult English speaker has a vocabulary of around thirty thousand words and speaks ten to twelve sounds per second. Most of us in modern America, apart from the very solitary and the very garrulous, speak anywhere from 7,500 to 22,500 words a day.* Grabbing these words, one every four hundred milliseconds on average, and arranging them in sequences that are edited and reviewed for grammar and appropriateness before they're spoken requires a symphony of neurons working quickly and precisely. Pronouncing (or signing) words in any language requires that your brain coordinate with your body in order to turn the electricity of nerve impulses into waves of sound (or, if you sign, of gesture and motion). So far, scientists have been able to draw only simple models of how the control of language toggles back and forth between the brain and the body.

Given the speeds involved, why aren't we better equipped to

---

*Precise figures for this are hard to come by, and the variability is immense. About 66 percent of Americans speak 7,500 to 22,500 words a day, while 40 percent speak 12,000 to 18,000 words a day.

put units of language in the right order? The problem is that sounds, words, and grammatical items aren't arranged in our brains as though on a library's shelves, with all the items ordered and catalogued by topics and authors. Rather, they're associated with one another in a matrix or a web. Some of these connections relate to the meanings of words; others relate to the sounds of those words. The web offers multiple ways to arrange these elements and many ways to arrange and use them in a linear fashion. They have to be arranged linearly because we have a mouth through which only one word at a time can come, in the same way that you have a lot of friends, all of whom know one another to varying degrees, but who can come into your house only one at a time through your front door.

In the 1950s, the psychologist Karl Lashley called the challenge of turning a disarrayed jumble of mental elements into a straight sequence the "problem of serial order in behavior." This was a challenge for many aspects of human behavior. He mentioned slips of the tongue as a good example of how getting things in order in time had to involve more than a linear set of responses to a sequence of stimuli. This was good news. Slips meant we weren't rats in mazes. In speaking, the serial ordering can fall apart across stretches of time. The other day I was listening to the radio and heard the expert being interviewed say, "You're not hearing over the phoine everybody's true voice." Instead of saying "phone" (which he clearly planned to do), he accidentally anticipated the vowel sound of "voice" and placed it in "phone." The problem of serial order suggests that many behaviors, including talking, are composed of continual efforts to plan and execute our actions. A full picture will be more complicated, but the simplest explanation for all verbal blunders, both the slips and the disfluencies, is that they occur as the brain shifts from planning to executing or back again.

Sentences also hide their internal structures, in the same way that skyscrapers hide their girders, their air-conditioning systems, their concrete pillars. We tend to think of the utterance that comes out of a person's mouth as a unitary thing, in the same way that a skyscraper appears monolithic. Yet in both cases what we perceive are the external characteristics. The building has thirty floors and it's made of glass and has odd balconies. The sentence has fifteen words of English, two of which are borrowed from Latin, and describes something that happened in the past.

If you ask an engineer what's going on, she'll tell you that the floor slabs inside the skyscraper are made of concrete, and that those slabs rest on steel beams that are connected to the central structural spine of the building, and that the slabs and beams and spine help stiffen the building and keep it from swaying during strong winds. Our brains work like those engineers. They make sense of a sentence's slabs and steel beams and the pressures on them. They know that sentences are composed of chunks of words that appear, on the surface, to be connected to each other in sequence, one after the other. They are actually arranged so that some chunks determine what other chunks mean. For instance, the sentence "I am not going to exploit for political purposes my opponent's youth and inexperience" is more than just a string of words. Though the phrases "for political purposes" and "my opponent's youth and experience" can be reversed in the sentence, neither can be moved to the front of the sentence—the resulting sentence sounds too odd. Thus, there's something about the verb "exploit" that has power over those phrases that requires them to follow, not precede.

Such chunks are the real building blocks of language; when you get enough chunks of the right kinds in the right relationship with one another, you've made a sentence. A speaker plans a sentence in these chunks, not in sentences or in single words. On the surface the sentence may look like a single unit. Yet most talking amounts to the accumulation of chunks. These natural chunks of language are called "constituents." In a sentence like "We think that a sentence exists as a unitary thing," the chunk "We think" seems to belong together more than the words "that a" do. So "We think" makes up a constituent.

Because we know something about this chunk-by-chunk accumulation, we know something about slips and disfluencies. For instance, slips are remarkably local in nature because we don't plan what to say too far in advance. Remember that spoonerisms don't happen over more distance than a phrase. It's also been noticed that disfluencies tend to occur more frequently at the edges of such chunks, not in the middle. And they occur before content words more often than before grammatical words (thus "the uh boat," not "uh the boat"). Why? Because at such moments a speaker is transitioning between planning and executing, which is where a pause is more necessary.

Conversely, because we know something about slips and disfluencies, we know something about the accumulating chunks. For instance, when you accidentally swap one word for another, you always choose a word of the same part of speech, which is why I heard someone say, "That's the cake on the icing" (where two nouns swap) and not, "That's the on icing the cake" (where a noun swaps with a preposition). Linguists use this regularity as evidence that before a person utters something, the brain is constructing a sort of frame with empty slots for words, and words can fit only into the slots designed for them. If they don't fit, they're kicked out, or the speaker notices the impending error and stops the sentence to revise it.

Slips never pop out willy-nilly; they follow the rules of English, or French, or Chinese, or whatever language the person is speaking. They are, in the term of the actuarial tables, "normal accidents." This has an intuitive appeal. If someone were trying to say "think quickly" and confused the two words, she would surely say "thick quinkly" and not "fxhamdx." Another example of a constraint on slips is that when a speaker swaps sounds between words, the sounds tend to come from the same place in the two words. This is why he'd say "chlodium soride," not "sochlo rideium."

Despite how widespread verbal blunders are, we recognize that each person blunders in a different way. We also know that while we can predict what blunders will sound like, we can't predict precisely when they'll occur. So it's tempting—and easy—to read all sorts of things into the bumps and hitches of a person's speaking. Thanks to Freud and Morelli, we take it as a given that a person's self has ways of getting noticed that he or she can't consciously control. We interpret all sorts of verbal blunders as if we were intellectual descendants of Freud. But we also owe a secret debt to Morelli, who also helped us extract information from noise, interruption, error, and silence. How someone talks provides precious information about their intentions and abilities in the future. Potential mates, along with voters, potential business partners, and new employers face the same dilemma. Before we commit our confidence, we want to know: will the client who pauses a bit too long in her speaking be late with her payments? Can you trust the boyfriend who can't decisively start a sentence to pack the heirloom china without tragedy? If you—if you—if you repeat words, would you be able to lead the men over the hill and take out the enemy pillbox? What do the actuarial tables say about the guy who forgets the punch line to the joke?

Informally, people try to use verbal blunders as information about traits—personality traits, intelligence, emotional tendencies, thinking style, and behavioral habits. We make these judgments all the time and probably don't realize we're doing it. When these judgments get turned into generalizations, they reinforce stereotypes. Take, for instance, the categories of "powerful" and "powerless" speaking styles.* As one might expect, the features of "powerless" speaking are "uh" and "um," as well as tag questions ("I think so, don't you?"), frequent use of intensifying adjectives ("so," "very"), hedges ("kinda," "I guess"), and politenesses. But certain styles of language are not intrinsically powerless or powerful, and such generalizations can be easily contradicted. For instance, Danielle Duez once showed that François Mitterand spoke more slowly as president than he did as a candidate—that is, the powerful man spoke "powerlessly." She deduced that challengers to power speak quickly in order to fit more ideas and critiques into a limited time span. The powerful, on the other hand, speak slowly, keeping the conversational ball and running down the proverbial clock.

Though verbal blunders may be unreliable measures of traits, they are fairly reliable gauges of states—states of mind, emotional states, and physical states. For instance, people who

---

*These categories were laid out by two anthropologists, William O'Barr and John Conley, who turned 150 hours of recorded court testimony into a script that's played by actors in front of mock juries, made of university students. The performances were then evaluated by the juries.

are forced to devote mental resources to other activities quickly jettison fluent speaking. To see how acting under time pressure changed a person's speech, a group of German scientists gave people a video game to play in which they had to navigate through an airport while asking questions of a robot helper device at the same time. As expected, whenever the players had to navigate through particularly tricky or distracting areas, they repaired sentences more frequently and used more word fragments. Because navigating increased the demands on their attention, it was more difficult to think and speak, and disfluency was a cognitive response, not an emotional one.

In law enforcement, verbal blunders are often used informally to assess states of mind. One snowy winter morning, I met Jerry Giorgio, a retired New York Police department homicide detective, to learn what the law enforcement descendants of Sherlock Holmes owe to Freud and Morelli.* Giorgio's a large man, barely contained behind the desk at the assistant district attorney's office where he now works, his tie neatly knotted, his irrepressible hands perpetually involved in telling his stories about bad guys and investigations on the streets of New York City. As a young man, before he became a cop in 1959, he pursued a film career. He still has a handsome ruggedness that would have suited him well depicting a small-town sheriff or a sea captain with a heart of gold. He became a detective in 1966 and worked on many homicide cases, becoming renowned for extracting confessions—without force but subtly manipulating the suspects nonetheless.

*Some of Giorgio's exploits were chronicled in *Street Stories: The World of Police Detectives,* by sociologist Robert Jackall, published in 2005 by Harvard University Press.

Giorgio didn't sit someone down unless he was certain about what the facts were, what jibed, what didn't fit—in other words, that the person he was talking to was the guy. But there was invariably still one crucial connection or piece of evidence missing, which was the most important one: the suspect with a weapon in hand at the scene of the crime. Giorgio would have already built a mosaic from other facts; he needed the suspect to confirm that this mosaic was, indeed, true. So Giorgio laid out the facts, piece by piece, then asked the person to reconcile the anomalies. Surprisingly, the suspect often obliged. Giorgio did it once, then again. Can I go? The guy would ask. "I'd say, just let me clear this one thing up, it won't take very long." The suspects didn't know it, but Giorgio was pushing them, slowly, to the point where two mosaics, two versions of the story, would emerge, two versions that were irreconcilable. He'd push the discrepancies in their face. And when he'd pushed far enough, they'd break. They'd cry. They'd confess.

At that moment of confession, a moment that always seemed to be approaching ineluctably, Giorgio says he listened to the suspects' voices most closely. Up to that point, many of them weren't under arrest, so technically they were free and could have walked out of the police station at any time. Giorgio wasn't listening to where a suspect stood in relation to the truth; he was trying to judge how close they were to spilling everything—or to walking out the door. He watched their faces and their movements. Is he agitated? Is he starting to move around in his chair? Does he uncross and cross his legs? Is he fidgeting with his hands in a way he wasn't doing before?

"Or he gets angry. 'You callin' me a fuckin' liar? You sayin' I'm lyin' to you?' I say, 'Ah, no, this is what I have here,' " and Giorgio gestured with his hands toward an imaginary pile of facts on his left, " 'and this is what we have here,' " and he gestured to a file on his right, " 'and I'm trying to make the two fit. And they don't fit.' "

Jerry Giorgio has a knack, an interpersonal gift. But police departments have begun to expect their staffs to have some acquaintance with the techniques that Giorgio uses, even if skills like his can't be entirely reproduced. Some experts have attempted to codify this know-how and train others in it. A number of training firms have developed specialized services: some focus on law enforcement; others specialize in shoplifting or retail store theft. One such firm is Wicklander-Zulawski, based near Chicago, which offers seminars on interviewing and interrogation.

Observing verbal blunders plays an important role in the company's approach. Liars are most under stress on their first attempts to lie—David Zulawski says it's like the opening day of a play. The words aren't scripted; the props are misplaced; no one knows where to stand. So liars, he says, will blunder at the beginning of their story. The further they get into the tale, the more confident they get, and the fewer blunders they make. If they have a chance to tell the lie several times, the telling gets smoother. That may be why interrogators isolate suspects and don't talk to them too much: the less practice suspects have in telling lies, the fresher their attempts will be.

Zulawski trains interrogators to listen for rising volume and increased pitch, which matches rising stress levels. In his model, a change in word choice is also important. For instance, "a gun" versus "the gun" indicates a varying level of familiarity with the gun. Repetitions of words and silences can indicate mental struggle. When a person diverges from his or her own speech style, then you know something's up. As Zulawski acknowledges, the interrogator still doesn't know what such interruptions mean. "All I know is that it was an oddity," Zulawski says, "and I want to go back to that point and see if it happens again. Is there a consistent response? A fluke? It might be. It could be a deception. It could mean a lot of little things."

But, he says, verbal blunders in and of themselves aren't significant, and the interrogator must interpret them. For instance, he has to consider the context of the conversation. "If I asked you right now, do you cheat on your taxes, and you say, 'Uh, uh,' I wouldn't think that was a cover for a lie," Zulawski told me. "I'd think it was a cover for confusion." On the other hand, "If we'd been talking about taxes and ethical dilemmas and I asked you the same question, then your 'uh' would more likely be a cover for deception."

A number of experiments have tried to map the typical behavior of liars, who toss their hands, twirl their pens, scratch their heads, talk more quickly, and keep eye contact a little longer. Why not use verbal blunders, as well as these other behaviors, as markers of deception? Because other subjects in the same experiments who weren't lying but whose emotions had been aroused when they had been blasted by noise also tossed their hands, twirled their hair, scratched their heads, and spoke in a different pitch. They also made verbal blunders. In other words, they sounded and acted like the liars did. So what the interrogator may be seeing and hearing is merely emotional arousal, not a speaker's self-indictment. If you rely only on Morelliesque tics and details, you'll uncover the inexperienced, nervous, and leaky liars—not the skilled ones. You might also pull in some innocent people who've never been in the hotseat before.

Despite the conflicting evidence, some researchers still maintain that stutters, pauses, "uh" and "um," and restarted sentences might be indicators of lying. In 1997, the Italian psychologists Luigi Anolli and Rita Ciceri wrote that blunders were vocal signs that a person was lying, because they "reveal [the subject's] lack of preparation and his/her weakness in coping with his/her own emotional reactions." In their view, a person fundamentally doesn't like to lie, and the blunders are signs of this emotional conflict. This approach to "vocal leakage" may assume too much. For one thing, do people actually prefer to tell the truth? One could argue convincingly that people are as likely to prefer social cohesion and tranquility and will tolerate telling and hearing omissions, white lies, and everyday spin to maintain that calm. Anolli and Ciceri's claim also assumes that liars are anxious because lying breaches a social contract, which causes shame, hence anxiety. But this explanation can't possibly be a universal across cultures, because such everyday social contracts are not universal.

Zulawski observes that blundering itself, or a certain number of errors, or certain types of errors, doesn't point directly at deceptive intent. What's more significant, he believes, is the frequency of errors in a stressful situation relative to a speaker's normal speaking style. Individuals vary widely in how much they blunder verbally, a fact that police officers and skilled interviewers recognize. The next time you're pulled over, the cop will often begin with a question that sounds like idle chit-chat: what a sunny day we're having; where are you going? But he or she is actually checking how you respond to something that presumably should be easy to answer. They start with the mundane in order to gauge how you give answers you don't have to think about. Theoretically, a person could confound an interrogator from the outset with liberal doses of "uh" and "um," like a jet spreading chaff to throw off a pursuing missile.

From here, how verbal blunders vary among individuals becomes stickier. It can be tempting to attribute a speaker's verbal blunders to his or her intelligence (or lack of it); only the cruelest misanthrope would blame *all* verbal blunders on a failure of smarts. The sociologist Erving Goffman offered a better distinction. He called some of them "knows better" errors and others "doesn't know better" errors. Both occur in abundance in our behavior, including our verbal lives.

The "doesn't know better" errors are caused by stupidity or lack of experience. These "boners" and "gaffes" (as Goffman dubs them) occur when someone violates the rules ignorantly. Boners provide "evidence of some failing in the intellectual grasp and achievement required within official or otherwise cultivated circles," Goffman writes. When a government official mispronounces a word outside his subject area, that's a boner. In 2002, then secretary of Health and Human Services, Tommy Thompson—not a health specialist—said, "We haven't had any attacks as of anybody receiving West Nile virus or encephalopoulus." A diplomat who addresses a prime minister as a president makes a boner, too.

A gaffe is a "breach in manners" that is "unintended and unknowing." In some circles, wearing white shoes after Labor Day is a gaffe; in others, a nongang member who wears gang colors as he walks down the wrong city street is making a gaffe that's potentially dangerous. Non-native speakers of a language like Spanish or French commit gaffes when they presume an intimacy that doesn't exist by using a familiar pronoun instead of a formal one such as, in Spanish, *tú* instead of *usted*.

The "knows better" errors represent a momentary, involuntary loss of control. The broadcast announcer who said, "We have a new Miss America, a lovely Georgia piece" committed a "knows better" error. The telecommunications expert who said "phoine" instead of "phone" made one, too, as does the baker who oversalts or the surgeon who undersews. Verbal blunders are the "knows better" errors, in the sense that they're accidents, inadvertent and unintentional, and outside of our control. To Goffman, slips and disfluencies are both "hitches in the smooth flow of syntactically connected words." That is, someone expects you to get something in order in time. When you don't, that's a blunder. One mark of the "knows better" fault is that the speaker knows, often immediately, when she's slipped. As a result, she corrects herself.

The naïveté or ignorance represented by the "doesn't know better" errors is easy to explain: someone didn't know the norm. On the other hand, the person who makes the "knows better" error does know the norm, yet couldn't prove or perform it. How many people have realized their shoes are on but their socks are still in their hands, or that they've put the child outside and poured a bowl of cereal for the dog? Competence doesn't always produce perfect performances—just ask Olympic athletes, who are highly practiced and coached athletes. Rather, you judge competence from other measures, such as repeated success. (On most mornings the dog goes outside and the child gets cereal.)

This doesn't answer the question of why perfectly competent, skilled, trained, intelligent people who can speak English, walk, open doors, play piano, or fly airplanes suddenly screw up. I'm fascinated by "knows better" errors of all types, because they're microinsurrections of our biochemical vassals. Against our control—and the pride of our control—our neurons rise up, invincible. We often treat our bodies and our selves as if they were nations under the control of a central government. From the perspective of the distant capital, the regions seem to be full of rebellion, all of it immune to surveillance, curfews, and punishment. But if you traveled to those areas, the tumult would seem less violent. You'd see that the uprisings don't threaten the entire nation but are more a response to local conditions. How should the capital respond? Not by becoming less tolerant of uprisings but putting into perspective their actual threat.

Curiously, "knows better" faults are often treated as "doesn't know better" ones. In the right circumstances, an honest slip of the tongue can appear to be (or made to be) a moral failing. This often happens in public life—indeed, it's an occupational hazard of living in the public eye. In 1865, before leaving to celebrate the retaking of Fort Sumter by the Union, the preacher and popular orator Henry Ward Beecher assured his listeners that the Union flag would fly over the fort "on Good Friday, on which occurred the resurrection of the Saviour"; the newspaper, *The World,* promptly criticized Beecher for the error.* Conversely, a person who makes a gaffe often tries to mitigate his or her stupidity by insisting after uttering the blunder that it was an inadvertent loss of control, an accident that anyone could have made. Tommy Thompson might claim that he of course knows the word "encephalitis"; it simply exited his mouth wrong. Claiming a Freudian slip can be convenient, too, because it blurs the line between the "knows better" and "doesn't know better" errors. If the Freudian slip represents the inten-

---

*The incident was mentioned by Richard Grant White, a popular American writer, in an 1875 article about slips, which he called "heterophemies." "A mental phenomenon so remarkable as the utterance by an intelligent being of just that which he does not mean to say, is surely worthy of careful inquiry as to its cause," he wrote.

tion of the unconscious self, it takes the conscious self, and what it could or could not know, off the hook.

What further complicates the way we manage our speech and live with verbal blunders is that we don't speak in a vacuum. Everything we say is part of a broader social context. Talking happens in a range of places, from the pulpit to the cereal aisle of the supermarket, and occurs within many contexts, from pillow talk to boardroom talk to baby talk. Different moods and settings shape what's said and how it's heard, determining the scope of our attention to verbal blunders as well as our tolerance for them. Some verbal blunders don't invariably register as errors: depending on who's talking, we might be willing to overlook them. The reverse also holds: many people correct their own speaking even when there's nothing audibly wrong. In Japanese culture, it's considered deferential to restart your sentences even if you know what you want to say.

Goffman noted that verbal blunders are as much sociological events as they are linguistic ones. Joseph Williams, an English professor at the University of Chicago, once illustrated this phenomenon for his fellow English teachers, who were always looking for the most productive (and efficient) way to respond to the errors that students make when they write. For his part, Williams wondered why some errors "excite this seeming fury while others, not obviously different in kind, seem to excite only moderate disapproval." Why, for instance, does mistaking "which" for "that" generate so much more attention from teachers, editors, and grammar mavens than "that" for "who"? Why does writing "should of," not "should have," get treated as a massive misfiring of grammatical pistons, when the error is simply a problem with spelling? In his essay "The Phenomenology of Error," Williams argued that errors don't exist only in texts, in writer's heads, or in the grammar books. They mainly exist in readers' experiences—hence the term "phenomenology," in reference to the subjectivity of error perception. Some readers "resonate" with language errors more than others.

He sweetened his point playfully. At the end of his essay, he revealed that he'd embedded about one hundred grammatical errors in the text. Many of them were the types of mistakes that student writers often make: split infinitives, misplaced apostrophes, dangling modifiers. As an experiment in expectations, he challenged readers to recall which errors they'd noted while reading without going back to search for the rest, and mail in the list to the editor of the journal. At one level, this was ivory tower fun and games. At another level, Williams had a serious point to make: the professor reading a student essay is cued to find errors. If she were reading the text in a professional journal, she would be less primed to notice errors.

Parents will recognize the parallax involved: when your kid trips, you're concerned. When the obnoxious neighbor kid trips, it's a hilarious pratfall. Goffman made the same observation: all grammatical faults may be something you hold a writer or speaker accountable for—a faultable. However, not all faultables are actual faults. That is, not everything that a teacher, editor, or transcriber directs a writer or speaker to change is, in fact, incorrect.* Moreover, quite often there are faults that never attract attention in the first place. Speakers them-

---

*There is also the degree of incorrectness: in writing, judgments about the serial comma ("apples, oranges, and plums" versus "apples, oranges and plums") will vary according to the stylistic domain, while the sentence "we gives up tobacco" will be judged grammatically incorrect whether one follows the *Chicago Manual of Style*, the Modern Language Association style guide, or the Associated Press style guide.

selves may want to fix something—which Goffman calls a "repairable"—that isn't necessarily technically wrong.

For a variety of reasons, we don't notice deviant speaking. But the converse can also be true: competent speaking isn't always beyond criticism. To put it another way, sometimes it's impossible to say something that won't be perceived as a problem. Take, for instance, the name of one of my favorite bands, Sigur Rós, which is from Iceland. I was first told that the bands' name was pronounced "Sigger Ross," which I said for years until someone gently pointed out that the Icelandic pronunciation sounds more like "Siyer Rouss" (rhymes with "gross"). No matter which version I choose to say, I always run the risk of being corrected. With "Siyer Rouss," someone can dislike the pretension of the "proper" Icelandic pronunciation. With "Sigger Ross," someone else might hate the American banalization. Or take the example of the young man asking the young woman to marry him. Should he ask smoothly and risk sounding rehearsed? Or should he stumble and blurt his question like the romantic fool that he really is, honest and passionate? As Goffman pointed out, a person can aim for the ideal delivery, but in some moments the best delivery is a blathering mess. As for me, I chose to propose as a blathering mess, and that's made all the difference.

# 4

## *What We, uh, Talk About When We Talk About "uh"*

Once people become aware of them, speech disfluencies come to represent weeds in the garden. Nails that hang us up. Bumps in the road. I like them because they're signs of the wild—like viruses and sexual attraction, they'll always slip out of our grasp, evading our thickest armor. But such wild things make a lot of people uncomfortable. Actors train to deliver lines clean of them. Teachers criticize students who utter them. At the Federal News Service, the transcribers complain about the powerful men and women who litter their speech with them. Rose Mary Woods, Richard Nixon's secretary, cleaned all the "uhs" and "ums" out of the transcripts of his taped conversations, along with the obscenities that littered the sentences. Likewise, the Presidential Recordings Program at the University of Virginia omits the "verbal debris" from transcriptions of presidential recordings. That is, unless the transcriber decides that a pause filler or repair "conveys any information about what the speaker was trying to say," as the introduction to the published edition of some of Lyndon Johnson's recordings puts it. Along with oral historians, an array of modern institutions—schools, the media, the legal system, religious institutions—work to stamp out verbal blunders.

Verbal blunders can also be seen (or heard) as yet another form of human behavior—not misbehavior. This view isn't incompatible with the purpose of producing clean transcripts, but people whose criticisms about deviant language have a moral charge don't accept the neutral view. Consider the facts, however: as a result of research over the last fifty years, we now know that anxious talkers have no monopoly on disfluencies, which pile up in people's unrehearsed speaking an average of two to twenty-six times every one hundred words. We know that longer utterances attract disfluencies. So do the beginnings of utterances, over their middles or ends. Men, young children, and older adults make them more often. So do people on the phone,* nonnative speakers of a language, and even people with their hands in their pockets. (Apparently gesturing reduces disfluency.) Speakers also say they feel more comfortable saying them around certain people: friends, family. In general, anyone who thinks or acts at the same time as they speak, especially under pressure, will blunder. Put a tape recorder in front of any of these folks, and you'll trap disfluencies like lint in a clothes dryer.

---

*In a study by Sharon Oviatt, two people talking on the telephone used the most disfluencies (8.83 per one hundred words), while a single person in a conversation with a computer used the fewest (1.74 per one hundred words), not just because the interlocutor was a machine but because the conversation was more restricted. She found that 60 to 70 percent of disfluencies could be eliminated if the human speaker's questions and responses were shorter and more structured.

Verbal blunders may be universal and profuse, but how people in a particular era conceive of speech, language, and communication also determines, in part, what faults are noticed, what faults acquire the status of "faultables," and what speakers are expected to do about them. Reverend Spooner had his name applied to a rare verbal blunder at a time when engineers and scientists were beginning to wrestle with how much of their thoughts and actions humans could control. And it's not a coincidence that Sigmund Freud's and Rudolf Meringer's study of speech errors tapped into an undercurrent of Vienna's fascination with social performances. In the same way, the conception of disfluencies as an aspect of normal communication arose after World War II out of an attempt to quantify human interactions so that they could be dissected, engineered, optimized.

The first scientist to count adult disfluencies was a Yale psychologist named George Mahl, who, in the 1950s, became interested in studying fear and anxiety in psychiatric patients. It was during the Cold War, and there was a climate of suspicion about undercover Communists and who might have been brainwashed by the enemy. One method for getting at a person's secret intentions or their cloaked meanings was a technique called "content analysis," which looked at patterns in word use to uncover what a person truly intended. The technique became integral to Cold War Kremlin watching, propaganda reading, and spy work and remains a key part of interrogations and analyses of evidence by law enforcement. For instance, if a new leader suddenly showed up in a foreign country that your country didn't have diplomatic relationships with, you might analyze the leader's speeches for clues about his priorities, his moral character, or his decision-making abilities. Though Mahl received money from the U.S. government, his research was confined to making psychiatry sessions more effective, as was that of his colleagues at Yale, who analyzed tape recordings of interviews to find out how their patients actually felt.

"Getting these tape recordings of therapy interviews was an eye opener for me," Mahl says. "We would have this material transcribed, and I noticed it being loaded with disfluencies." Because content analysis required clean, unbroken sentences, the hesitations, repetitions, pause fillers, and other fragments of speaking were scrubbed out of the transcripts. Though his work was little noted at the time, Mahl recognized the potential value of the real, verbatim transcripts and he determined to study how people actually talked. Their dross became Mahl's treasure.

When we met, George Mahl was an active, spry eighty-seven-year-old who had just finished a singing lesson when he picked me up at the New Haven train station. He lived in nearby North Haven, Connecticut, and intrepidly drove his station wagon several times a week to the Yale campus to work out at the gym and attend lectures. With his red suspenders, a white beard, and white hair, he looked like a cross between Burl Ives and Moses. During World War II, he worked as a psychologist in an army hospital where psychosomatic medicine, the notion that some physical ailments had psychological causes, was in fashion. Back at Yale after the war, Mahl wrote a dissertation about peptic ulcers caused by anxiety and in 1947 joined the Yale faculty and studied stomach-acid secretions in dogs and macaques. Some of his psychologist colleagues would record interviews with patients, have the interviews transcribed, and use the transcripts for analysis.

"I looked at the transcripts that we were getting, and I saw all this, quote, garbage," Mahl said. The analysts cleaned the transcripts so that counting words was easier, but Mahl was fascinated by what he came to call "speech disturbances"— everything that was cleaned out. "I thought—that's where the gem is," Mahl told me. "To study fear and anxiety, I'm not going to start counting sentences where the patient talks about being frightened or being anxious. I'm going to study the speech process itself, because I think speech disruption is a much better indicator of anxiety."

Content analysis didn't sit well with Mahl—he didn't like how it assumed a one-to-one relationship between a word and some intention. Simply because a patient says "fear" doesn't mean he's afraid, just as someone who doesn't say "fear" isn't afraid. To Mahl's way of thinking, some language use doesn't "mean" anything at all; in some situations any word could provoke the same response. If a piano were tumbling out of a window, a person could shout "Piano!" or "Look out!" or "Geronimo!" to get people's attention. This was what he called the "instrumental" aspect of language. Content analysis overlooked this aspect in lieu of counting words and noting their literal meanings. To Mahl, this wasn't sufficiently probing. Furthermore, in the case of anxiety—a negative emotion—a patient was unlikely to address it so directly that an analyst couldn't mistake it for something else. So rather than relying on a therapist's perceptions or the patient's own (often unreliable) self-reports, Mahl turned to speech disturbances as a reliable, unobtrusive, and objective way to check and measure the moment-to-moment fluctuations of a patient's emotional state.

For instance, when a Russian immigrant told the therapist about a pogrom he'd witnessed as a child:

"My uncle had his throat cut," the patient said. "And my

uncle . . . ah, he wasn't killed, but they tortured him. They took him and they slit his throat right . . . the skin . . . just cut the skin around like this."

"Who did that?" the therapist asked.

"Mmm . . . hulligan . . . holigan . . . huligans, whatever you call them."

"The who?"

"The . . . ah . . . you know the . . . ah . . . sss . . . he was in . . . the . . . he . . . was dri . . . traveling from one town to the oth . . . next and—"

"Mhm," the therapist said.

"He was stopped by a couple . . . ah . . . if you know the situation in the south . . ."

"Were . . . were they . . . were they Russians or were they Bolsheviks?"

"Yes. Yeah . . . mujik . . . mujiks . . . peasants."

Mahl related this scene in "Everyday Disturbances in Spontaneous Speech," an essay that explored how flustered speech (not only slips, as Freud would have it, but other hesitations and self-interruptions, too) might be therapeutically useful. A therapist measuring disturbances at the start of therapy and again at the end might have an objective measure of the therapy's success. More immediately, a therapist could note that when a patient spoke in a flustered way, it meant he or she had ventured too near a repressed emotion. That would be a clue to the therapist that a mother lode of therapeutically useful emotion lay nearby.

Once, Mahl asked a patient where he was going for vacation. "Oh, to B," the patient replied. "I have a friend. . . . well, I planned first to go to A," then rambled on about vacation choices. Then Mahl commented, "You said, 'I have a friend.' "

"Well," the patient said, "I was referring to L., a woman at Z. We bedded together and became close friends." By noting the sentence repair, Mahl had opened the patient to talking more about the woman, who turned out to be ten years older than the patient, and whom he called "prudish, stern, and remote." Mahl reported that this conversation led to a breakthrough when the young man realized that his attachment to his mother had shaped his attractions to other women. "Left unremarked," Mahl wrote, "the sentence completion would have enabled the patient to avoid this oedipal material."

Though it wasn't an original way of using verbal blundering, Mahl thought if he could collect enough of these flustered moments he could correlate them with other instrumental measures. Yet "flustered speech" was too crude a category to be useful for such a grand project. What's the difference between the nephew of the tortured uncle who said "uh . . . uh . . . uh" and the oedipal son who changed his mind about vacation spots? Were they anxious in different ways? Were they anxious at all?

Mahl realized that the patient's speech swarmed with interesting bits and pieces: the repetitions of words, the attempts to pronounce a word correctly, the pause fillers, the sentences that start in one place but head in another direction. So he developed a more detailed taxonomy of speech disturbances, which is still used today and is his most enduring contribution to the study of disfluencies. His list included the "ah" (for consistency I'll relabel these "uh" and "um," except in direct quotes from Mahl), the sentence change, the word repetition, the stutter (which was to be a repetition of a single sound or syllable), the omission of a word or part of a word, the incomplete sentence, the slip of the tongue, and the "incoherent intruding sound" (one such sound made by the patient with the uncle was "sss").

With financial support from the U.S. Public Health Service, Mahl recorded interactions between psychiatrists and patients on twelve-inch tape reels and set up a room where trained secretaries turned the recorded speech into text. Later Mahl coded the transcripts, counting all the disfluencies and marking them up with a red pencil. His plan: correlate speech disturbances with stomach acid levels due to anxiety, then develop a diagnostic tool for dealing with stress.

Long before he concluded his research, however, something interesting happened. The patients, the interviewers, the research assistants, the secretaries, and even Mahl himself were shocked that perfect prose didn't come out of their mouths when they spoke. Some became angry or ashamed. Others disavowed their own speaking or questioned the secretaries' accuracy. It was as if Mahl had revealed them to be dirty or ill—indeed, much of speech education in the early twentieth century had taught the need for "verbal hygiene." People not only hadn't been aware of how they spoke; they believed that they spoke in prose, all of their sentences starting with a capital letter, finishing with a punctuation mark, and flowing unceasingly between letter and punctuation like a river to the sea. That, Mahl had to tell them, was a fantasy, a dream.

Mahl became so absorbed by the realities of speech as people interacted with one another that, in 1952, he began recording a radio talk show hosted by Tex McCrary and his wife, a former bathing beauty, Jinx Falkenburg. Tex and Jinx would interview celebrities live from the Waldorf-Astoria, which gave Mahl access to the most interesting blunderers of all: the celebrity blunderers.

One time Jinx asked Edward R. Murrow, the radio broadcaster, what six people he would invite to dinner.

"One . . . one would certainly be Sir Winston Churchill. A

second would be H. G. Wells. A third one would be Heinrich Heine. The fourth one, Marcus Aurelius. The fifth, Mr. Lincoln. And the sixth, now it gets really difficult, Jinx . . . ah . . . the sixth, I think, would be Beethoven," Murrow said.

"Murrow had been talking along very fluently," Mahl remembered, "and then Jinx said, 'They're all men,' and his speech fell apart."

"You know something? You selected all men," Jinx told Murrow.

"I wonder why that was," Murrow said. "I haven't a clue. I don't know why. I—"

"No woman in history, or currently, would interest you?"

"No, no. Th . . . this . . . ah . . . ah . . . you trapped me somehow. I don't know how you did it, but . . . ah . . . ah . . . this—"

Murrow worried about what "some psychiatrist" would make of his confusion. Mahl believes that Murrow must have been afraid that he'd tipped people off to his male chauvinism or even some latent homosexuality. "I'm embarrassed," Murrow admitted. Then he regained what Mahl called his "characteristic fluent speech."

With his recordings and a room full of transcribing secretaries, Mahl was the first to discover that people say "uh" more frequently when they're talking to an interviewer on a telephone than when they're face-to-face. It's not because of any inherent property of the technology. Rather, the speaker's disfluency is an ingredient of the face-to-face interactions.

Mahl also recognized very early in his research that disfluent individuals fall into one of two groups: they either change their sentences, or they say "uh" and "um" and repeat words.

Intuitively, you can see what personality types correspond with these two patterns. Sentence changers are the people who burst ahead, confident, speaking in a fluid stream of words. If they don't like the way the sentence is going, no problem—they rethink it and start over as fluidly. Even if there's nothing wrong, they often rush to double back and dive into rephrasing as easily as they first phrased it.

Then there are people who say "uh" and "um." These are the planners, the crafters, the forestallers. Mahl called them "ah-ers." He told me that he had once studied his own speech patterns, thinking himself a frequent uh-er and repeater. To his surprise, he found that he's a sentence changer. (After listening to the tape of our conversation, I concur—Mahl, mostly umless, spoke in rolling, ongoing sentences that he would restart now and then but invariably managed to keep comprehensible.)

Because he had also asked his patients to fill out standard personality questionnaires, Mahl could sort the traits of the uh-ers and sentence changers. Uh-ers reported being "unusually self-conscious" and "worry quite a bit over possible misfortunes." They rated themselves as distractable and careful, and reported that they'd been weaned early. They tended to come from strict families, with a preponderance of strict fathers. Meanwhile, sentence-changers considered themselves shy public speakers and easily embarrassed. Individuals from this group also agreed with the statement that "It is not always a good thing to be frank," and thought that it was easy for others to see what was going on with their emotions.

Subsequent to Mahl, researchers have confirmed in more sophisticated ways that the verbal blundering clusters in several types, almost as if there are species of talkers. When Liz Shriberg (the speech researcher who gave the robot Flakey his "uh") was working on her dissertation at Berkeley in the 1990s, she plotted how many of each type of disfluency each of her subjects made. At first she couldn't make sense of the resulting graph, whose random-seeming data points only seemed to confirm that individuals varied widely in the ways they showed their delays. Both groups were equally disfluent overall and spoke sentences of the same length.

But when she inspected her data, two distinct groups emerged. Those in one group tended to say "uh" and "um" and also repeat words but didn't restart their sentences or accidentally choose the wrong word. She called them "repeaters." Members of the second group were exactly the opposite: they tended to substitute the wrong words and restart their sentences, but they didn't fill pauses or repeat words quite as frequently. Shriberg called them "deleters." Deleters differed from repeaters in one other regard: they spoke more words per second and, as a result, were more disfluent per unit of time.

This dichotomy is useful, especially if one were, like Shriberg, designing automatic speech recognition software. It's not enough to lump all speakers together, averaging their disfluencies. We might want the systems to "profile" a speaker as one or the other. Beyond this immediate application, the dichotomy might point to cognitive qualities we might someday be able to make sense of and measure. When Shriberg noticed that the deleters repaired and restarted their sentences more often, she mused about their cognitive profiles—how the spikes in certain blunders and the absence of others might disclose something about deleters' cognitive traits and how they went about solving problems. To justify an approach in which blundering style may indicate cognitive traits, she noted that timing, planning, and executing occur in many other activities. If you were to ask someone to draw a picture, for example, some will stop to scratch their heads and gaze out the window. Others will dive in, begin drawing, and quickly exhaust the erasers on their pencils.

This difference may reflect variations of cognitive style—in how a person solves problems, how she accepts new information, and how she monitors her own behavior. If you speak quickly and repair more often, there's something about you that causes you to monitor less while you're speaking. This allows you to sound stylistically as if you're moving ahead even though you're actually moving backward. If you're speaking more slowly, you could be monitoring yourself more. Does that reflect some underlying personality trait, say, of being a more responsible person?

Such inferences are intriguing, but beyond a plethora of anecdotes, psychologists so far have little solid evidence that such variation in blundering points to personal traits. In the only comprehensive study to date, college students were tape-recorded at random intervals for three days with computer-controlled microcassette recorders they wore on their belts. The researchers, at the University of Texas at Austin, James Pennebaker and Matthias Mehl, counted students' word choices, mostly nouns, adjectives, negative words, personal pronouns, and other content items. They also transcribed "uhs" and "ums," swear words, and filler words (such as "like"). Before the taping, the students took a personality test that measures what psychologists call the "big five" personality traits: extraversion (how much stimulus from people and situations a person can handle), agreeableness (to what degree a person defers to others), conscientiousness (how organized and careful a person is), openness (how open a person is to new experiences and ideas), and emotional stability (how a person responds to stress). They also took tests to measure their levels of depression and self-esteem.

Of the disfluencies, Pennebaker and Mehl counted only "uhs" and "ums." Hence, the only correlations they calculated were between personality variables and those pause fillers, the most common disfluencies. Contrary to the stereotypical expectations, the students who rated themselves depressed or introverted didn't say "uh" or "um" more frequently. And when snippets of their recordings were played to independent judges, the speakers who said "uh" and "um" more often weren't rated more depressed, either. Otherwise, there were no meaningful correlations between the frequency of "uh" and "um" and personality traits. Whether they were extroverts, introverts, neurotics, nice kids, open kids, or responsible kids, their personality traits didn't correlate with more (or less) use of "uh" and "um" at all. Only in one dimension did anything significant turn up: people who said "uh" and "um" were rated as more conscientious by the judges, as were those who used fillers like "well" and "so."

Pennebaker and Mehl did, however, find evidence that supports an observation that George Mahl also made: that each person consistently blunders in a way that's unique to him or her. Over the course of the three days, the recordings showed that each student tended to say the same number of "uhs" and "ums." If their pause fillers were counted at Time 1 and then again four weeks later, the students would be blundering at roughly the same rate. There were only two other features of their speech that were more stable than this: their swearing and their use of filler words ("well," "like," "so"). In casual listening we can often hear speakers' distinctive speech patterns when their disfluencies become excessive—the novelist who repeats every word at the beginning of each phrase ("the the the the book has been received well and and and and it generated a lot of discussion . . .") or the computer scientist who begins each sentence with a long string of "uhs" ("uh uh uh uh uh I'm always entertained by the dogs in the park").

The scientific work that would link disfluency patterns with personality traits hasn't yet been done—it would require experiments that can measure reaction times in milliseconds, not a crude instrument like a personality questionnaire. Until then, the question of some link remains wide open.

Perhaps George Mahl's most interesting finding in those early days of disfluency research was that anxious people don't say "uh" or "um" more. That is, a person's use of pause fillers didn't correlate with his or her level of anxiety. At first he was disappointed—he had hoped to measure anxiety with pause fillers. Then he made another finding: if he counted all eight of his speech disturbance types, subtracted the "uhs" and "ums" from the total, then calculated this number relative to the total words a person had spoken, the ratio was highly correlated with anxious moments. In other words, "uh" and "um" didn't correlate with anxiety, but all the *other* disfluencies did.

This has been Mahl's most enduring finding. It isn't widely known, though, and flies against the conventional wisdom. If you ask a typical person why speakers say "uh," he or she will probably reply that it's because they're anxious. Not so, said Mahl. To measure anxiety accurately, listen to all of their other verbal blunders.

Heather Bortfeld, a psychologist at Texas A&M University,

and her colleagues have confirmed this finding. In a study published in 2001, they analyzed the conversations between pairs of people and drew a stunning picture of all the factors that influence a person's disfluency. Each pair was assigned the task of arranging a set of picture cards, with one person directing the other person to do the actual arranging. The pairs were mixed by gender, age, and familiarity—that is, there were males partnered with males, females with females, and females with males; some of the pairs were strangers, while others were married, and some were age peers while others were young-old pairs.

Bortfeld found that the oldest people in the group, the seventy-year-olds, spoke more disfluently than the people in their twenties. This wasn't surprising—it's long been known that older adults are more disfluent than younger adults. Bortfeld also found that men said "uh" and "um" much more than women did, making them more disfluent than women overall. Men also restarted more sentences and repeated more words. Surprisingly, the married couples blundered as much as the strangers. If you've cherished the notion that you blunder more with people you don't know, you'll have to give that up.

So what determines how much someone blunders? In the study Bortfeld found that the more active member of the pair, the person directing the other person, made the most blunders. Presumably this was because they were trying to manage thinking and speaking simultaneously. Both men and women in the director's role were more disfluent than their partners. She found, too, that their disfluencies (the pause fillers, silent pauses, repetitions, and repairs) were more frequent at the beginning of the sentences. This is where the brain is between planning and executing. Thus, people are more disfluent when there's an additional cognitive load, such as a distraction, an additional task, or an emotional response. The anxious state of an uh-er may be the local, most visible reason for his hesitation. The deeper reason is a cognitive one.

In Bortfeld's study, this heavier cognitive load came not only from the social roles but from some aspects of the tasks themselves. Each pair of speakers had two sets of cards to arrange, one showing abstract shapes and one with children's faces. Each director spoke more disfluently when arranging cards with abstract shapes than the ones with faces. Bortfeld concluded that the more serious problems with talking and acting at the same time are indicated by word repeats and sentence restarts. As Mahl had also found, "uh" and "um" aren't reliable symptoms of a brain under stress.

Bortfeld says she first noticed disfluencies as a junior in college when she was living in Madrid, where people said "eh," not "uh." She realized she was going to have to learn how to fill her pauses like the natives did in order to be treated as a native speaker. (In fact, children must learn how to use pause fillers as adults do—it doesn't come naturally.) There is a right way and a wrong way to be disfluent, and the right way seemed to be a matter of linguistic ease as well as convention. "Uh" is one of the easiest sounds to make in English, so it makes sense that the Spanish equivalent, "eh," would be the sound of the neutral vowel in that language as well, the one that can be pronounced with a relaxed tongue and jaw. The pause fillers of many languages sound so similar because the relaxed tongues and jaws that make them are also similar. Yet each language trains its speakers in a slightly different set of vowels, making for slight phonetic differences among its pause fillers, too.

During and immediately after World War II, scientists and engineers embarked on ambitious plans in information design, communication systems, and artificial intelligence. One goal was to calculate, control, and mobilize the nation's resources to wage modern war. During the Cold War, a massive war with the Soviet Union seemed imminent. The mobilizations of World War II had also created an optimistic, even utopian sense that societies could be quickly improved and modernized via scientific methods. On the civilian side of things, researchers tried to reduce the unpredictable clutter of human activity to formulas. By quantifying the human world, they figured they could predict it. By teasing out the rules that govern human behavior, they could engineer better schools, prisons, and cities.

Mahl's work was part of this wave of interest in communication and information theory that sought more advanced "command and control" technologies. Take, for instance, the problem of how to hit a moving airplane with an anti-aircraft gun, which involved calculating not only the arc of the shell, the firing speed of the gun, and the speed and direction of the plane but the ways that smaller, faster fighter planes and bombers might zigzag to avoid getting hit. To solve the problem, Norbert Wiener of MIT developed sophisticated algorithms that relied on real-time data from radar (itself a new technology) to tweak a set of tracking orders and compensate for the zigzag.* As the scope of research into the dynamics of communication broadened from an individual's speaking in isolation to the inter-

---

*Norbert Wiener, whose life is discussed in a recent biography, *Dark Hero of the Information Age,* pioneered this method.

action between individuals, the focus also shifted from the self to the transmission of information signals. Disfluencies were treated as noise in signals that disrupted communication.

Social engineering put language under the microscope as well, and scientists began to observe a range of communicative behaviors in humans and animals. Some tried to figure out the universal algorithms that underlie all languages, in order to build computers that could translate from one language to another. Others tried to teach human language to primates or investigated the communication of dolphins.

Frieda Goldman-Eisler was a psychiatrist who pioneered the study of pauses and hesitating in speaking—later dubbed "pausology." A former student of Freud's from Austria, she arrived in London in 1940 and worked menial jobs at Maudsley Hospital, a prominent psychiatric hospital in Camberwell, England, until she was eventually appointed as a therapist there. A year later she met and married Paul Eisler, an Austrian engineer who was trying to find a market for the electronic circuit board he'd invented. She published widely and was eventually appointed to the faculty of University College, London.

One of Goldman-Eisler's strengths was her curiosity and willingness to try new ideas. (One of her graduate students, Brian Butterworth, now a neuropsychologist at University College, said she tried to instill the same values in him when they ate lunch at the Indian restaurant around the corner: she always ordered curries for Butterworth, expecting him to try hotter and hotter concoctions.) In the 1940s, she discovered the work of Eliot Chapple, a Harvard anthropologist who was timing human behavior to explore the basic temporal principles of human interactions, such as how long two individuals talked to each other, how much time they spent saying certain things, and how much time they were silent. He'd invented a device called the "chappleograph," a typewriter through which a paper tape moved at a constant rate; the observer pressed certain keys when events started and ended, then went back and calculated the time interval from the marks. By measuring gestures, head nods, and body postures as well as speaking, he was able to capture the texture of interaction more closely, especially its use of silences.

Goldman-Eisler first used the chappleograph to measure breathing behavior, especially among psychiatric patients, the population she knew best. This led her to look at their pauses in speaking, which were related to their thinking. What were they thinking, anyway? How could anyone ever figure that out? In her formulation, speaking was a peripheral activity related to a central activity: thought. "If activity in conversation, if vocal action, is a peripheral phenomenon," she wondered, "might not absence of activity indicate the presence of central activity?"

In other words, pauses in speech pointed to thinking—not, as had been previously thought, a lack of thinking, a gap between two thoughts, some psychic tension, or embarrassment. The pauses were parts of the cycles of thinking and speaking that involved sequences of planning what to say, then actually saying them. Goldman-Eisler discovered these cycles when she asked subjects to describe some pictures. On the first attempt, half of what her subjects said came out in phrases less than three words long. Longer phrases were fairly rare: those with ten or more words occurred only 10 percent of the time. Perhaps, she thought, this would change if the speakers had more practice. Indeed, subjects who rehearsed used fewer short phrases and fewer medium-length phrases. Yet they increased their long phrases (those with ten words or more) a mere 5 percent. Even with practice, speech remained stubbornly fragmented—two-thirds of speaking, Goldman-Eisler concluded, came in chunks of less than six words apiece.*

We commonly think that some people speak faster than others, but Goldman-Eisler found that someone who sounds like a fast speaker simply uses shorter pauses. Speed has more to do with the amount of time left between sounds than how quickly the sounds are spoken, which is a fairly constant ten to twelve sounds per second.

She also found that speakers paused strategically, at moments in sentences that presented them with more choices. The more predictable the next word or phrase was, the less likely a speaker was to pause. The notion that the length of a pause, whether it was silent or filled, equaled the length of the mental delay itself became the basis for observations of many types of talkers. In the 1990s, Stanley Schachter, a psychologist at Columbia University, looked at how professors spoke in lectures. He wanted to investigate the notion that speakers are disfluent when they're deciding, choosing, or selecting the next increment of language they're going to say. Since academic knowledge varies across fields, and since professors communicate that knowledge with language, their speaking should be different. One particularly common form of speaking is lecturing, which was also easy for Schachter to study.

Indeed, in their lectures humanities professors said "you know" and "uh" more frequently than social science professors—4.85 "uhs" per minute to the social scientist's 3.84. Before the social scientists erupt in huzzahs, however,

---

*Swedish researcher Robert Eklund has observed that about half of ten-word utterances are fluent, but fluent twenty-word utterances are very rare.

they should know that they blundered more than the hard scientists, 3.84 per minute to 1.39. On the whole, humanists said "uh" at a higher rate than the others.*

Humanists also said "uh" more frequently, at 4.76 per one hundred words, and they said it more frequently than the social scientists (2.67 per hundred words), who outstripped the hard scientists (1.47 per hundred words).

Why was this the case? What might these patterns say about the people who choose different fields? Schachter interviewed the professors in their offices, where they all blundered at rates similar to each other; only in lectures did their blundering profiles diverge. Schachter surmised that it was the content of their lectures and ultimately the shape of knowledge in the professors' respective disciplines that led them to blunder as they did, not who they were as individuals.

Thus, it was no surprise that the humanists blundered more: their field gave them more thoughts and ideas to express, and they hesitated and paused more often because they had more options for self-expression. Their hesitations didn't reflect their level of certainty; it reflected their creativity. By contrast, what the scientists had to say seemed to be more cut and dried. It wouldn't be the first time that passionate disfluency would be romanticized, or science stereotyped as cold and uncreative. To be fair to both sets of speakers, Schachter doesn't rule out the

---

*This can be confirmed by a quick visit to the Michigan Corpus of Academic Spoken English, which archives transcripts of various spoken performances. When I visited, "uh" turned up 1,317 times and "um" 1,308 times in humanities and arts lectures, but only 423 and 331 times (respectively) in biology lectures and 292 and 65 times in engineering and physical science lectures. The number of lectures in each field was about the same. The corpus is online at http://micase.umdl.umich.edu/m/micase/.

possibility that professors deliberately train in the acceptable level of disfluency in their field—in other words, whether or not the humanities are more creative, it's important that practitioners act (and sound) as if they are. As odd as it sounds, community norms shaped the blundering.

Goldman-Eisler's idea that delay often indicates active decision making found a darker expression in the work of Basil Bernstein, a British sociologist, who applied it to a problem in educational reform in the 1960s. It was a time when educators in the United States and the United Kingdom were attempting to predict how a child's language performance could predict his or her success in school. In the United States, psychologists focused on the supposedly "impoverished" language of African American children, while in the United Kingdom, they looked at class differences.

To Bernstein, longer pauses seemed to be a sign of greater language resources. After all, one paused to think, and part of thinking involved planning what to say based on one's stash of words. He hypothesized that working-class students would pause less than middle-class students. His findings confirmed this notion. Even among the middle-class boys, the ones with the higher IQ paused longer. Because they had more complex sentence structures and larger vocabularies at their mental fingertips, Bernstein supposed that the boys had to pause to riffle through their verbal riches. By contrast, the working-class boys had an empty cupboard, so they could speak more quickly. Here was the language deficit that endangered their educations, Bernstein concluded. If we fill their verbal larders, they'll be more successful in school.

This conclusion set off a firestorm that's never really sub-sided. Though he was well-meaning, Bernstein had overlooked a crucial point that had also escaped Goldman-Eisler: the rates of speech, hesitations, and length of pauses may have depended as much on the norms of the boys' communities as on their own mental processes. What Bernstein counted had more to do with environment than with intelligence, vocabulary, or cognitive style. His conclusions pointed out the pitfalls of doing class-based research that comes with hidden assumptions about class.

Bernstein's research also showed, albeit inadvertently, how one group's norms for speaking aren't always greeted happily by another group. In America, we encounter regional dialects all the time, as well as ethnic or racial forms of speaking. We readily link accents with cultural identity. And while we hold stereotypes about aspects of speech style—for instance, North-erners speak quickly; Southerners speak more slowly—we tend not to think that other stylistic characteristics, such as pausing, may be shaped in communities, too.*

In the United States, we often admire people for their brilliance when they're merely glib and smooth. Yet if we're interested in other qualities, such as honesty, authenticity, and charisma, then glib, uninterrupted speaking may not be what we want to hear. In fact, we might want to begin to mistrust per-

---

*In 1931, the linguist Edward Sapir, who was also interested in the link between language style and personality, warned against inferring that a man with a "strained or raucous voice" is "coarse-grained," because he might come from a place where people shout a lot.

fect fluency. In the 1960s, Walter Weintraub, a psychiatrist at the University of Maryland School of Medicine, developed a method for analyzing the personality traits of political leaders through their speech styles. After listening to millions of words by public figures, Weintraub concluded that true fluency is a chimera. "While several sentences of spontaneous and fluent ad-libbing are possible, lengthy impromptu remarks free of qualifications and hesitation are extremely rare," he wrote.*

Yet the notion that speaking is usually—and should properly be—hitch free remains deeply ingrained in ideas about language. For instance, the communications research literature is filled with studies confirming that research subjects perceive disfluent subjects negatively. Their messages are corroded, their character impugned. However, these subjects are almost always college students in large speech courses, where their attitudes about disfluencies may already have been altered. Such research isn't well equipped to understand what happens on the speaker's side of things. As a result, the research serves only to confirm the existence of a stereotype, not uncover anything remarkable about human communication.

These types of studies cannot account for the large number of disfluencies in spontaneous talking or conversation, which are permeated with halts, interruptions, backtracks, repetitions, and grammatical tangents. In 1994, the Scottish speech researcher Robin Lickley found a disfluent phenomenon every 9.4 words, if "well" and "sort of" were not counted.

---

*Goldman-Eisler noted the fluid imagery at play in the notion of fluency: "Many words relating to speech derive from descriptions of water in motion, such as 'gush, spout, stream, torrent of speech, floodgates of speech,' etc." She added that "the facts, however, show these images to be illusory."

Every 36.8 words, the speaker repeated a word, mostly a word like "the," "that," "was," "of," or other function words. Every 44 words, there was an attempt to fix a word or a sentence that the speaker had already embarked on. Pause fillers occurred once every 33 words. Most of these, about 74 percent, were "um." Many fewer, or 24 percent, were "uh."

A bigger problem for the idea that disfluencies limit, block, or negate communication is a group of experiments showing the opposite. Repeated words don't impede word recognition, and "uh" can actually speed recognition (for some reason, "um" provides no such benefit). Disfluencies can also help listeners determine what new information is contained in a sentence and can also help them parse ambiguous sentences. Such advantages are measured in milliseconds—but so are any actual disadvantages.

The idea that speaking is smooth and unbroken results, in part, from the fact that we don't hear the fragments. They simply don't register. "Speech may be peppered with the various disturbances," Mahl wrote, "but most of them escape the awareness of both speaker and listener. Only when they occur at relatively rapid rates and are 'bunched' does the listener perceive them, sensing an episode of 'flustered' speech." For instance, normal speakers usually repeat sounds at the beginnings of words, not in the middle of them, which can be a sign of chronic stuttering. Making more than ten disfluencies per one hundred words (not counting editing words like "well" and "like") may be a sign of organic disorder like aphasia or dementia.

This presents additional questions: Why are we such inattentive listeners? And should we worried about it? One reason for this is that humans are evolved to be that way; it's only slightly an exaggeration to say that we do it for the sake of survival. In order to hear what someone says, we filter out noise all the time: party chatter, the traffic, the rumble of the train, regional accents, and even "uh" and "um" (which tend to be said at a lower pitch anyway, so they're more easily tuned out). We filter them out so unconsciously that even scientists who study verbal blunders admit that they don't always hear completely. Robin Lickley says that he's often had the experience of pulling out a fluent snippet of conversation from tapes only to find a disfluency in it. "I've realized there's something in there I didn't notice before—this disfluency just appears."

On the other hand, the experts also admit that after they've learned to tune in to disfluencies, it requires a deliberate effort to ignore them. Dan O'Connell, a retired psycholinguist, spent more than thirty years studying pause and hesitations in people's speaking. As a result, "when I'm speaking with people in a cocktail situation or an academic situation," he told me, "I make it a very deliberate decision, I do not listen for these things. I think that's profoundly impolite. I simply refuse to do it. If something comes up that you can't ignore, then we joke about it and talk about it." When it comes time to be a scientist, he looks at his watch, often in lectures. "I sit there with my sweep on my watch and count per minute. If that person begins to say something intelligent, I shift into my other mode of listening. That's the way I do that. Just for fun. It's really a matter of mental hygiene."

The truth is, our language systems don't have to work perfectly; they simply have to be good enough. Part of the way we deal with the complexity of language is to make guesses— ever so brief, and with low stakes—about what's coming next. Such predictions can be a weakness: what happens when a listener predicts incorrectly? Or when he or she needs time to recover from an infelicitous prediction? For the most part, predictions are a strength; they keep us from getting overly hung up on noise and other errors in the signal. They also allow us to patch any gaps. This is how some disfluencies aid predictions, in the way that an "um" in the right place signals to the listener that he or she should pay more attention. Far from hindering communication, some disfluencies lubricate it. Their function has little to do with how we feel about them.

Social considerations also filter our listening: our ears perk for everything a president says, but we pay less attention to what the ordinary working person says. Erving Goffman argued that listeners notice verbal blunders according to the social role that the speakers are expected to play. When the blunder indicates a deviation from the assigned social role, listeners are more likely to notice them. Formal speaking situations are one such situation. (So are experimental situations.) Differences in social status trigger more attention, as well. The blunders aren't themselves inherently funny; when the janitor says "this venereal institution," you probably won't laugh quite as hard as when the governor says it (as Ohio governor James A. Rhodes did in 1964). When ordinary people are on television, the audience has the same high expectations for their speaking. "And are you enjoying your honeymoon?" the announcer asks the newlywed. "I'm enjoying every inch of it!" the young woman exclaims, and the laughter from the audience breaks slowly, then engulfs her, as she puts her finger to her forehead, her eyes ablaze. In general, Goffman says, audiences are "on the prowl for faultables"—and what puts them on the prowl is an important but unanswered question.

. . .

The converse issue is just as interesting: Why do we seem to be such lackadaisical, inattentive speakers? Why do we let such things slip past our lips? We do, in fact, monitor our speaking, and we often fix it, too. As a result, the failure to be fluent isn't a failure of knowing how to speak. After all, Rudolf Meringer found that 75 percent of sound slips and 53 percent of word slips were caught by speakers. And as the conversational analysis pioneer Harvey Sacks and his colleagues noted, "Even casual inspection of talk interaction finds self-correction vastly more common than other-correction." (We correct ourselves more than we correct one another.) It's not at all uncommon to hear someone say, "Sure enough ten minutes later the bell r— the doorbell rang."

In the parlance of speech science, the fixing is called a "repair." Willem Levelt provided a basic anatomy of the repair's three parts: there's the original sentence (1), interrupted by some moment of editing (2), then the repair itself (3). From adult speakers who were describing visual patterns, Levelt gathered examples like these:

| go from left again to | uh | pink again to blue |
|---|---|---|
| 1 | 2 | 3 |

Levelt marked several crucial moments in the sentence with numbers. It's easy to find examples in verbatim transcripts of prominent media figures we listen to all the time. Take this excerpt from a 2006 interview with Garrison Keillor and Robert Altman, when Altman's movie *A Prairie Home Companion* had been released. The interviewer asked how Altman as a director had treated Keillor, who replied:

No. I was alarmed at how—at how indulgent he—he is
as—as a director. He's very, very precise about—about
camera movement and—and he knows exactly where—
where he's going at all times. But as far as, you know, the
facial expressions, you know, of an actor and—and how
you do something.

The verbatim transcript makes Keillor seem disfluent,
though anyone who's heard him on the radio knows that his
stumble has some charm. Keillor repeats himself and pauses,
but until "of an actor and," he hasn't repaired. Until that point
he's doubtlessly been monitoring his speech. But at "of an actor
and" he decides that he needs to repair. This is something we
learn how to do when we are as young as two or three years old.
The older we get, the more we repair, and the more complex the
repairs become. Levelt found other reasons that people
repaired. Sometimes it was because the information was incorrect; sometimes the speaker was trying to avoid social awkward-
ness.

Of the many reasons for repairs, the greatest number occur
because a speaker anticipates that he or she is about to make an
error, say something ungrammatical, or perhaps make a slip of
the tongue. A slightly less common reason is that the speaker
realizes that the information needs to be less ambiguous.
Finally, people interrupt themselves and start again because
they want to present something in a different order. We can't be
certain that Keillor was about to make a speech error—more
likely he was trying to keep his answer short, to make it fit into
the conversation.

In conversation and other types of spontaneous talking, people tend to stop speaking as soon as they've detected a mis-

pronunciation, a slip of the tongue, something inappropriate, or any deviation from what they planned to say. Consider this exchange between Larry King and Charlie Rose (on Rose's show) about Ted Turner and Jane Fonda:

LARRY KING: Yeah. Ted would—Ted was—anybody who knows Ted would have to say they miss him. You have to miss him.
CHARLIE ROSE: What happened to him and Jane?
LARRY KING: You know, they're the best of friends.
CHARLIE ROSE: Yeah.

In King's first sentence, he starts and stops the sentence twice because he's obviously having a difficult time selecting the most appropriate thing to say about Turner. Now, speakers usually finish the word that they're saying ("Ted would—Ted was"), unless the word itself wasn't intended. This happens so regularly that Levelt called it the "Main Interruption Rule." It indicates that a speaker will "stop the flow of speech immediately upon detecting trouble." This is what led Oprah Winfrey to say on her show, to one of the young men who had turned his father in for bank robbery, "I can see that, you know, I mean, obviously, all of you are up—upset about it, and you are still very much emotionally impacted by it." (Levelt might note that Oprah didn't need to interrupt "upset" if it was the word she wanted.)

Levelt also found another pattern in repairs. It seems that speakers are more likely to detect trouble or make a change when it occurs toward the end of a phrase, clause, or other chunk of language. In "go left again to uh pink to blue," the interruption occurs at the end of a chunk. Likewise, when Rush

Limbaugh said of Democrats, "Some of them tried to couch it in—in, oh, disguised ways, but you strip all that away and they were clearly trying to make the case." Here the repair occurs toward the end of the clause.

In Levelt's example,

| go from left again to | uh | pink again to blue |
|---|---|---|
| 1 | 2 | 3 |

he calls moment 2 the "editing term." This appeared in Tiger Woods's response to a question about the origin of his personal discipline. He replied, "I get that—you know, people think I get that from my dad." In Levelt's parlance "uh" and "um" are editing terms. "You know," "sort of," "rather," "well," "I mean," and "kind of" are, too. According to Levelt, these editing terms have several uses—after all, why not simply remain silent? A speaker may not want to be interrupted, so he prefers to keep a pause filled with sound. He may also use the editing term as an opportunity to make his meaning more clear, or to comment on the mistake itself. In Levelt's sample of adult Dutch speakers, 42 percent of repairs had no editing term. When people repaired to make a message more appropriate, rather than to make the language more specific, they used "uhs," "ums," and other editing terms only 28 percent of the time. On the other hand, if a speaker repaired in order to correct a statement, 62 percent of the repairs used an editing term.

In Levelt's data, "uh" was the most frequent editing term, used in 30 percent of all repairs. The earlier that a speaker detected a problem, the more likely he or she was to use "uh." Though the theories about the meanings of "uh" and "um" vary widely, Levelt is content to say that the pause filler basically means "I've temporarily forgotten X." Searching for "uh" and "um" among transcripts on LexisNexis turns up very few of them—not surprisingly, given that transcription services like the Federal News Service routinely clean them up. However, there are a few that sneak in, such as this sentence from a Chinese expert speaking on National Public Radio: "And now people have their own, uh, some of them have their own independent income."

In Levelt's sentence, the last moment in the anatomy of the repair is marked "3":

| go from left again to | uh | pink again to blue |
|---|---|---|
| 1 | 2 | 3 |

It is the repair proper, where the speaker picks up the sentence again.

Interestingly, seeing actual examples of repairs allows one to see how strong the urge is to create grammatical sentences. Take this snippet of an interview with Diane Sawyer, in which she described the play *Angels in America:* "It is. It is. It's a great play. And as we know, it really—it rocked Broadway. It really brought people into the theater who had never come before." Even though the sentence looks disrupted by her repair, "it really—it rocked," it follows another pattern in repairs: the words after the interruption have to give closure to the most important chunk of language before the interruption. Sawyer didn't say, "It really—rocked Broadway." Rather, to create this continuity, she backtracked to the beginning of the clause and repeated the entire thing. This drive to completion is what creates many instances of repetitions, whether of words or phrases.

Unfortunately, the self-monitoring mechanism of the average

person as well as the professional talker doesn't block all the instances of disfluency or errors. It can't. As Levelt puts it so colorfully, "The meshes of a speaker's trouble net are too wide to catch all the queer fish in his own speech." Depending on where in the utterance the problem is perceived, what the social situation is, what type of problem it is (a sound versus a word, for example), or whether it will be disruptive for the listener, a speaker's monitor or self-editing mechanism catches things— more or less. About half of the errors in the speech samples that Levelt studied weren't, in fact, caught or corrected at all. That's not to say the speaker didn't hear them; perhaps they just neglected to stop. Other speakers were inordinately fond of stopping. In about a quarter of all the repairs that Levelt studied, he couldn't discern any reasons why the speaker interrupted him- or herself—some speakers are so quick to fix (or are self-monitoring so sensitively) that no queer fish are ever heard.

Fifty years of research into speech disfluencies and the normal aspects of spontaneous human speaking have demonstrated that many of our norms for "good speaking" do not parallel the biological imperatives of language itself. Those standard-bearers who insist that speaking should be faultless and interruption free can't account for the fact that we don't perceive most verbal blunders, and they can't explain the sheer numbers of faults, except to attribute carelessness, ignorance, lack of preparation, or some other deficit to speakers. Not only do the prescriptive tastes of society diverge from the biological reality of language. But language remains steadfast; norms, though, shift and evolve. This is clearly on display in the story of what may be the most noticed disfluency of all: "um."

# 5

## A Brief History of "Um"

New members of the Canadian diplomatic corps play a ball game as they stand in a circle. Whoever holds the ball must talk, unrehearsed, on a random topic. As soon as the person says "uh" or "um," he or she must throw the ball to someone else. The winner is the one who holds the ball the longest. (The long-running BBC game show, *Just a Minute*, is based on a similar premise; competitors attempt to speak on randomly assigned topics as long as possible without hesitating, repeating words, or switching topics. "Uh" is one sign of hesitating.)* New German foreign service officers play for multilin-

---

*From a *Just a Minute* transcript from February 16, 1970, chosen at random:

NICHOLAS PARSONS: The blarney stone is a piece of rock in a castle in a village outside Cork in Southern Ireland. It is considered that if you manage to kiss this particular er blarney stone . . .
[*Buzz*]
CLEMENT FREUD: Derek . . .
DEREK NIMMO: Hesitation.

gual stakes. They train to avoid pause fillers in the speeches they give in German *(uh, um)* as well as in English ("uh," "um") and French *(euh)*.

One could find many other scenes where people are trained to provide smooth, unbroken speech, and where "uh" and "um" are censored, derided, mocked, and erased—as are the people who say them. The attitude of the amateur public-speaking organization, Toastmasters, is not uncommon. Each club assigns a person, the "ah-counter," to collect a nickel for each time a club member giving a speech says "uh" or "um." (Most clubs cap the fine at fifty cents per speaker.) As Ralph Smedley, the Toast-master's founder, wrote, "Mannerisms are not limited to physical posture. Many enter into speech itself. My favorite aversion is the 'grunt'—the 'ah' and the 'er-r' with which many speakers fill in the gaps between their words. It is a bad habit and should be broken by every speaker—even by every conversationalist."

Such distaste for "uh" and "um" isn't merely a judgment about a person's speech; it's a deeper judgment about how much control he should have over his self-presentation and his identity. Not surprisingly, the battle against "uh" and "um" figures prominently in our lives with language at school and at work. My friend Sara, who's now in graduate school in economics, had a second-grade teacher who refused to listen to her talk until she could start a sentence without "um." It was an unattractive habit in such a gifted girl, the teacher said. Kristin felt a little embarrassed, but she now says that "more than anything I was frustrated—with myself, I think, not the teacher." She had to pause "for a really long time" to prevent the forbidden word.

---

NICHOLAS PARSONS: Unfair!
DEREK NIMMO: With great pleasure, hesitation!

Even among a more open-minded New Agey crowd, "um" isn't acceptable. Lee Glickstein, a California-based public-speaking and presentation guru and founder of Speaking Circles International, used to tell students not to say "um." But the admonition wasn't effective. People kept saying "um." And the proscription made them even more self-conscious and nervous. "So we don't talk about 'ums,' " Glickstein told me. He believes that when you're fully present with the person you're speaking with, you say "uh" or "um" much less. You don't eliminate it entirely—Glickstein said "uh" several times when we were on the phone, though he noticed it immediately and chided himself. If you find yourself saying "um," he suggested converting it into a slow "yum," to make yourself more conscious of what you're saying. "When you start hearing yourself go 'um,' " Glickstein recommended, "start saying 'yum,' and turn your 'ums' to 'yums, um, umm, yummm, mmmm, mmmm.' " By meditating on them, Glickstein said, a speaker should eventually be able to turn "mmmms" to what he calls "rich stillness."

Where does this aesthetic of umlessness come from? How did it become so ingrained that it seems to be a biblical commandment? Assuming that nothing short of archaeology was required, I began digging for its origin at the very root of Western ideas about language and eloquence, among the rhetoricians of ancient Greece and Rome. What did they have to say about "uh" and "um"?

These writers said plenty about good speaking that's rhythmic and smooth. But they didn't mention pause fillers at all. In *On Rhetoric,* Aristotle urges an orator to choose words well, to craft beautiful metaphors, and to use the right rhythm and speak grammatically. In his day, most oratory was extemporaneous, not prepared ahead of time. Around 400 BCE, if one sat long enough in the Athenian marketplace, the Agora, or in the assembly on Pnyx Hill, or in the Theater of Dionysus, one was bound to hear people say "uh" and "um." Yet Aristotle doesn't instruct speakers to avoid a hesitant style. Nor does he mention "uh" or "um" (or whatever the ancient Greek equivalent would have been).*

Almost four hundred years later, ancient Roman teachers of oratory described their likes and dislikes in terms of boldness and confidence. In *De Oratore*, one of Cicero's works of oratorical instruction, Crassus, a character in the dialogue, describes a good speech as intelligible and perspicacious, graceful, and suited to the topic. Those who speak the best, he explains, appear to have lost their sense of shame about speaking. This allows them to begin their speeches without timidity. Not everyone can be an accomplished speaker, Crassus warns. Some individuals are "so hesitating in their speech, so inharmonious in their tone of voice," he says, that no amount of oratorical training can redeem them from their own incompetence. Cicero himself was known for starting a speech weakly. In a passage that Cicero's biographer Anthony Everitt takes as Cicero's description of himself, Crassus says, "Indeed, what I often observe in you I very frequently experience in myself, that I turn pale in the outset of my speech, and feel a tremor through my whole thoughts, as it were, and limbs."

---

*Christopher Johnstone, who studies the history of ancient rhetoric, also notes that the venues for speeches in Athens were sizable enough to require speakers to train to speak loudly and to use other ways (such as pausing) to take advantage of these spaces' acoustic designs.

Trembling, pale, confused, some of the orators of Athens and Rome stumbled through their speeches—and were noticed and criticized for doing so. Later in *De Oratore*, another character, Sulpicius, criticizes Antonius's performance at a trial for starting too slowly. "What timidity was there! What distrust! What a degree of hesitation and slowness of speech!" Sulpicius himself is accused of speaking too slowly, "owing to his genius." However, he is still "somewhat too redundant." It's safe to say that Cicero, reflecting the aesthetic of his time, was attuned to speed and fluidity in oratory. Yet he doesn't record particular faults. And he doesn't mention pause fillers.

Even Quintilian, a Roman rhetorician who stressed the value of the delivery of a speech, seems not to have heard the Latin equivalent of "uh" or "um." In his oratorical textbook, *Institutes of Oratory*, he urged orators to practice delivering pleasing-sounding speeches. To Quintilian, "pronouncing well" consisted of a varied tone and an equal rhythm, "so that our speech may not proceed by starts . . . as a person halts in walking from having legs of unequal length." He noticed bad speakers who suck air through their teeth, pant, cough, spit on their audience and speak through their nostrils, and he believed that orators should not be "dull sounding, gross, bawling, hard, stiff, inefficient, thick, or, on the contrary, thin, weak, squeaking, small, soft, effeminate."

To Quintilian's ears, a speaker's worst fault was to speak in a singing tone. "I know not," he moaned, "whether it is more to be condemned for its absurdity or for its offensiveness." Such preferences were Quintilian's as much as they belonged to the tastes of his era. But he didn't say a thing about the beauty of the umless.

It would be a fallacy to think that the ancient Greeks and Romans didn't say "um" simply because they appear not to have recorded it—the evidence that they heard and wrote it down may have been lost. They likely said "um" for all the reasons that we do: they had to delay when they explained difficult or new things, or they had other demands put on planning what to say. The neural substrate of the brain that leads to the cycles between planning to act and executing an action have been in place for a long time, perhaps millions of years. Meanwhile, the structure of human language has been around for at least one hundred thousand years. Some people may think that "uh" and "um" are creatures of the twentieth century, the products of young sex-addled minds corroded by drugs and hip-hop. More accurately, it's the twentieth century that made us call "uh" and "um" ugly. (They've been there all along.)

It's not that the ancients were insensitive to deviant or disfluent speaking—but in their wisdom, they had other reasons for not noting "uh" and "um." They did notice abnormal talking, particularly if it had a medical cause. According to the historian Ynez Violé O'Neill, the earliest description of speechlessness appears in an Egyptian surgical text, written on papyrus, that dates from 3000 to 2500 BCE. A list of forty-eight case histories, it describes several individuals with head injuries who couldn't talk.

The Old Testament also noted speechlessness and speech impediments—Moses responds to the burning bush, "Who am I, that I should go to Pharoah? I am a man of feeble speech and a slow tongue." Homer included them in the *Iliad* and the *Odyssey* (Penelope loses her speech when she hears the suitors' plot to kill her son, Telemachus), and they appeared in tragedies like *Oedipus at Colonus* by Sophocles. In his natural history texts, Aristotle discussed why humans speak (and why animals don't). He even referred to imperfections in children's speech, but he didn't single out "uh" and "um." A later text, *Problems*, generally attributed to Aristotle but whose true authorship is a mystery, discusses *ischnophonos* (hesitancy in speech), *traylos* (lisping), and *psellos* (stammering). *Ischnophonos* comes closest to what we might call "hemming and hawing." But it might also refer to an inability to select words, as might befall someone with aphasia, a language disorder caused by stroke or trauma. In either case, the writer, whoever he was, doesn't illustrate with details.

The *Oxford English Dictionary* first notes "hem," an alternate spelling of "um," in 1526, citing John Skelton, an English rhetorician and translator, who wrote, "Hem, syr yet beware of Had I wyste!" "Um" also appears as "hum," "uh" as "haw," defined as "an utterance marking hesitation." According to the *OED*, the first written use of "haw" comes in 1679, where a woman is described as having "a little haugh in her speech." "Hum" is even older, dating to 1469. The dictionary calls it "an articulate vocal murmur uttered with closed lips in a pause of speaking from hesitation, embarrassment, or affectation." Shakespeare uses it in *The Winter's Tale,* in Leontes's misogynistic tirade against Hermione, saying that she can't be called both good and honest. "These shrugs, these hums and ha's, when you have said she's goodly, come between ere you can say she's honest."

On the job, people who may have noticed "uh" and "um" didn't write them down either. Consider the notes taken during court proceedings by scribes using quill pens that periodically needed to be dipped in ink. At top speed, scribes wrote about 30 words a minute. They were still outpaced by brisk talkers putting out 250 words a minute. So there may have been a technical reason that the gaps, falterings, and backtrackings of spontaneous speaking by judges, clients, lawyers, plaintiffs, or defendants weren't recorded. Even when defendants were questioned after they'd been flogged, the scribes filtered out the blunders, according to Daniel Collins, a linguist at the Ohio State University who has studied trial transcripts from medieval Russia. Collins knows of a few cases where there is evidence that someone stopped talking or became muddled, but the reason for including such random details isn't noted, and is now—like nearly every other verbal blunder ever spoken—lost to time.

If the aesthetic of umlessness doesn't appear to have its roots in classical ideas about speaking well, perhaps its origin is more contemporary: in the tensions and battles about English in America. In the 1800s, as the United States left behind its status as a colony, Americans of all social classes struggled to sort out an emerging American dialect from the British one. As in other countries growing into their nationhood, language became a matter of national character. Commentators and educators sought to define and impose a uniform dialect on the range of American vernaculars, institute standards for spelling and pronunciation, write authoritative dictionaries and books of English usage, and establish teaching methods.

By the 1850s, language became a matter of social character. In burgeoning cities, people of different classes and backgrounds mingled, some of whom had taken advantage of American society's openness to aspiring to higher social status. In this context, nonstandard language was less marked by regional dialect than by the vulgarities, slang, and colloquialisms that the lower classes used. New standards of civility and manners were not only forced on language: twenty-eight different manuals outlining etiquette appeared in the 1830s, thirty-six in the 1840s, and thirty-eight in the 1850s. They encouraged their readers to adopt the manners of metropolitan society, not only to secure success in one's social climbing but because etiquette was seen as crucial for civil society and democracy itself.

By the early twentieth century, it was recognized that any person had a number of social roles to play, particularly those who lived in booming commercial metropolises. For someone to speak in many different contexts—chatting colloquially in the morning, giving a lecture in the afternoon, telling genteel humorous tales after dinner, and talking to clerks, children, city officials, men, women, and workmen in between—was an expected part of daily life. How could people keep track of all these performances of different sorts of selves?

Language as marker of identity and social status is not unique to America. But America's vigor and pragmatism, the ferment of its diverse society, and its openness to opportunity created an environment in which people considered language mutable. In America it remains largely true that if you change what you say and how you say it, you change who you are. Before plastic surgery allowed you to change yourself physically, books, clubs, teachers, and therapists taught you to alter your accent and hide your true origins, build your vocabulary, read more literature, or discipline your grammar.

So could "uh" and "um" have been useful shibboleths for Americans who reserved the right to make judgments about a person's place in society based on their language?* Did increasingly rigid rules that looked down on ribald humor, swearing, poor spelling, and accents also extend to "uh" and "um"?

If this had been true, you'd expect to find umlessness championed in the vast American literature aimed at improving speech. But if the numerous handbooks and textbooks on rhetoric, oratory, speech, elocution, and reading performances published in America and Great Britain in the eighteenth, nineteenth, and early twentieth centuries were full of dictates about how to speak and write properly, they said nothing about "uh" or "um." Books like *The Philosophy of the Human Voice* by James Rush (1827), *A Plea for the Queen's English* by Henry Alford (1864), and *The Science and Art of Elocution, or How to Read and Speak* by Frank Fenno (1878) offer small armies of rules, admonitions, and exercises that stand ready to march on grammatical deviance and phonetic ugliness. Page after page contain pronunciation charts, vowel graphs, consonant tables, even musical staffs, along with grotesque diagrams of a cross-sectioned larynx, mouth, and tongue, as if learning the relevant anatomy would unlock the secret of perfect enunciation. Indeed, some elocution books taught myriad methods of disciplining the body, now mostly forgotten: illustrations showing the beauty of holding the left hand to the forehead, clasping both hands to the chest, turning the wrist and ankle just so. Other volumes are filled with model speeches to practice reading aloud, as well as lists of good words—to be recited for pro-

---

*The Old Testament book of Judges tells how the Gileadites tried to identify their enemies among hordes fleeing a battle. Anyone who wanted to escape had to say "shibboleth" (meaning "flood water"). The test was designed to expose foes from the land of Ephraim, who couldn't pronounce the *"sh"* in the word. Those who could say only "sibboleth" were killed, and the Bible says forty-two thousand Ephraimites died that day.

nunciation practice and memorized to make one's vocabulary sparkle—in contrast to hearty lists of bad ones—slang, vulgarisms, and regionalisms, all to be avoided.

To pore through linguistic jeremiads by the so-called verbal critics of the nineteenth century who struggled to hold the tide against the language rot they perceived is to be struck by the lack of strictures against "uh" and "um." They are also not mentioned in books of etiquette written for young American men and women, with sections on how to be polite to your elders, courteous, serene, and self-disciplined. Elocution books offered detailed grammatical recipes for creating specific rhetorical effects with pauses, for instance, to "pause after the nominative when it consists of more than one word." However mind-crushing the rules were, none of the books prohibited "uh," "ah," "um," "hum," "haugh," or "haw."

Even when cultural critics raged against American decadence at the dawn of the twentieth century, pause fillers didn't seem to qualify as symptoms of the end of civilization. In 1869, the American neurologist George Beard began to popularize a malady of nervous exhaustion, labeling it "neurasthenia." If you couldn't sleep, were thirsty, irritable, or had noises in your ears, you were neurasthenic, overstimulated by modern life down to your very molecules. You were nervous, literally, in your bones. The disorder was caused by the increasing speed of modern life, the explosion of new ideas, trains, and other new machines. What was called "progress" provoked civilization's inevitable decline—or so people like Beard worried. One symptom of American decline was decrepit language, phonetic decay, and degenerate speaking: nervous people spoke more quickly, clipped their words, and dropped their "g's." Beard apparently overlooked "uh" and "um."

Because oratory was so popular in nineteenth-century America, the elocutionary educations of famous American orators were also widely read. These stories took the form of moral tales of bad speech habits overcome by the power of will and the exercise of discipline. Yet for all their egalitarian fervor, none of them mentions the pause fillers. Henry Ward Beecher's childhood problem was his garbled speaking. "When Henry is sent to me with a message," his aunt once said, "I always have to make him say it three times. The first time I have no manner of an idea than if he spoke Choctaw; the second, I catch now and then a word; and by the third time, I begin to understand." At Sunday school he was left in the catechismal dust by other children's brilliant recitations. His sister described him as "blushing, stammering, confused and hopelessly miserable stuck on some sand-bank, . . . his mouth choking up with the long words which he hopelessly miscalled." To cure himself Beecher tramped around in the woods and shouted vowels into the trees, transforming himself into one of the most popular orators of his day.*

---

*This story is clearly modeled on the story of Demosthenes, considered by some to be the greatest ancient Greek orator. Some say Demosthenes had a speech impediment that he cured by filling his mouth with pebbles and shouting to the waves; Plutarch describes the young Demosthenes as having a "weakness in his voice" and a "shortness of breath" that fragmented his sentences and "much obscured the sense and meaning of what he spoke." His story of verbal rags to riches has been a model for the biography of orators ever since.

The earliest admonition against "uh" that I was able to find comes from a long poem, *Urania: A Rhymed Lesson,* written in 1846 by Oliver Wendell Holmes (the father of the Supreme Court justice Oliver Wendell Holmes Jr.). Holmes was thirty-seven years old and a professor of anatomy and physiology at Dartmouth College when he wrote the 749-line poem that contains a number of lines concerning proper speech, including these:

> Once more: speak clearly, if you speak at all;
> Carve every word before you let it fall;
> Don't, like a lecturer or dramatic star,
> Try over-hard to roll the British R;
> Do put your accents in the proper spot;
> Don't,—Let me beg you,—don't say "How" for "What?"
> And when you stick on conversation's burrs,
> Don't strew the pathway with those dreadful urs.

Holmes's spelling of "uh" as "ur" is a variant of the British spelling, "er." That he rhymes "urs" and "burrs" suggests not so much a lax rhyme as a pronunciation of "burr" that sounded like "buh."

In Britain, meanwhile, they were often spelling "uh" as "haw," and using it as the linguistic marker for a cretinous gentleman (not, as we do, for an industrial-age dropout), so that snooty inbred aristocrats were said to speak an affected "haw-haw dialect." In Edward Bulwer-Lytton's 1841 novel, *Night and Morning,* a stranger visits Robert Beaufort to deliver the unseemly news that Beaufort's deceased brother had been secretly married, thereby entitling the brother's widow and two sons to the estate that Robert thought was his. " 'It is false!' cried Mr. Beaufort, finding a voice at length, and springing to his feet. 'And who are you, sir? and what do you mean by—' 'Hush!' said the stranger, perfectly unconcerned, and regaining the dignity of his haw-haw enunciation; 'better not let the servants hear aunything.' "

Other people affecting the "haw" of the upper class were said to suffer from "haw-hawism." In 1853, Robert Smith Surtees published his comic novel about fox-hunting escapades, *Mr. Sponge's Sporting Tour,* in which Lord Scamperdale, a foolish whiskered bachelor, hems and haws. " 'Ha—he—hum,' " says Lord Scamperdale. " 'Meet at the Court,' mumbled his lordship—'meet at the court—ha—he—ha—hum—no; got no foxes.' " In 1939, the Nazi apologist William Joyce was nicknamed "Lord Haw-Haw" for speaking what was described as the "English of the haw-haw, damit-get-out-of-my-way variety" (a description given to another British citizen broadcasting for the Nazis), which no doubt added a note of class consciousness to the detestation heaped upon the man, who was executed for treason in 1946.

One might assume from the written record that pause fillers were used only by the British, not by Americans. But Mark Twain's writing is full of evidence that nineteenth-century Americans used pause fillers. Well-known for having an ear sensitive to the rhythms of talk and the peculiarities of American dialects, Twain used many pause fillers in his dialogue. George Mahl did a little study of *Tom Sawyer,* published in 1876, in which Tom, Huck, Becky, Aunt Polly, the schoolteacher, Joe Harper, Muff Potter, Mrs. Harper, and an anonymous playmate all repeat themselves and restart their sentences in situations of emotional distress. Only Tom says "uh," usually when he's trying to remember his Bible verses.

We have evidence of American umming with the oldest extant recording of Thomas Edison's voice, which dates to 1888, the year that Edison was presenting a phonograph known as his "perfected phonograph." Unlike his first version from ten years earlier, this one reproduced a person's voice more faithfully, using cylinders that were replaceable and transportable. Though no specific accounts exist, we suspect that the recording came from one of the public exhibitions of the phonograph, such as the one at New York's Electric Club on West 22nd Street, on May 12, 1888. Members of the industrial elite, military leaders (such as General Gabriel Sherman), and politicians attended. In another room, Edison, forty-one years old at the time, recorded and played back his voice. In that particular exhibition at the New York club, it's not known what Edison recorded, but he may have described a trip around the world, something he often did to illustrate how the phonograph could capture even foreign words. When you click on the button that plays the digital file of the recording, rattles and hisses seem to come from a million miles away—as different from a modern recording as a pinhole camera is from a digital one. Here's the beginning of the transcript.* (For easier reading, I've put the pause fillers in bold.)

*Digital recording available at the Edison National Historic Site Web site.

**Uh,** now, Mr. Blaine, as you've been nearly around the world, I'll take you around the world on the phonograph. I'll not charge you anything. I'll take you on a steamer, **eh,** a Cunard steamer to Liverpool, and from Liverpool to London, from London on the London & Brighton Railroad to Brighton, and from Brighton we'll go on those little two-cent steamers across the English Channel to Calais. And from Calais we'll go on the chemin du fer du nord. I can't give you the exact Parisian pronunciation of this railroad, but I guess you'll understand it. We'll get into Paris and make for the, **uh,** Grand Hotel. And then in the morning we'll go to our bankers and get you some money on our letters of credit.

They continue through Europe, then into the Red Sea via the Suez Canal, "and then to, **uh,** Bombay" where "we'll probably get the, **uh,** cholera," then to Calcutta, Singapore, Hong Kong, then to San Francisco, then by train back to New York. Edison signs off, "**Uh,** goodbye, Edison."*

Given what we know about Edison's technical perfectionism—he often threw out disks and cylinders marred by slight flaws, and he believed that recording for the phonograph required a special voice, which he didn't possess—his willingness to overlook an inaugural "uh" suggests that the project of purging public speech of "uh" and "um" hadn't yet gotten under way. Our aesthetic of umlessness wouldn't crystallize for

---

*Gerald Fabris, Curator of Sound Recordings at the Edision National Historic Site, also speculated that "Mr. Blaine" might have seen the Republican politician, James G. Blaine, who had traveled in Europe in 1887 and 1888 and was living in New York during late 1888. There is no evidence that Edison ever met James Blaine.

another thirty years, not until Edison's invention brought speaking back to listeners and provided the first incontrovertible evidence of their own imperfections.

Early in his attempts to design a phonograph, Edison projected glowing promises about the future of spoken communication. He foresaw the phonograph transforming business when businessmen could talk to each other "in perfect privacy" by sending wax cylinders back and forth, their secretaries producing transcripts on the newly invented typewriter that would contain "every break and pause, every hesitation or confident affirmation" captured by the wax. Though he obviously overestimated the willingness of readers to read verbatim transcripts, Edison promised that the new technology would give people new ways to listen to speaking in terms of speaking, not the conventions of writing. "We shall now know for the first time what a conversation really is," he wrote. "The phonograph, in one sense, knows more than we do ourselves."

Gramophones, phonographs, wax cylinders, resin discs, telephones, microphones, then wire recordings and radio broadcasts, then talking pictures: these new technologies let people hear speech as it really was for the first time—an activity that happened in time, dynamic and not frozen in writing. As early as the 1890s, a nickel would buy an opportunity to hear prerecorded speeches on gramophones in entertainment arcades, and by 1908, Edison had sold more than one million gramophones. These were used in homes to listen to prerecorded wax cylinders but also to make the first home recordings, which a person did by talking into the gramophone's horn. These recordings (and eventually broadcasts) detached speech from the speaker's body, and they divorced speaking from actual face-to-face situations where speakers interacted with listeners. The technology also captured the stopping, repeating, and retreating of talking so that people could replay and scrutinize speech. Disembodied and nailed down, speaking became a new sort of object.

The prohibition against "um" probably grew into a general expectation of flawless speaking with the advent of the radio. The popularity of the technology exploded in the 1920s in a way that contemporary Americans who witnessed the rise of the Internet would recognize. "All of a sudden it hit us," a newspaper reporter wrote. For instance, in August 1921, there were two new broadcasting stations; nearly a year later, in May 1922, there were ninety-nine. Ordinary consumers waited hours to purchase radio receivers, "only to be told when they finally reached the counter that they might place an order and it would be filled when possible," according to an editorial in the first issue of *Radio Broadcast* that month. Between 1922 and 1924, the Radio Corporation of America made more than eighty-three million dollars selling more than a million "radio music boxes." Starting in the eastern United States, the radio craze eventually swept west, where isolated listeners and huge distances made radio even more popular. Radio stations received fan mail from shut-ins, remote ranchers, farmers, and gold diggers. "I am keeping bees in an abandoned lumber camp sole alone," one man from Washington wrote. "Radio is my only comfort—it keeps me from going mad."

But the electronic hardware didn't come with instructions about how people should use it. In the same way that e-mail etiquette has shakily coalesced, the standards about how to speak on the radio took time to develop. Faced with a solitary microphone, not the shining faces of a real live audience, the earliest radio performers (many of whom were veteran actors) experienced "mike fright." Radio also highlighted the weaknesses of speakers and was a merciless test for the speakers of the "rough-and-ready, catch-as-can school" (wrote the *Saturday Evening Post* in 1924) who couldn't employ devices (the facial expression, the shifted posture) that kept the attention of physical audiences. In the first stage show broadcast by New York's WJZ in February 1922, Ed Wynn, a comedian, was so struck by the silence that followed all his jokes that his performance began to falter. The producer ran through the building, assembling in the studio everyone he could find—electricians, janitors, telephone operators—to give Wynn a real audience. Once he heard their responses and saw their faces, Wynn was able to keep performing.

One impact of these technologies of the voice was that people developed new standards of speaking for them. In the age of recording and broadcasting, a "good speaker" had a different style of voice. T. H. Pear, a British psychologist, described the speechifying of the preelectric era as taking place in halls with "bad acoustic qualities" as "bored or fidgety" audiences sat in uncomfortable chairs and were occasionally woken up by a speaker shouting, "Ladies and gentlemen!" In such settings the style of speaking was slow, overarticulated, and often "childishly simple." Important words were SHOUTED! And important thoughts. Were broken. Into pieces. By dramatic. Pauses.

Microphones gave speakers the ability to speak at a volume more suited to face-to-face conversation. Early radio orators didn't grasp this at first—until they discovered that booming oratory could blow out a microphone. Speaking at a normal volume meant speaking at a normal pace, since the speaker didn't need to pause as often to gather huge breaths. It also made sentences sound more connected, uninterrupted by gulps of air. Robert West, in his radio handbook, *So-o-o-o You're Going on the Air!,* called the preelectric orators "leather-lunged word hurlers who depended on stentorian power to carry their voices to three counties at one time." Once electromagnetism displaced sound waves in the air as the vehicle of the voice, the elocutionary standards of the nineteenth century were rendered obsolete.

The elocution manuals had provided elaborate instructions about when to pause and how long to do it. It was a mechanical necessity—the orators needed a space in which to take a breath. Yet that same pause may have given the speaker a moment to plan what to say next. When the need to project the voice disappeared, so did the luxury of the pause. In this way the utilitarian pauses of oratory might have become the useless hesitations of the electrically amplified public speaker. It was in these hesitant moments that the "ums" are likely to have been spoken and recognized.

Provided with new opportunities to hear real speaking, people began to prize umlessness. James Winans, a professor of speech communication at Cornell University, was one of the first to extol the conversational style and help transform "oratory" into "public speaking." His textbook *Public Speaking,* published in 1915, was also the earliest textbook I found that explicitly advised against saying "uh" and "um." (A few textbooks quoted only Oliver Wendell Holmes's *Urania*.) Though the speaking style that he recommended was informal, it was less interactive than actual conversations. "Hesitation is especially annoying when the gaps are filled with urs and uhs," he wrote. "Grunting is no part of thinking." To emphasize his point, he quotes Holmes's poem, which dictated against those "dreadful urs."

Hesitation was a common handicap of the unrehearsed speaker, who also erred by speaking too quickly. Winans urged the speaker not to confuse pauses—which he said provide natural boundaries between topics—with hesitation. "We pause to think; we hesitate because we cannot think," Winans said bitingly. "Nothing is more tiresome to an audience than a hesitating, halting delivery."

Teachers of public speaking as far back as Quintilian had cautioned the speaker against hesitating. They advocated a style that would later be labeled masculine, controlled, and strong. Now the hesitant style had a name, and, thanks to the technology, it had a symptom. No longer referred to vaguely as "stammering," hesitant speaking could be prevented if speakers followed this simple directive: don't say "uh" or "um."

This admonition lodged in the culture of language with remarkable speed and emerged as a key standard for speaking in the electric age. It's not clear whether other cultures share the umless aesthetic that Americans acquired in the early twentieth century. But we can safely suppose that in other parts of the world, technologies would also have made "uh" and "um" perceptible by throwing the fleeting sounds of interruption up to our ears so they were impossible to ignore. Recording, amplifying, and replaying human speech allowed it to be sent across time and through space. This not only transformed captured sound into a commodity, it enabled ways of listening to the aspects of the human voice that had once vanished in the air, overriding the natural filters that kept the "uhs" and "ums" of daily life beyond the limits of people's conscious attention.

People must have heard pause fillers so frequently that by

the late 1920s, "uh" and "um" seemed unhygienic. In 1928, a public-speaking professor, Wilmer E. Stevens, published the first rating scale for grading student speeches or judging speech contests that included the absence of pause fillers as a sign of prized fluency. "Consider the flow of the speaker's words," the scale reads. "Notice tendency to block, repeat, stutter, or to say 'ah.'"

Writing in 1931 about the psychology of public speaking, T. H. Pear ranted against "er," saying it exemplified the halting, fragmented style of speaking that now seemed to be cropping up everywhere. "How much time is given, in many secondary schools, to the writing—and speaking of Latin by boys and girls who cannot speak English coherently in public for two minutes?" he wrote, then mimicked the educated gentleman who's grown up into an average speaker who begins his speech with "I'm sure—er—we're all very—er—*grate*ful—to the—er—speaker . . . for his interesting and—er—suggestive—er . . . talk." Pear was incensed. "Cannot the generation which has added flying to the accomplishments of the human race do better than this?" he ranted. "What is the reason? Nervousness? A foolish, misleading word. Self-consciousness? A little better, but is complete anaesthesia the highest aim of civilisation?"

As the conventions of the public sphere invaded the private sphere, the dictates against "uh" and "um" in normal, spontaneous conversation also made inroads. Beginning in the 1920s, the arbiters of well-mannered society denounced "uh" and "um" as frequently as the arbiters of the well-spoken did. In 1928, in *Manners: American Etiquette,* Helen Hathaway cautioned against "ah" and "er" as "little mannerisms" and "peculiarities of speech." "Well-educated and well-bred people are always the simplest in every way," she observed. "Puncturing our sentences with *ah*'s and *er*'s, mincing our words, employing affected tones and gestures, are tricks annoying even to our friends and positively repellant to strangers."

Even in that most intimate of twentieth-century conversational settings, the therapist's office, "uh" and "um" were frowned upon. In his 1959 *Mannerisms of Speech and Gestures in Everyday Life,* Sandor Feldman, a psychiatrist, noted the mannerism as "a crutch" among his patients, whose "moaning-like 'er . . . er . . . er . . .' is annoying, draws the conversation out to great length, and makes the listener, who is far ahead of the speaker, wait." Unfortunately, Feldman was convinced of the link between "er" and anxiety: "One can say that whenever this mannerism is used for one reason or another there is anxiety present."

Given that other disfluencies, particularly restarted sentences and repeated words, indicate mental disorganization, cognitive load, and anxiety more readily (as George Mahl and Heather Bortfeld, among others, have shown), it is curious that "uh" and "um" are considered the sine qua non of hesitant speaking and disorganized thinking. Though "uh" and "um" are more frequent, sentence repairs and word repetitions clog their share of sentences, too. So why did "uh" and "um" become the shorthand for anxiety and disorganization? Why does their presence make us panic in a way that other disfluencies don't?

It may be that "uh" and "um" became the emblem of a disorganized self. If the aesthetic of umlessness applied only to public speaking, one might say that orators were most concerned with pleasing their listeners by leaving out such disfluencies.

Yet umlessness was taught as the norm for private and intimate spheres of life. The only rule left unwritten was "don't say 'um' when you're talking to yourself."

This persistence suggests other worries were attached to "uh" and "um" uniquely. For the last century, sociologists have argued that identity is neither essential nor fixed in complex industrialized societies. The modern identity, they say, is performed. Individuals must navigate a variety of settings, interact with many different people, and play diverse roles to achieve a shifting set of goals. The aesthetic of umlessness may have emerged as a response to this demanding modern conception of self. Perhaps saying "um" was a sign that a person couldn't keep their social performances in order and thus wasn't fit for this social world. "Um" represented a breakdown of the bureaucracy in your head.

Umlessness isn't a natural preference—left to our own devices, we naturally ignore most "ums." People began to prefer umlessness in public speaking and conversation around the same time they began to value order, organization, planning, and efficiency in an increasingly complex and urbanizing society. People worked hard to keep control of how they performed socially, and they prized and admired others who did the same. We prefer in speakers what we prefer in our individual selves.

Frederick Houk Law, a lecturer at New York University and head of the department of English at Stuyvesant High School, wrote an eight-part textbook, *Mastery of Speech*, that linked success in the dizzyingly complex social life of modernizing America with talking; he specifically mentioned "uh" and "um." Published in 1918 and intended for men and women, *Mastery of Speech* gave how-to advice on a range of interactions: "how to dictate to a stenographer," "how to talk to a private secretary," "how to ask for a loan," "how to speak to unfortunates," "how to talk to public officials." Law outlined what's at stake in the hypothetical biographies of "Henry" and "Jim," both of whom are equally privileged. But Henry is rich, while Jim is stuck in his mediocre job. The reason? "[JIM] IS A POOR SPEAKER."

Henry's a good speaker because he "can talk to any man at any time, and he meets everyone in exactly the right way." He can act as a boss, a colleague, a citizen, a bystander, a customer, a client, and a parent all in sequence, keeping track of these performances of a social self in his repertoire and shuffling the right one out at the appropriate moment. Saying "uh" or "um" signals that one doesn't, in fact, have control over these performances. "Lack of fluency may be caused by bashfulness or by fear of your audience," Law wrote. "You have somehow formed the habit of saying 'Well, now,' 'and-a-a-a-a,' 'n-o-w,' 'er-er-er-er,' and various other expressions. Resolve firmly to break the habit and to speak fluently." The message is clear: if you say "uh" or "um," you're doomed to live the life of Jim, not Henry.

After the pioneering work of George Mahl and Freida Goldman-Eisler in the 1950s, it took some time for the study of pauses, pause fillers, and other disfluencies to be seen as valuable. But once sociologists, psychologists, linguists, speech pathologists, and communication theorists started to plumb the depths of "um," they explained the universe of pause fillers in myriad ways. Some said an ummer was searching his memory for a word. Others concluded that the ummer was uncertain. In the view of some, the ummer was trying to decide what to say or how to say it. For others, it was a way to keep a place in a conversation, while others thought it was a way to signal that one wanted to take the next turn. Others said the opposite, that the ummer wanted to give up the turn. Meanwhile, in the popular mind, umming was simply a bad habit, akin to spitting or picking one's nose.

Some communication theorists argued that the umming public speaker discredited himself and his message; others found evidence (usually by surveying college students in one's own speech classes where umlessness is insisted upon, which means one is surveying a biased sample) that it discredited the speaker but didn't interfere with the message itself. Some theorists think that "um" invited others to speak, or requested help finishing a sentence, or invited a listener to think about what the speaker was about to say, or was simply another way of being polite.

One of the most far-reaching conclusions about "um" comes from Herb Clark, a psychologist at Stanford, who submits "uh" and "um" to exhaustive exegesis. A slim man in his midsixties, Clark keeps an electric kettle and a row of tea boxes for visitors to his office. Because of what he studies, it's hard not to notice how he speaks: he's a fast talker, not given to much umming, though his sentences often shift midway through an idea. The effect isn't distracting. When I transcribed our interviews, I realized how deliberately he places his "ums" and his repetitions, often adding a commentary, sometimes as brief as a single word, on his own pause.

Which turns out to be the heart of his argument about "uh" and "um." Clark argues that when people talk, they produce two parallel streams of information he calls "tracks." One is the "primary track," where the subject of the conversation—the football game, a novel, dinner—travels. The other is the "collateral track," interjected with the speaker's commentary on his or her primary track. Editing comments ("sort of"), moments of self-consciousness ("what was I saying?"), even dramatic asides ("as if I cared") all belong to the collateral track. The collateral track coordinates the primary track in one person's speech but also coordinates the communication between two speakers.

Clark likes to use the metaphor of a waltz to describe this communication—that is, as a dance in which participants provide subtle cues to each other about how and where to move. When someone forgets a word in the middle of a sentence and says, "I'm trying to think of this word but it's not coming to me," she's coordinating the conversation by explaining why her primary track has faltered. When she repairs and then apologizes for interrupting herself, she's coordinating as well. For most of us, this happens at a fairly unconscious level—we're just trying to keep the conversation going—but someone like Clark, practiced at controlling his collateral track, can manage this subordinate conversation with great consideration for his listener. Far from being distracting, his speech seems to embrace the listener in warmth.

For Clark, "uh" and "um" are valuable tools in this waltz-like communication, and they function more like words than conversational grunts. Not only do they sound as if they're being used deliberately, they seem to have two distinct meanings. With Jean Fox Tree, Clark's former student, now a psychologist at the University of California, Santa Cruz, Clark examined about 170,000 words of transcribed conversations between adults, 5,000 words of calls to telephone answering machines, 2.7 million words of telephone conversations, and thousands of words of storytelling. Clark and Fox Tree discovered that "uh" and "um" always preceded some notable pause or delay in both the monologues and conversations. They figure that speakers are deliberately signaling the upcoming delay in the sentence, and doing so with "uh" or "um." As Clark likes to put it, the "uh" isn't the problem; it's the solution to the problem.

Clark and Fox Tree also argued that "uh" and "um" have two different meanings. In their study, "uh" appeared more often before a short pause, "um" before a longer pause. Not only do speakers have control of "uh" and "um" (as demonstrated by the fact that some people can learn to stop saying them) but their internal speech monitors could deftly foretell how long a delay was likely to be. That formed the basis of whether or not to use "uh" or "um."

Whether or not one agrees with Clark and Fox Tree's perspective, the notion of conversation as waltz suggests a reason that some novice public speakers say "um" too much. They may be using the word to try to interact with their listeners, and since they get no feedback they can use, they keep saying "um" to no avail.

From the listeners' perspective, what's annoying about this is that there's no way to signal, we're with you, keep going, you're doing fine. A flood of "ums" is like a continual cry for help by someone who can't help him- or herself. In a 1988 *Psychology Today* article about speaking as communication, psychologist Michael Motley offered a way of circumventing this frantic flood drawn from his public speaking classes. He begins a conversation with the speaker and tells the rest of the audience to leave the room. Once the speaker is confident in the conversation he or she is having with Motley, the rest of the audience returns until the speaker is interacting with all of them.

Clark pulled out his laptop and set it on a low table so he could flip through sound files in his collection. He clicked on a file of a twenty-second-long string that he'd excised from a radio interview with a man who was saying, "They-yah . . . And-uh . . . But-uh . . . But-uh . . . Some-uh . . . And-uh . . . As-uh . . . Don't-uh . . . Right-uh . . . Some-uh . . . It's-uh . . . It's-uh . . . The-uh . . . We-um . . . Airplanes-um."* It sounded like someone getting punched in the stomach each time he begins to talk. Clark had excised all the "uhs," which were all attached to other words, saying, "His strategy is to attach the 'uh' to the previous word, always. He doesn't just get but. Uh. He gets buttah." On the whole he's found huge variation among speakers, some who speak as few as 1.2 fillers for every thousand words, others who speak as many as 88 per thousand words.

Clark's research has sparked controversy about whether "uh" and "um" are symptoms of delay or (as he argues) signals of delay. Liz Shriberg thinks they're symptoms. For her, the patterns of "uh" and "um" may result more from the relationship between language and the brain than what an individual intends to say. "I think it's hard to get inside the heads of listeners," she told me. For instance, Shriberg has found evidence that "um" is used outside of larger clauses, while "uh" is used more frequently inside of clauses. This is because "um" is associated with the same strong change in intonation that marks the edge of a clause.

To someone who stumbles onto Clark and Fox Tree's work

---

*Some sound artists have produced pieces editing out words and leaving only disfluencies, laughter, throat clearing, and other vocal marginalia. The Books, an electronic folk group, have a fifty-five-second piece called "ps," and the Seattle-based composer, David Hahn, turned a recorded interview between a journalist and a CEO into a piece called "Corporate Coitus." Hahn used the "ums" and "uhs" as "compositional building blocks" to create a piece with the crescendos of sexual intercourse.

after a lifetime of valuing umlessness, the psychologists can seem to be advocating wayward speech. In 2002, when one of Clark's articles in the journal *Cognition* was picked up in the mainstream media, he received a pile of angry mail. "I recently uh read an uh article by Amanda—ah—Onion about you and Jean ah Fox uh Tree," one man wrote in an e-mail. "Then the other day I saw this ah cartoon of 'Beetle Bailey' and it uh dawned on me that uh that is what uh you are uh trying to do. Have all of us ah become idiots uh like the uh poor uh guy in the cartoon, you know." He accused Clark and Fox Tree of failing as professors to teach proper communication. Instead, he said, they were teaching "mere conversation" and letting people off the hook for their bad habits.

The writer couldn't know that Clark's notions about using language in public are fairly conventional, and he holds high standards for his students' writing. When he talks to curious reporters, he makes it a point to recommend that public speakers honor their audience by removing "uh" and "um" from their speeches, just as one wouldn't wear flip-flops to a formal occasion. At home you can wear flip-flops and say "um" all you like. As for Fox Tree, she wasn't very pleased when her daughter came home from nursery school saying "like," and when her students go for job interviews, she tells them not to say "uh" or "um," either. Those words signal delay, and in such situations you want to appear on the ball, quick-witted. But with your friends? In an informal situation? Um away.*

This pragmatic attitude is a healthy one: uphold the stan-

---

*As for "like," Fox Tree would recommend you don't say it, though she argues that "like" has a different function than "uh" and "um" (they are not used interchangeably in stories that a person has told once, then been asked

dards of umlessness that are so deeply ingrained in our culture, but exempt spontaneous conversation, ordinary talking, and all but the most formal situations from them. It may even hold out promise for a new standard for public speaking. Speakers might be able to train to exploit their collateral track—to draw listeners to them, right there, in a specific moment, and really say what's on their mind.

Otherwise, how can speakers be made more fluent—more umless? If people have to pay money for each "uh" or "um," repeated word, or interrupted sentence, their fluency will increase. Verbal reprimands help. So do electric shocks. Gesturing with the hands apparently keeps one fluent, and tying down someone's right arm makes them disfluent, and even more so when their other arm's strapped down. As Nicholas Christenfeld, a psychologist at the University of California, San Diego, puts it, "When people talk, no matter what the content or purpose of their speech, they tend to do two things. They wave their arms about and they say 'uh.' " One might skip the electricity and shouting and simply order a person to stop interrupting themselves, which works—but only for a short time, because the reprimand won't stick.

A person's fluency can also be increased by reducing the amount of stress he or she feels. Paradoxically, some people can be more fluent if they feel more stressed—if someone considers a task to be more important, he or she may talk with more care.

---

to repeat). Fox Tree has found that speakers use "like" for a meaningful purpose, which is to qualify or "soften" the information that follows.

The use of "um" and "uh" is a tactic of speakers who are speaking self-consciously, argue Christenfeld and a colleague, Beth Creager. They observed drinkers in bars and found that drinking alcohol reduced "um," though the method is somewhat impractical for everyday use: to become fully umless, a drinker would need to drink nineteen beers.

It appears that every type of spoken disfluency also exists in signed language. In Deaf culture, slips of the hand are opportunities to make a joke or feel embarrassed, and signers who often fill their pauses are considered distracted. To make the sign for "um" in American Sign Language, hold your dominant hand in front of you, palm facing up, your five fingers slightly apart. Now circle your forearm away from you and return it, repeating the gesture. Cathy Williams, a sign language interpreter, was once at a convention signing for a speaker who repeatedly said "um." Normally, she'd leave it out, but the speaker used it so much that it was a distinctive mark of his style. So she signed it. As the speech went on and Williams kept making this sign, a deaf person in the audience became agitated, apparently distracted. After the presentation he confronted her, and the next day he followed her around the convention hall, shouting at her (in sign) that she was a terrible interpreter. Williams explained that she was obliged to sign the speaker's style. "It was so noticeable with that speaker," Williams says, "that if I was going to give the message accurately I had to include the 'um.'"

In other words, to get rid of the "um," it's necessary to understand that it means something, not that it means nothing. For Doreen Hamilton, a communication guru who works with Lee Glickstein, speakers can eliminate their "uhs" and "ums" if they understand why the pause fillers are significant to them.

"Conscious or not, when an 'um' is uttered it is a signal that uncertainty and anxiety is lurking around the corner," she once told workshop facilitators. "Stepping into the silence and letting go of the filler is courageous." Even as the "um" remains, its meaning will change.

# 6

## *Well Spoken*

In the absence of any precise knowledge about Toastmasters, I long assumed they were men who met for ceremonial drunkenness. Secret handshakes wouldn't have surprised me. Hats with tassels. Go-carts.

But they turned out to be seekers. Toastmasters, a self-help public-speaking club founded more than eighty years ago, is to public speaking what General Electric is to lightbulbs. The market for public speaking improvement is substantial, mostly because in many corporations and other organizations employees can rise only if they can present information effectively. The yellow pages of the phone book are filled with speaking coaches and trainers, and Web sites abound with books, videos, and DVDs. Yet it's an industry that operates without oversight or certification—there's no licensing board or national exam, and no one really knows how many coaches or classes are out there. As a result, when people try to make good on their promise to get better at speaking in public, it's natural that they'd turn to the known name.

Founded in 1924, Toastmasters International currently has about two hundred thousand members in 180 countries; 52 percent are women (before 1973, when segregation by gender was banned, there were all-women groups called Toastmistresses), and 82 percent have a college degree. Its influence is widespread—it's said that millions have done the program. All told, there are about 10,000 clubs, 150 of them affiliated with churches, 2,453 affiliated with companies, and 71 sponsored by prisons, where inmates learn to make arguments and deliver speeches. Thirty percent of the club's membership lives outside the United States, and the bulk of the club's recent growth occurred in Asia and the Middle East, where people want to practice speaking English. In the 1920s, people joined Toastmasters to make themselves more competitive in face-to-face business relationships. Today, non-English speakers abroad want to make it in the global business world that depends on English.

The overall ethos of the club is optimistic self-improvement. What Toastmasters train to do, we all train to do at some level: produce speeches that are smooth and well-practiced, reflecting the tone of the board room more than the tumult of the soapbox or the fire of the pulpit. On a continuum of the raw and the cooked, the good Toastmaster speech is fully cooked, the product of a voice, a vocabulary, and even a body that's fully under control and disciplined. According to the accounts, the training works. In 2000, a graduate student at the University of Nevada named Ellen Beth Levine Bremen surveyed 343 Toastmasters to see what the program had done for them. Fifty-one percent of the people who responded said that they felt their speaking had improved—they considered the quality of their voice, their eye contact, body posture, and hand gestures to be better. Forty percent said that their fear of public speaking was "significantly reduced," but only 15 percent of the respondents agreed with other statements such as "I am better at using humorous material," "I am an improved impromptu speaker," "I have become a better and more organized speaker," and "I use fewer 'ahs and ums.' "

The self-help benefits of Toastmasters are most dramatically apparent, both figuratively and literally, in prisons. As the *Wall Street Journal* reported in 1993, members of prison-sponsored clubs find their way out of lives of crime. In one medium-security Louisiana prison, the Phelps Correctional Center in Dequincy, only one of eighty Toastmaster members returned to jail (well below the national recidivism rate at the time of 70 percent). Prisoners find new ways to talk to prison staff and set themselves apart from other inmates. "In prison you're surrounded by illiterate people who are not so pleasant or cultured," said one prisoner, Michael Bryant, who had stabbed a man. "We try to stay away from that. We use words like 'assuage,' 'phantasmagoric' and 'castigate' all the time." Some of the members had been educated before prison but most had discovered Toastmasters and the intellectual challenges of performance and persuasion while behind bars. Said one warden: "They're so used to lying, they can give speeches with so much feeling."

One Atlanta prisoner's faith in the power of speaking turned Toastmasters' true-blue American optimism into a convict's delusions of innocence. "If all the people in here spoke better, they wouldn't be here," said Michael Damien, who had joined Toastmasters to prepare for the (inevitable, he said) overturning of his life sentence for murder. He expects that when he's finally released, he'll be talking to reporters. "Toastmasters is helping me prepare."

. . . .

At their annual conference, Toastmasters International holds an international public-speaking contest, which it bills as the "World Series of public speaking, the Olympics of oratory, the final bout for the heavyweight title of World Champion of Public Speaking." It's been held every year since 1938 except for 1944 and 1945. In 2004, I went to the contest, which was held in Reno, not to hear the contestants as much as to listen for verbal blunders in a social context. Toastmasters prepare for speeches intensively, even for relatively informal presentations. Practice, they believe, is the key to good speaking. (Other approaches to public speaking, such as Lee Glickstein's, are closer to jazz improvisation; do come prepared but don't map out every sentence, pause, or joke; do be prepared to be with your listeners in their moment.) I wanted to see what standard Toastmasters train for. Given their level of preparation, do they make room for errors, and if so, what kind? How do Toastmasters define what makes a good speaker—and how do they frame what they treat as verbal blunders and what are they willing to let slide?

I needed a guide to the contest and was lucky to find David Brooks, who won the championship in 1990 and proudly bears the title "World Champion of Public Speaking" on his Web site. He's an expert on the contest and is so fond of talking about its history and strategies for winning and what life is like as a World Champion that I wondered, as I listened to him, what he talked about before he won. He's a tall, slim man, about fifty years old, with a broad wave of graying hair that sweeps boyishly across his face. In his baritone voice, Brooks speaks quickly and crisply, a slight trace of Dallas, his hometown, in his vowels. Obeying his Toastmaster training, he doesn't say "uh" or "um" and rarely restarts a sentence, though he often repeats words at the beginning of sentences. ("By God, these guys learn how to get rid of [ums and uhs]," Herb Clark told me. "Often at some other expense. They have to go do other things to deal with the problems they usually use 'uh' and 'um' for.") A former high school journalism teacher and public relations director, Brooks makes his living as a professional speaker and loves language protectively. When the waiter serving us breakfast said, "Very well, guys," Brooks muttered, "Good. It should be good." He might have rolled his eyes a little. "Some people overcorrect."

His winning speech in 1990 was an old-fashioned jeremiad, calling his audience back to moral values that American society had abandoned. Probably no one repented, but it didn't matter: Brooks won the championship. After seven more years of building a business as a professional speaker, delivering uplifting keynote addresses and day-long seminars on good writing and speaking, he made the jump to becoming a professional speaker, traveling to Bahrain, Ireland, and Hong Kong. He's also a championship guru, an avid student of the contest who advises contestants every year. In Austin, Texas, where he lives, he's not well known outside of Toastmaster circles, but thousands of Toastmasters all over the world revere him. In Reno well-wishers mobbed him. "I guess I'm a rock star," he said with reluctant delight.

The road to Reno began about 2,500 years ago in ancient Greece, where Athenians developed a tradition of using persuasive language, or rhetoric, to shape the course of events, to claim power, and to mete out justice and shame. The first handbooks for public speaking appeared in the fifth century BCE by two Sicilian authors, Corax and Tisias, to help ordinary men plead their own cases in court. Itinerant teachers of various subjects, including rhetoric, called the sophists, brought these handbooks to Athens; the sophists were the first in Greece to teach for hire. Works by Aristotle (384–322 BCE), Isocrates (436–338 BCE), and Plato (429–347 BCE) also taught and debated the precepts of persuasive language. Although many Greek thinkers believed that the ability to wield words was an inborn talent, others believed it could be taught and practiced in public venues—an egalitarianism that was a founding tenet of Athenian democracy. Toastmasters is an heir to this Greek tradition, particularly to the strain that treats rhetoric as a craft—a skill that you can learn, perhaps not in a few weeks, but with the long, hard work of nearly embarrassing yourself to death with every phrase and gesture.

People now tend to think of ancient rhetoric as a noble pursuit but find contemporary forms of persuasive language—advertising and propaganda, most of all—to be inconvenient at least and dangerous at worst. The ancient Greeks, who were afraid that the persuasive language they prized might work too well, first voiced these same fears. Around 414 BCE, the early rhetorician Gorgias warned that speech could charm, like witchcraft. It also worked like a drug, creating emotions in listeners that they couldn't control. "For just as different drugs dispel different secretions . . . so also in the case of speeches, some distress, others delight, some cause fear, others make the hearer bold, and some drug and bewitch the soul with a kind of evil persuasion." Gorgias made these comparisons in a famous speech that excused Helen of Troy for giving in to Paris, because Helen had been as susceptible to persuasive language as to violent force or even falling in love.

Ancient Rome inherited the Greek rhetorical tradition, and Cicero and Quintilian became its most eminent teachers of rhetoric and oratory. Cicero fought political and rhetorical battles to defeat conspirators trying to overthrow the Roman Republic, while Quintilian, born about eighty years later, practiced law and wrote about how to properly educate the good speaker. These Greek and Roman conventions were adapted in medieval Europe, then again in colonial America, where they were transformed by life in a frontier democracy, practiced in frontier churches, infused with African American traditions, and were even influenced by Native American oratory. In the twentieth century, urbanization and the importance of business, as well as the rise of the mass media, also changed how people spoke and wrote.

One of the most durable ancient conventions of speech was a speaker's style. Cicero considered the ability to produce sentences thick with imagery and allusions to be the Roman orator's essential tool. Embellishing a subject was the central task of eloquence, he said, which could make the smallest thing seem significant or the best thing not very good at all. Perhaps Cicero, who honed his skills arguing legal cases, found that it was effective to overwhelm listeners with metaphors, poetic images, repetition, and artful deviations from proper grammar. By his own admission, Cicero wasn't a fluent speaker—he was prone to nervousness when he began a speech—but he knew how to articulate the importance of patriotism to the Roman Republic. In Cicero's world, copious speaking was put in service of patriotic goals, hence its virtue—in other words, copiousness was not essentially more beautiful or persuasive than other styles, but it became associated with desirable social values and their prestige.

Through the Middle Ages and Renaissance, people wrote Latin and the European vernaculars in the same highly ornate, profuse style, which was thick with stylistic flourishes, classical references, and accumulations of language. For five hundred years, it was the dominant style, taught in schools and perpetuated by the hierarchy of the Roman church. Speakers and writers were trained in the art of profusion, or what was called "copiousness" or "amplification." It was associated with fertility, wealth, education, and other characteristics of the powerful and wealthy.

In early America, speech making was an everyday activity, practiced as much by the hangman as the head of the local literary society. Even the condemned orated from the scaffold, a noose looped around their necks. Before many people knew how to read and before public schools were established, newspapers were often read aloud in public, and storytelling, plays, and lectures were popular forms of entertainment. The United States had an oral culture whose robustness stood, as a sort of political metaphor, for the life of the country itself. But frontier life, a lively democracy, and eventually the mass market placed new demands on traditions of speechmaking.

Americans developed a wide distaste for the verbally florid around the Civil War. The critic Edmund Wilson called it "the cultivation of brevity." Two rising stars of the new prose style were Abraham Lincoln (in the Gettysburg Address) and Ulysses Grant (in the *Personal Memoirs of Ulysses S. Grant*). Wilson argued that their style was a response to the political exigencies of the times, because "they had no time in which to waste words." The plainer style, with its spare words and faster pace, was considered efficient and functional, the language of action and decision in the political crisis of secession and the subse-

quent war. After the war, the telegraph, the train, and Green-
wich Mean Time accelerated the pace of daily life, which sim-
plified the overblown conventions of speech and writing. In this
environment leaders needed to direct their constituencies
to action quickly; deliberation or reflection now seemed like a
luxury.*

A plainer, more muscular style of language was also now
being used for advertising and business, as the ordinary man
and woman, not the classically (and leisurely) educated,
became targets for the sales pitches of the industrial age. Men
such as self-help guru Dale Carnegie expressed the urgency of
the time in public speaking handbooks he wrote for YMCA
schools. "We are in a hurry," Carnegie wrote. "This is the age of
automobiles and aeroplanes and wireless. We are nervous.
Have you anything to say? All right, let's have it at once. Get
through with it and sit down."

Ralph Smedley recognized the need for speed and directness as
well. In 1903, as a college senior, he wrote an essay for the Illinois Wesleyan University newspaper about whether four years
of college were too many. He decided they were not—but then,
he argued, people should seek education for their whole lives.
After graduating with a bachelor of science degree in 1903, he
worked for the YMCA in Bloomington, Illinois, where he founded

*A wide-ranging account of conceptions of time during the late nine-
teenth and early twentieth centuries and their impact on art, literature, and
diplomacy is *The Culture of Time and Space, 1888–1918,* by Stephen Kern.
Kern argues that World War I was precipitated by a failure of rulers' and
diplomats' decision making to account for and keep pace with diplomatic
telegram messages.

a speech club for boys.* One can clearly see the outlines of the Greek rhetoricians in his precepts, as well as those of Quintilian, who defined the good speaker as "a good man speaking well." As the Toastmasters official history tells it, Smedley spent the next twenty years as a YMCA employee, moving from city to city and becoming a sort of oratorical Johnny Appleseed, planting a public-speaking club wherever he landed. In Freeport, Illinois, for example, he established a club for professional men whose first meeting, held on March 27, 1907, was conceived as a mock farming convention. Though most of the men had had no farming background, they gave hearty speeches like "Corn is king" and "The hog, his nature and values."

By Smedley's time, old-style oratory was mostly gone, surviving in preaching traditions, barnstorming lawyers, and politicians' stump speeches. In its place rose a new form, with a style all its own: "public speaking." Smedley and Carnegie† believed that the voice of the common man was needed in the business world as well as the political sphere. "In the days when pianos and bathrooms were luxuries, men regarded ability in speaking as a peculiar gift, needed only by the lawyer, clergyman, or statesman," Carnegie once wrote. "Today we have come to realize that it is the indispensable weapon of those who would forge ahead in the keen competition of business."

When Smedley launched his first club, continuing educa-

---

*Smedley's college course work included trigonometry, rhetoric, Greek, German, chemistry, American literature, essay, geology, biology, calculus, psychology, French, logic, history, sociology, and philosophy. He also studied for a semester for a master's degree in Greek.

†Eventually the two men headed in different directions, Smedley toward establishing nonprofit clubs around the world, Carnegie toward building a for-profit consulting company.

tion for adults was growing more popular, and the YMCA was at the fore of this movement.* Smedley's goal: create a nonschool venue where adults could learn new professional skills or other topics in a fun atmosphere. Responsibilities for leading meetings and speaking rotated among the members, who were expected to critique one another's speeches. In his memoir, Smedley recalled that not all of his YMCA bosses saw the value of his clubs. They treated them "as a sort of peculiarity—an idiosyncrasy—of Smedley's," he wrote. In 1922, after years of traveling in various cities and setting up a club in each one, he finally settled in Santa Ana, California. There he established a club whose agenda has passed to every Toastmasters' meeting since: business announcements, then five-minute prepared speeches, and ten minutes for evaluation of each speech. In 1934, the organization added a round of on-the-spot speeches about current events, called "Table Topics," to give all members a chance to speak.

Smedley's basic premise: you should talk to an audience as you would talk to one person. He called the style "amplified conversation." It was more interactive than the old-school bombast; you didn't exhort, perorate, shout, goad, lash, or incite your audience. Instead you spoke to them—ideally, with them. It was an after-dinner style, spoken by the sated to the sated, not rallying the troops into battle. It was pragmatic, suited to the rise of Rotary, Kiwanis, and Lions Clubs in the 1920s, as well as the prominence of chambers of commerce, whose weekly lunch and dinner meetings were venues where

*Smedley also held this opinion. As a senior in college, he wrote, "Education is to prepare man not only for usefulness in this life, but for blessedness in the life to come."

speakers reaffirmed the values of the organization. Though one's audience consisted of one's peers, a speaker didn't speak informally, use slang, or clip his pronunciation. In a semi-intimate, matter-of-fact way, you told your friends what they already felt, knew, and held dear.

Smedley also taught rules for delivery, lists of do's and don't's that brought skills to a wide range of students in a brief amount of time. Smedley's lists were like vitamin injections to boost a person's eloquence. The list of do's included brevity and making eye contact; don't's included avoiding controversial topics and saying "um." As Barnet Baskerville notes in *The People's Voice*, a history of oratory in America, in the decades before the rise of "public speaking" and commercial values, people had read model speeches collected in anthologies and histories of oratory. By the 1920s, few people had time for a drawing-room sort of self-education. A person had to learn the formula for a good speech, then hit the lecterns.

Smedley and Carnegie weren't alone in transforming oratory for the booster age. James Winans at Cornell revived the study of speaking in colleges and also promoted the conversational style. All of them helped adapt public speaking from the political and religious sphere to the business one. At its most practical, Toastmasters would make an individual more competitive in his business and his service club, where he might be called to speak upon anything at any moment. A man could at least survive a request to say a few words—public speaking was no reason for swoons or heart palpitations.

In the hands of the Toastmasters, public speaking took a turn away from the moral education of the oratorical training of the past. Despite how Socrates chastened the Sophists in Athens for teaching the youth tricks with language, making them more powerful than they were wise and good, the classical rhetorical training had focused on educating the speechmaker—and inculcating them with the community's moral values. The education of the orator was the education of a soul, and a citizen. Demagogues and charlatans might still exist, but you could hunt them down. After all, when you created good speakers you also created listeners who could discern insidious rhetoric and resist its intoxication. Oratory once attempted to build and reaffirm community. Smedley made it all about the sale.

"All talking is selling," Smedley once wrote, "and all selling involves talking, whether it's written or oral. In all our talking, we are attempting to 'sell' information or ideas or inspiration, or some other intangible." In a Calvinist framework, economic success had been a sign that God had chosen you. Now, it was almost as if you had only to learn the principles of speaking well in public to show that you, too, were one of the chosen.

Reno was dry and hot but occasional raindrops splashed down from lone clouds overhead as I headed to the Hilton casino. When I arrived, I went straight to the convention and an awards ceremony in the hotel's ballroom, where a string of emcees with impressive voices read lists of names and made each one ring like a philosophical truth. One set of awards went to people who'd passed the first ring of fire in the Toastmasters' world: preparing and delivering a series of ten speeches. In 2004, 19,608 people voluntarily did what many Americans say they fear more than death itself. And each of them paid forty dollars (a basic membership fee) for the privilege of doing so.

Most of the exercises in this basic speech sequence focus on delivery. (Later courses teach more specialized skills.) First there's the Ice-Breaker, then Be in Earnest. Organize Your Speech helps a speaker organize her thinking, Show What You Mean works on gestures and body language, Vocal Variety explores different ways to use the voice, then Work with Words expands a speaker's vocabulary range. Apply Your Skills gets a person to combine the techniques, and he or she raises the stakes in Make it Persuasive. Speak with Knowledge is an informational talk. The apogee of the Toastmasters basic training comes in the final speech, Inspire Your Audience, in which you "select a topic about which you feel strongly, analyze your audience's mood and feelings, and inspire them using all the skills you have developed." It was this basic speech, five to seven minutes long, that contestants in the world championship would be giving.*

One part of the Toastmasters training is eliminating "uh" and "um." Once speakers became sensitized to its presence, a public-speaking coach or teacher could get them to catch it before it came out of their mouths. Militance is one word you could use to describe the Toastmasters' attitude about the pause filler. Before one convention event, I chatted with a Toastmaster from New Jersey, a longtime member who sold chemicals for a living. I said something like, "the errors people make when they, uh, speak."

"You just said 'uh,' " he interrupted. Pause.

"I did, you know," I admitted. "But conversation is different from formal speaking."

"You're right, you're right," my new friend said. He leaned

---

*The list of basic speeches has since changed slightly.

closer. "They say not to say it," he said sheepishly. "I say it sometimes."

After the ceremony, I met John Hunt, a Texan friend of David Brooks and an old Toastmasters hand, who had a flattop haircut and was wearing a flannel shirt. An employee for a federal agency, he first became involved in Toastmasters to "improve my writing and leadership skills," he said, adding that "I already was a ham." (According to Bremen's survey, 50 percent of Toastmasters members said they joined "to improve public speaking skills for professional purposes" and 23 percent said they joined to improve speaking skills for "self-esteem and personal reasons.")

According to Hunt, Toastmasters helps people's confidence as speakers. "People know their errors," he says. "When someone finishes a speech, they know all the places they should have changed. But they need someone to tell them what they did right. And sometimes the hardest thing to do is to evaluate positively. We work on this all the time. The hardest thing to do is to figure out what your peers have done well. Our job is to say, You got up. You spoke. You made sense. Let's do that again. That's how we sucker people into doing more speeches. It's the same dynamic as in gambling," he said, gesturing toward the hotel's casino. "You put in a nickel. Nothing. You put in another nickel. You get four back. Are you going to continue?"


I wandered up to a small bookstore that had been set up for the convention, where piles of Toastmasters paraphernalia were on sale: T-shirts, caps, bumper stickers, ashtrays, sun visors, and coffee mugs, all of them printed with the Toastmasters logo (a globe framed by two gavels and bearing a "T"). There were also official Toastmaster trophies and plaques and stacks of work-books for speeches. I hoped they'd sell refrigerator magnets with Ralph Smedley standing beatifically at a podium, a sort of oratorical kitsch, but I couldn't find any. Yet rank-and-file members I met didn't appear to go in for genuine founder worship, either. I heard only one Toastmaster mention Smedley by name, and that was to complain about how the judges who evaluate the championship speeches are "brainwashed" in Smedley's teachings.

All of the brochures radiated a Horatio Alger appeal. It's a bewitching message: anyone who applies him- or herself has the innate ability to be an engaging and witty speaker. Ralph Smedley believed, in a by-your-bootstraps classic American sort of way, that eloquence can be yours—if you're willing to work for it. This begged the question of where your eloquence was, if you didn't have it now. Carnegie located it in childhood. Children had a natural eloquence, he argued, which they lost—or that was stolen from them. "You were born with the ability to express yourself," he once wrote. "A little child four years of age is able to express anger and love and joy without any drill in public speaking." How do they get ruined? Carnegie claimed that they are robbed of their natural spontaneity by society, school, and authorities, which turns them into adults who are reluctant, anxious, and slow.

If the World Championship of Public Speaking represents the verbal barnstorming side of Toastmasters, then David Brooks is the barnstormer's barnstormer. One of the most knowledgeable students of the contest, he studies patterns and trends in judging and spends hours watching videos of past contests. He has an impressive stash of facts and anecdotes about the championship, which he says he couldn't win today with his 1990 speech, because the standards keep changing. In the 1980s, contestants started venturing beyond their lecterns, which was a shocking innovation in its day; as I see in Reno, they range the stage like boxers. Brooks says their moves are mapped out on paper and timed to the second.

Though Toastmasters prize a speaker's control of his or her setting, voice, and body, they're also connoisseurs of risk; like acrobats they know a genuinely dangerous stunt when they see one. Brooks likes to tell stories about his own flubs, costume mistakes, and equipment failures. In 1990, a hundred people told him not to wear the "Texas tuxedo" he wanted to wear— string tie, blue jeans (usually starched and pressed), and cowboy boots. Such an outfit was a radical informality. "And after I won, the same hundred people told me it was a great idea," Brooks says.

In 1999, Craig Valentine gave a speech that contained a dialogue between him and his conscience, back and forth. "It starts slow but becomes rapid fire. It was so"—Brooks paused, in awe still—"tightly constructed, like you were listening to two different people. I thought: this is like crossing a highwire without a net." Valentine won. (He is now a motivational speaker and president of a consulting firm.) Two years later, a contestant from Boston named Darren LaCroix, a stand-up comic who joined Toastmasters to get more time onstage, opened with the line, "Have you ever had an idea," and then fell face-first on the floor, where he stayed while he said his opening lines. The basic Toastmasters speech is highly formalized; after the opener, the speaker acknowledges the emcee and the audience. LaCroix did this prone. "He had the courage to stay there, to play it out seconds after what anyone should have done," Brooks said. "He won the contest in that first minute."

"Today's American audiences want information in an entertainment package," Brooks added. In Europe and Asia, adults don't need a stand-up comedy routine to be tricked into learning. "In Europe, you can stand behind a lectern and read from notes and most people will like it," he says. "I spoke at Volvo once in Sweden and when it was all over, they said, 'We like you. You're not a typical American speaker. You have knowledge, and you can give it to us in a format that's not an over-the-top style.' An American style is not a compliment— that means you're showy, and preachy, but light on content."

The night before the contest, he invited me to eat dinner with three other world champions who were in Reno. Going through the buffet line, they joshed one another constantly like regular guys after a day of gambling. Once they sat down at the table their magnetism and charm was so strong I could hardly eat. Along with Brooks and LaCroix was Ed Tate, who had been a successful professional speaker before his championship, and Jim Key, a lanky man with a shaved head who won in 2003. The son of a minister, he was inspired by management guru Zig Ziglar to take up inspirational speaking. He placed second in 2001 and 2002, then in 2003, asked Brooks to be his coach. That year, Key won.

Ed Tate (the 2000 champion) is an intense African-American man who used to be a computer executive and corporate trainer. Now he's a professional speaker whose client list reads like the Fortune 500. All four always seem to be on the look-out for ways to leverage their champion status—Key wants to leave his day job, Brooks likes to travel overseas to speak to audiences at companies and Toastmaster conventions, while

Tate and LaCroix upped their speaking fees and now ask more than seventy-five hundred dollars per speech. LaCroix, a short, bald man in rimless glasses, explains that's how years of investment are paying off. "I used to drive two and a half hours to Portland, Maine, for five minutes onstage, and now I get paid extremely well for a one-hour keynote," he said. "It's not for the one hour—it's for all the two-and-a-half-hour drives which allowed me to develop a skill to change the way an audience thinks in an hour. That's our value—when we're done talking, the audience will have changed the way they think."

They talked about their favorite audiences. "Women," LaCroix said immediately. Of course, I said, if you're a public-speaking rock star and they're showing up at your hotel door. I was joking, but LaCroix corrected me. "It's not about that, it's about what they're like in audiences," he said. "Women are more boisterous, they're more open with their laughter. I'd rather speak to an all-female audience—"

"Hear, hear," Tate said.

"—than mixed or all men."

"When I started my career, I'd speak in front of anybody," Tate said. "You want me to do that? I'll do that. But now it's very limited. I'm at a place in my career where I can choose my assignments."

"The women want to love you more," LaCroix added. "The guys are like, 'I should be the one up there.' The women see you up there, and they're like, 'Hey, let's have fun.' "


The next morning, the day of the contest, I caught up with David Brooks and Jim Key wading into groups of admirers, laughing, signing autographs. Around them people were filtering into their seats in the vast ballroom buzzing with two thousand anxious Toastmasters. The day before, I had seen some videos of previous contests, but the videos hadn't prepared me for the tension in the room, or how distant the chairs seemed from the broad stage, or how the room, hung with black curtains, felt like an immense cave.

The contest began promptly (Toastmasters are very punctual) with the emcee introducing former world champions from the audience; Brooks rose from his reserved seat, tossed a graceful wave, and smiled a large grin, an image that was projected onto two twenty-foot video screens. Tate, LaCroix, and Key had a moment, too, as did Dana LaMon, the 1992 champion.

The emcee explained the rules. The audience can't talk. We may laugh and clap, but talking's forbidden. Toastmasters pride themselves on being the model audience—the evening before, the champions told me their most favorite audiences in the whole world were other Toastmasters, who listen best and laugh the loudest. Securing the room's borders is key for cementing the bond between the speaker and the audience. Once the contest begins, the doors are closed, and no one is allowed in or out.

And then the first speaker was announced. One by one the contestants came onstage for their seven minutes, most of them reaching center stage with a fake lope that comedians use to signal enthusiasm. Everyone smiled. Because the speeches are designed for multipurpose appeal, the ones that day were tied to no current events. They're all mother, home, and heaven. David Brooks had prepared me for this. Critics of the contest, he said, frequently complain about its intellectual shallowness. It was true: the speeches were perfectly, faultlessly delivered, and they were vacuous. Though the anecdotes were winning and the specifics shown, not told, the underlying messages were polished smooth, like rocks in an eternal river: love your children and listen to them, because they know the truth about existence. Persevere; don't abandon your dreams. You should live by your values. Have fun. All of it proved that speakers can deliver a speech flawlessly yet move their audience no farther than if they'd stood wordlessly on the stage.

But who really knows why the eighteen judges score as they do? Even David Brooks doesn't predict that the winning speaker will be a large, red-nosed man in a tuxedo whose speech, all 779 words and seven minutes, twenty-four seconds of it, featured dogs, car crashes, two men nicknamed "Fat Dad," a toppled statue of Mary Poppins, love, a death by cancer, and a chair.

It was also the only speech with verbal blunders.

The winner was Randy Harvey, a fifty-three-year-old human resources director in a school district near Eugene, Oregon, who comes from a long line of storytellers from Oklahoma. He practiced his speech, "Lessons from Fat Dad," three to four times a day for seven weeks in his head and gave it about twenty-five times to various Toastmasters clubs. His speaking style resembles Garrison Keillor's brand of urban corn pone and came, he told me, from sitting on a porch as a kid with his grandfather who was drinking whiskey and "just spinning these yarns." The stories would change, based on who was listening and how much he'd drunk. Fat Dad was a nickname first given to Harvey's great-grandfather. Harvey's father, the third Fat Dad, was also a constant storyteller. By the time young Harvey left home at eighteen, he knew all the versions to tell of his tales, a Fat Dad on the rise.

Growing up poor and rising far gave Harvey various ways to talk to people. His great-grandmother was Cherokee; his mother worked as a secretary; his father once did time for armed robbery. "We're what you'd call white trash," he says with a merry air. He's worked so hard to put this past behind him, he can hardly now sit back to enjoy what he's built. He has a PhD in educational administration, is a private detective, runs a labor consulting business, and is slated to finish a law degree in two years. Most of the time he plays the methodical, logical professional. But storytelling, he says, has helped him the most. "The reality is," he told me, "if you tell people a story, you capture their attention."

I admired Harvey's artful omission of specific details—the color of the car, the smell of pipe tobacco—which invited the listeners to interact with his speech, making it their own. I also liked his aw-shucks delivery. At least it was genuine corn pone. And the speech genuinely moved me, exactly because it was a story, not a sermon. He could have written a speech that aggrandized himself, or told of the ups and downs of his career, but he opted for sweetness. I told him all this. And, I added, you were the only contestant who blundered. At first he was shocked—he reminded me he grew up uneducated, of course he might not have used words correctly. I don't mean those kinds of errors, I said, explaining Goffman's "knows better" and "doesn't know better" errors. I meant the "knows better" errors, the ones that would be noted by an audience that prizes control.

Harvey immediately wanted to know what I'd heard. One was early in the speech, I said, when you're describing buffing the car, when you stumbled on the word "hand." But you quickly recovered and kept going. Harvey nodded, Yes, that was one moment. The other, I told him, was when you said, "It was like ice water being thrown on you in a cold shower" instead of "in a hot shower."

Harvey explained that both moments involved recent additions to the speech that he hadn't practiced that much. He also felt proud that his speech had broken with Toastmaster tradition. No one had won the contest with a speech in which someone dies, and he was happy to point out that, in his speech, two people had died.

"Toastmasters don't expect you to be a perfect speaker," he said. "They can be technically perfect in their pronunciation and their body language, but the message has to ring."

# 7

## The Birth of Bloopers

In 1952, on a live television broadcast, the actress Betty Furness tried to open the door of a Westinghouse refrigerator during a commercial break on *The Rube Goldberg Show*. She pulled. She yanked. But the door stayed shut. "Who's the comedian?" she muttered through her teeth.

A professional, Furness continued to talk about the appliance's virtues, tugging on its door, as the camera pulled in so tightly on her face that it loomed in the screen. Witnessing the prop failure and Furness's frustration was the producer of the show, a veteran radio producer, talent agent, and television pioneer who in that moment envisioned an empire of books and records built on the embarrassed tongues of broadcasters, performers, and celebrities flubbing their way through their appearances, a blooper franchise that would live on, making people laugh, long after he was gone. When Kermit Schafer died in 1979 at the age of sixty-four, he'd made millions of dollars putting out thirty records, a dozen books, a bunch of television shows, and a movie, *Pardon My Blooper*. He sold the rights to the "bloopers" trademark to television empresario Dick

Clark, whose production company continues to assemble and air blooper shows until the present day.

Schafer was the first to transform other people's flustered speaking, slips of the tongue, and inadvertent solecisms from television and radio broadcasts into gold. In his hands, a blooper wasn't just a mistake. It was a noteworthy event, a slice of everyday media life, otherwise evanescent, that he shined up for display. There was the Vick's 44 Cough Syrup commercial that guaranteed "You'll never get any better!" Or as the stumbling newscaster said, "Also keeping an eye on the Woodstock Rock Festival was New York's governor Rockin Nelsenfeller." In Kermit Schafer's many blooper books, the bloopers are listed one after another, three or four lines of text separated by a space, then another blooper. A disc jockey said, "COCM Stereo Land now presents popular Hawaiian favorite Don Ho with Tiny Boobies . . . uh . . . Tiny Bubbles." Ralph Nader, who was investigating false nutritional claims by food manufacturers, came on *The Mike Douglas Show* and announced they were "looking into some of the claims made by a leading booby foob company." A Canadian announcer said, "This is the Dominion Network of the Canadian Broad Corping Castration." An actress announced that "the fog was as thick as seepoop."

Why did blooper humor work? Because it stripped the dignity from public figures and celebrities. Bloopers also split the media persona from the actual human being, puncturing the performance and with it the cool persona. Bloopers weren't attached to a single figure, as spoonerisms were linked to Reverend Spooner; the blunderers Schafer depicted were frequently anonymous, and each blooper incident offered something to dissect.

In some bloopers, you can catch the mistake right off; in others, you must discern the off-color meaning in a perfectly innocent statement. In either case, you had to listen intently, even aggressively, not passively. By carving out the moment of interest, the blooper targeted your attention, and in so doing taught a way to listen to and watch the new broadcast media. The phonograph (in the early 1900s), radio (in the 1920s), and television (in the 1950s) brought the public and commercial spheres into the privacy of people's homes in successive waves, each more penetrating than the last. Suddenly people had access to public figures, such as Franklin Roosevelt in his fireside radio chats, not as public speakers but as talkers; just as suddenly, advertisers had access to them. Unanswered questions abounded about the news bulletins and constant entertainment. Should the devices be turned on all the time in the background of home life? Should they be turned on at special times? Was it entertainment or education? Who were the announcers and other figures of the emerging media elite, and could they be trusted? Why should they be trusted at all?

To people who wanted to duck the broadcasting juggernaut by finding its faults, Schafer became a hero.

Kermit Schafer was born in 1914 in Brooklyn, New York, where he was a boyhood friend of Allen Funt, creator of the radio show *Candid Microphone* and the television show *Candid Camera.* Working separately, Schafer and Funt were among the first to help us appreciate twists of unscripted reality—especially if they were caught on film or video or tape. Before World War II, Schafer worked mainly in radio, though in 1940, he produced a television special of *Babes in Arms* for NBC. After spending four years in the U.S. Air Force as an entertainment director, he went back to television. His blooper fascination began as a hobby; he collected fluffs and outtakes from military training films and played them for friends. But it was his work producing Allen Funt's *Candid Microphone* album that showed him that bloopers had commercial promise.

Schafer's first production was a 1953 book, *Your Slip Is Showing*, which he followed in the same year with a record, *Radio Bloopers*. It sold 4.75 million copies.* His LP, *Pardon My Blooper!*, volume 1, hit number 9 in 1954, and volume 2 hit number 12 the same year. The bloopers were such hot commodities that by 1956, at least two other records by imitators had been released: *Excuse My Fluff* by Don Meyer and *Slips, Fluffs, Boners* by Roy Freeman. Schafer claimed to have coined the word "blooper," but the word was already in use. (He did trademark it, however.) Since the 1920s, it had referred to the howl or whoop from a radio picking up interference, which made a "blooper," a radio set that regularly made the noise.

To feed the demand for bloopers, Schafer trawled the media world. He produced records such as *All Time Great Bloopers, Citizen's Bloopers, Funny Bones, 100 Super Duper Bloopers, Best of Bloopers, Washington Bloopers, Comedy of Errors, Slipped Disks, Prize Bloopers, Super Bloopers, Off the Record, Station Breaks, Funny Boners,* and *Foot 'n Mouth Club*. He told interviewers that he wanted a quote from Alexander Pope carved on his gravestone: "To forgive is human; to err, divine."†

Schafer also became a regular visitor on talk shows. Broadcast live into the 1960s, they were verdant with mistakes, long

---

*As of 1976, it was the seventeenth-highest cumulatively selling record in the world, selling 250,000 fewer than The Monkees and 750,000 more than a John F. Kennedy memorial album.

†Pope's original line reads, "To err is human/to forgive, divine."

after other shows where Schafer had found bloopers were pre-recorded. Once shows were prerecorded, bloopers were edited as outtakes and set aside; these snips of tape eventually found themselves in Schafer's hands. He appeared with Johnny Carson, Dinah Shore, David Frost, Dick Cavett, and Mike Douglas to hand out a gold figurine with its hands over its lips, the Bloopy, an award given to actors prone to gaffing. His collections included bloopers from the hosts themselves, such as the time that Merv Griffin told a guest, "We sure thank you for taking time out from your busy sexual . . . I mean schedule." There's also the time that Johnny Carson said, "Here's how to relieve an upsex stomach . . . I mean an upsep stomach . . . with Sex Lax . . . Ex-Lax!"

In his publicity photos, Schafer often posed as the secret listener perpetually on post. Bloopers are more appealing when they're freshly captured, like fish. But Schafer also played with the image of the ham radio operator—the amateur who spreads international goodwill—and of spies eavesdropping on enemy governments. Pictures accompanying a profile of him published in *Magnetic Film and Tape Recording* in 1955 show Kermit and his wife, Mickey, a former model, seated side by side at tape recorders with earphones on, presumably scanning the airwaves from their home, high on a hill in New York State.

His mountaintop aerie, the profile reported, "is a veritable listening post and monitoring station for radio and television Bloopers," and the house is "entirely wired with audio circuits to allow recording or listening to be done anywhere." Timed circuits turned on recorders to tape certain shows, and Kermit could control the television from bed. The whole thing was playfully calculated to look as if Schafer was turning technology back on the industry itself.

Schafer crafted his image as a watchdog of the airwaves, tirelessly roaming the frequencies, protecting his fans and listeners not from the Communists but from broadcasters' errant control. "When someone commits a Blooper on the air," the profile wrote, "he is less concerned with all the people who heard it than with the man who might have been listening—that man being Kermit Schafer."

In truth, the king of bloopers wasn't really a snoop. Schafer claimed that his collections were authentic, "gathered from video tapes, kinescopes, sound tracks, off-the-air recordings, and other bona fide sources." But Schafer was a deft manipulator of "authentic" and "bona fide." His 1974 feature-length movie, *Pardon My Blooper!* splices film clips to create the sense of being present at the exact moment of blundering, which had been caught only on audio. One scene juxtaposes a shot of a church and a troop of nuns with a woman's voice announcing "our peter-pulling contest at St. Taffy's Church."

However, many of his radio bloopers were re-creations or reenactments. Schafer claimed to have a recording of the first slip ever made on the radio: CBS's Harry von Zell in 1931 making a birthday tribute to the president of the United States, Hoobert Heever. Schafer may have had the original recording, which was likely made on a wire recorder. But the quality of its sound would have been lower than it sounds on *Pardon My Blooper!* because Schafer had rerecorded it using a voiceover actor. A consummate entertainer, he was always willing to opt for the laugh over the truth. In his book *Blooper Tube* he claims to have been the first producer to blow the whistle on deceptive quiz and game shows in the late 1950s. He himself had produced some shows and told a United Press reporter, "You can't run a panel or quiz show without some planted answers and ad libs." Schafer always told the truth about the lies that television tells.

The blooper products married older forms of straight-up language humor to that old standby, the sexual innuendo. If bloopers are regular slips of the tongue into which sexual content has been read by an alert, attentive listener, then Kermit Schafer had a stereotypically masculine sense of humor. Bloopers clearly bear the mark of *Playboy* magazine. In fact, late in his life Schafer adopted the swinger's garb: leather jacket, sunglasses, gold chain.

Not surprisingly, the bloopers that Schafer seems proudest of (and so gives central billing to) are decidedly blue. Veiled jokes about boobs, dicks, balls, and butts outnumber jokes about shit, death, drugs, or race. It must have provided quite a kick to a generation worried about Communist infiltrators to realize that obscene material was being inadvertently broadcast directly into their homes. For every ten interviews with a newly-wed woman ("Are you staying in Los Angeles for a while?" "Yes." "At a hotel?" "Oh, no, we have relations in the Valley"), every thirty inadvertent titty jokes ("Stay tuned for Dickens's immortal classic, the Sale of Two Titties!"), and every forty close calls with obscenity ("Just drop by the colonel's place for delicious finger lickin' Kenfucky fried chicken"), there's only one or two about race, and none about Communists or events on the national political scene (though political figures like Adlai Stevenson, Senator William Fulbright, and then vice president Richard Nixon appear).

Bloopers also represented a new kind of dialect humor for the media age. American humorists used to mock how African

Americans, Jews, Mexicans, Germans, and hillbillies talked, making fun of the recent arrivals, the people who didn't know the rules. Bloopers made fun of another new American group: people on TV, whether part of an emerging media elite or of the anonymous American street. Bloopers were funny because they played out a kind of identity slapstick, peeling off the mask of the media persona to reveal the errant human being beneath.

Dwight Eisenhower was often mocked for his rambling sentences, though he didn't appear in Schafer's blooper books. A parody of the Gettysburg Address à la Ike ("I haven't checked this figures but eighty-seven years ago, I think it was, a number of individuals organized a governmental set up here in the country, I believe it covered certain eastern areas. . . .") ran in the Virginia City *Territorial Enterprise,* a Nevada newspaper, and mock reports from the Society for the Completion of Thoughts and Sentences also ran in *The New Republic.* All this because Ike tended to repair his sentences, interrupting himself so he sounded like "Well, it wasn't on his desk yet. It was a report that had—well, he didn't know whether it was a report. It was a study—he had—as he had seen it—and it had been going back and forth—and they had been going at it for a long time. And it wasn't ready at this moment—at least, for publication—and its eventual destiny—he had forgotten the details."

Eisenhower was the first television president: he campaigned via television, held the first televised press conference, and hired a television consultant.* His persistent

*"What do the Republicans think the White House is, a box of corn flakes?" came the sarcastic question from Adlai Stevenson, the Democratic candidate.

self-interruptions and repairs—many of which were televised and transcribed—made people suspect that he wasn't up to the intellectual demands of the presidency. Until the 1970s, historians thought he'd played the role with neither catastrophe nor stunning success. Later scholars began to wonder if he had deliberately employed syntactic loop-de-loops as a hallmark of his style. As new historical materials became available (and as the memory of his blundering faded), a consensus emerged: Eisenhower may not have been a rousing speaker, but he wielded his ambiguity deliberately in order to fend off the tough questions. That took rhetorical skill.

For instance, before one press conference, Eisenhower's press secretary, James Hagerty, was concerned that reporters would ask Eisenhower whether or not the United States would use atomic weapons against China to defend American allies in Taiwan.

"Don't worry, Jim," Eisenhower said. "If that question comes up, I'll just confuse them."*

Ike had a linguistic foil: Adlai Stevenson, a Democrat and governor of Illinois who ran against Eisenhower in 1952 and 1956. Though Stevenson was a paragon of public eloquence, he suffered in the nascent television age because he refused to pay attention to the new rules. If Eisenhower was mocked for his "garbled syntax" (the single most common phrase used to describe Eisenhower's speaking style), then Stevenson had a reputation for speaking too loftily. Sometimes his reputation worked to his advantage—people admired him, even those who eventually voted for his opponent. His own adviser, George Ball, criticized him for spending so much time writing and rewriting his speeches, not shaking hands or greeting local dig-

---

*Which he did.

nitaries. In both of his national campaigns, Stevenson refused to shorten his speeches for television. On election night, in 1952, he held a televised fireside chat, which he'd agreed to begrudgingly. But he'd spent so much time reworking his text ("We used to tell him that he would rather write than be president," Ball wrote in his memoir) that it outgrew the allotted time. The networks cut him off five minutes before he was finished.

The American tradition of public speech in the political sphere holds that the powerful are also the eloquent. But as television displaced the face-to-face meeting as the exemplary venue in which communication takes place, it gave more power to the succinct, the catchy, and the glib. What Stevenson didn't grasp was that mass media was also mass interaction. His eloquence was never extemporaneous, for example, even though he was credited with raising the intellectual level of presidential campaigns. (It was during the 1952 campaign that the epithet "egghead" was invented for him. He responded with a good-natured play on a famous line from Karl Marx: "Eggheads of the world, unite! You have nothing to lose but your yolks!") By contrast, Eisenhower often faced reporters without a script, expecting to speak spontaneously about questions they lobbed to him.

Yet those transcripts were transcribed verbatim and then provided to the press, often after being cleaned up by James Hagerty. Otherwise, unedited transcripts made Eisenhower's speaking look awkward. In his memoir, Arthur Larson, Eisenhower's speechwriter, defended the president's style of speech as an artifact of these transcripts. "Before anybody makes fun of the alleged garbled syntax of Eisenhower's answers as literally reported syllable by syllable in the papers," Larson wrote, "let him just once read an equally literal stenographic transcript of something he himself has said, in a congressional hearing, or in an extemporaneous speech, or on a witness stand." As George Mahl's experimental subjects knew, the faithfully transcribed speech makes the speaker look like a garbler.

So what was Eisenhower actually like as a speaker? In August 1957, a young scholar of political communication, Thomas C. Kennedy, sat about six feet away from Eisenhower, who was giving a speech to greet new Republican staff members of Congress. (Kennedy was also headed to Congress to do research.) By that point, Kennedy had spent fifteen years evaluating student speeches, so he couldn't help but evaluate the man standing at the podium, who, to Kennedy, didn't at all resemble the president known for his gnarled self-interrupting style: he moved from side to side, occasionally gesturing with his right hand, and once or twice looked at the ground to recall his next topic. His voice was loud enough (Kennedy opined), and it rose and fell appropriately. That day he didn't repair, wasn't ungrammatical, and didn't deviate from standard English. "In the classroom," Kennedy wrote in the crisp analytical article he published later, "its equal would earn a solid A."


Meredith Conover started working for Schafer in 1977, when his blooper empire had grown to include a Dial-a-Blooper hotline, a mail-order business, and plans for a game show. She would come into the office around 8:40; Schafer showed up at 9, and the phones started ringing. Johnny Carson. Milton Berle. Merv Griffin. After more than forty years in broadcasting, he knew everybody. "They wanted him to have the material—it was good free advertising," Conover said. "People used to send outtakes all the time. There was so much stuff, you couldn't believe."

By then the public's appetite for bloopers had dwindled, and

Schafer's records weren't selling as they used to. A California disc jockey, Barry Hansen (better known as Dr. Demento) told me that in the 1970s, when broadcasters began to speak more casually, broadcast blunders became less worthy of notice. The faults, in other words, became faultables less readily. And as humor became more raw and openly sexual, the comedy of sexual innuendoes dissipated, as if all the entendres and ambiguities had resolved themselves.

Kermit and Mickey were then living in Coral Gables, Florida, in a two-and-a-half-acre estate with a swimming pool, a tennis court, a studio, and a seven-bedroom modernist manse. They no longer pretended to surveil the airwaves but lived quiet lives, driving a Ford station wagon and going out for Chinese food. They had no children, but they had a spaniel named Muffin and a cat named Fluffin (as in muffing and fluffing lines).

In 1978, a young woman named Laurie Hannan-Anton, a music student at the University of Miami, was working at a Pier One when a polite, pudgy elderly man with gray hair came into the store. He asked her how the blooper book they had for sale was doing. Laurie asked him why he wanted to know.

"Because I'm Kermit," he said.

"Prove it," she said.

He took out his driver's license, and there it was. They became friends (she collected frog trinkets and was fascinated by someone named Kermit), and he asked her to write music for his theme song, "Blooper Man." He'd already written the words. Anton wrote a song for the electric piano that, by mixing croon and jingle, the nightclub and the circus, perfectly sums up Schafer's career. Only on the chorus does the calliope slapstick come out: "Bloop, bloop, bloop, everybody bloops, and it can even happen to you/Bloop, bloop, bloop, everybody bloops, and once you do it it's hard to undo." The song sums up the history of the slip of the tongue from Sigmund Freud to Schafer himself ("Then along came Schafer/whom we shout hip, hip, hooray for/ Blooper Man is his name/Bloopers are the name of his game") and ends with a blooper:

"This conclee—
This conclu—
This co—"
(pause)
"That is all."

The next year, Kermit died, and his estate eventually set up a foundation in Kermit's and Mickey's names at the University of Miami to give scholarships to students in broadcast media and comedy. We have Schafer to thank, along with Allen Funt, for giving us a taste for metareality, whether it was fake life interfering with real life (in the case of *Candid Microphone* and *Candid Camera*) or daily life erupting through the performances (in the case of bloopers). The Blooper Man's genetic material can be found in reality television as well as in the blooper outtakes on a DVD's special features. It also lived on when Dick Clark bought the rights to the term "blooper" and agreed to honor Kermit's memory in each show.

While Americans had found humor in bloopers, the studios found treasure. Schafer's radio bloopers and military-film outtakes began their lives as trash, unwanted scraps of tape and other media that no one wanted. When the studios realized that they were sitting on gold mines of material, they wised up, and thanks to Schafer's invention of the "blooper," they had a way to repackage the detritus of performances for sale. Al Schwartz, the executive producer of Dick Clark's blooper shows and specials since 1980, including the show *TV's Bloopers and Practical Jokes,* said that a minute of blooper video could cost a few thousand dollars for rebroadcast rights and up to $10,000 once actors, writers, and directors received their fees. Now, he said, the studios can ask as much as $10,000 just for the rebroadcast fees for a minute-long clip. News bloopers are cheap; so are animal bloopers. But bloopers of stars are the most expensive. "The most successful bloopers were the ones that stars made," Schwartz said, "because people liked to see people who are on a pedestal show their human qualities."

Today legal restrictions against showing people's faces on television without their permission means that Dick Clark Productions employs blooper researchers to find out who owns a certain clip and get their permission to use the blooper. The researchers can spend three weeks to three months finding bloopers and getting legal clearances for a one-hour show.

Inevitably, a certain amount of blooper material that can't be cleared goes into an "outtake outtakes" pile, where it waits for its Kermit Schafer to arrive.

# 8

# *Slips in the Limelight*

In the late 1950s, the MIT linguist Noam Chomsky launched a revolution in the study of language by asking, How do babies learn language? The prevailing idea—that children learn by parroting their parents—couldn't explain why children develop language so quickly, or why they say novel things they've never heard before. As Chomsky argued, there must be basic shapes and formulas of language embedded in human brains by evolution and triggered early in life.

The new linguistics focused on these basic building blocks and the templates for assembling them, calling them "language competence," since the blocks and plans made up everything speakers could potentially do with their languages—how you make words, how you put sentences together, how you recognize ungrammatical sentences. Linguists explored this competence and where it came from. Less interesting to them was what people actually say (or sign), which are instances of "language performance." In the new linguistics, language wasn't what a speaker does. It's what a speaker knows.*

Chomsky's basic insight—that the forests of language must come from mental seeds—fundamentally altered how we think about language learning, child psychology, cognitive science, artificial intelligence, and the evolution of the mind. However, by exploring only competence, linguists ignored a number of interesting everyday features of language, such as how men and women speak differently, or how languages change when speakers come into contact, or where slang comes from. Also irrelevant were slips of the tongue.

In 1965, Chomsky brushed away real speakers—and speech errors—with a sentence that's often quoted in full because it gives a taste of his characteristically brusque way of prescribing what linguists should do. "Linguistic theory," he asserted, "is concerned primarily with an ideal speaker-listener, in a completely homogeneous speech community, who knows its language perfectly and is unaffected by such grammatically irrelevant conditions as memory limitations, distractions, shifts of attention and interest, and errors (random or characteristic)." In other words, slips of the tongue had no place in the science because they were random anomalies. As random, they had nothing to offer the study of language.

A great irony in the study of slips of the tongue is that Chomsky's ideas about language, ostensibly hostile to slips, eventually revived scientists' interest in speakers' inadvertent waywardness.

---

*The opposite of competence in this sense isn't incompetence; it's performance. Thus, knowledge of a language, as Chomsky refers to it, isn't what you learn in school but what you already have in your brain—therefore, linguists say you *know* it.

The most direct reason was that Chomsky freed linguists to philosophize and speculate about language as an abstraction in the mind. The American linguists who preceded him refused to consider language abstractly, or to suppose that unseen mental processes were at work. If a mental process couldn't be observed or recorded, they refused to talk about it. Sticklers about evidence, they considered any discussion of "mind" to be unscientific. Chomsky changed all that by providing a theory of language in the mind, permitting linguists to talk about unseen mental processes and creating a distinction between what a speaker knows and what a speaker does. This paradigm shift transformed the occasional lapse from a mere curio into evidence that a scientist could ponder; it put on a pedestal what had been kicked around just a short time before. Of course, Chomsky hadn't intended to provoke interest in speech errors, and he probably would have preferred linguists stay away from slips. But slips were so attractive because through them you could see how the knowing and doing of language were connected—that is, how basic shapes and formulas in the brain turned (or did not turn) into actual words.

What really cemented slips' new status was that they could best illuminate some of Chomsky's own ideas and smooth some persistent wrinkles in his approach. For example, he had posited the existence of basic blocks of language that one couldn't see or perceive. Slips gave voice to these units. Take the slip "glear plue sky" (for "clear blue sky"). In this slip, entire sounds don't move; rather, it's a subpart of a sound, called a "feature," which moves. The feature involved in "glear plue sky" determines whether the vocal cords vibrate when the consonant is pronounced, which is called "voicing." In the slip itself, the voicing feature disattaches from the "b" (the voiced), leaving it as "p" (unvoiced). Then the feature attaches to the "k" (unvoiced), making it "g" (voiced). One could accept the existence of what were known as "phonological features" on faith. Or one could look for evidence. Slips of the tongue, in these instances and in many others, were evidence. They allowed linguists to read the hidden architecture of language.

Well into the 1970s, there was a small boomlet of interest in slips of the tongue—a slip renaissance. People's tongues weren't slipping more; the renaissance was made up of scientists who married slips of the tongue to Chomskyan ideas about language. These ideas had also attracted psychologists, who brought their own long tradition of studying slips that stretched from H. Heath Bawden to Karl Lashley, and when they quoted Rudolf Meringer, it gave deeper historical roots to what linguists were trying to do.

All this raised the profile of verbal blunders—and of verbal blunderers themselves. For many, slips came to stand for the creative potential of language in its purest form: using a finite number of basic building blocks, the human mind was ineluctably driven to combine those blocks in an infinite number of ways. Only a slice of them would be "correct." Slips amounted to the untapped potential lying dormant in our minds. Cognitive scientist Gary Dell expressed the attitude succinctly: "Slips of the tongue can be seen as products of the productivity of language," he wrote. "A slip is an unintended novelty."

Scientific interest in slips of the tongue might have bubbled along tepidly if a UCLA linguist named Victoria Fromkin hadn't arrived to turn up the heat. With her forceful personality and politically astute manner, she persistently explained to linguists why slips mattered. A child of Russian immigrants who grew up in New Jersey and California, Fromkin was from her teens a civil rights and labor activist. She was also an accidental scientist, as she told an oral historian; she went to grad school in linguistics at the age of thirty-eight, encouraged by a friend of a friend. Her belief in social justice might have made her especially attentive to language that would otherwise be forgotten or mocked: for her, all language was meaningful, and everything could be studied. The fact that she began her scholarly career relatively later in life might also have made her more successful in spreading new ideas.

Among linguists, Fromkin is famous for her personal energy, enthusiasm, and her deep sense of right and wrong. Her adviser, phonetician Peter Ladefoged, called her "the mother of all linguists" in an obituary in 2001. Her linguistics textbook, *An Introduction to Language*, has sold nearly a million copies and been translated into Portuguese, Japanese, Swedish, Chinese, Korean, Hindi, and Dutch. One of her more colorful affiliations was with Sid and Marty Krofft, the producers of psychedelic kids' television shows such as *Sigmund and the Sea Monsters* and *H. R. Pufnstuf*. In the 1970s, Fromkin was contacted by the Kroffts to invent a language for the character of Chaka, the apelike Pakuni character on *Land of the Lost*. She based Chaka's language on sounds from West African languages she'd studied (including Hausa, Twi, and Yoruba) and wowed her students when she told them she invented Paku, its six hundred words, and its simple grammar—she claimed that five hundred undergraduates once gave her a standing ovation. With Fromkin's credentials (in 1978, she was named the vice chancellor at UCLA, the first woman to hold the title), she didn't need a TV or movie career, but she was hired as a consultant. Her first client was the Volvo Corporation, which wanted to know how to pronounce "volvo" (Americans pronounced it too much like "vulva," and Fromkin recommended the company promote itself as "vahlvo"), and later she invented a vampire language for the Wesley Snipes movie *Blade*, which involved teaching the actress Traci Lords her vampire lines by telephone.

Among linguists, Fromkin is best known for her work on slips of the tongue. In 1971, she published a landmark paper of the slip renaissance, "The Non-anomalous Nature of Anomalous Utterances." It was the first paper to argue—and in grand fashion—why slips (such as "I'm going to buy a new broof keese today" or "take it out to the porch—uh, veranda") were relevant to linguists. Though Fromkin was a fan of Chomsky, her title was a challenge to his view of errors: if slips fell into discernible patterns, how could they be random? And if they weren't random, what accounted for the patterns? Here she also presented a model of how speech actually occurred, which she called an "utterance generator." It showed how a meaning that a speaker wanted to express began with an intended idea and ended with commands that muscles of the mouth move to produce sound. The utterance generator itself is a graphic of boxes, triangles, and arrows that appeared in an academic article. Unlike other models, however, this one was derived entirely from the predictable dynamics that slips of the tongue revealed.*

In 1973, she published a collection of classic articles on slips from Freud, Wells, and others, putting her 1971 paper last in the book, suggesting that the science of slips had a venerable

---

*It didn't remain current for long; other models, built on speech errors, superseded it.

history (and perhaps that she was its heir). She sponsored a conference in Vienna on the state of the science and spoke at New
College, Oxford University, about Spooner. At scientific meetings, people who lectured after her blundered more than they
normally would. "This produced amusement and strange looks
directed toward me," she once wrote, "as if I had special psychic powers manipulating the audience to provide support for
my contentions."

She also encouraged people to collect slips of the tongue,
teaching them how to do it. By 1971, Fromkin already had her
own stash of six hundred slips, such as "lumber sparty" for
"slumber party," "smart smoking" instead of "start smoking,"
and "moptimal number" for "optimal number." In a file cabinet
in a back office in the UCLA linguistics department is her collection, built over thirty years. One morning, Carson Schütze, a
tall, lanky German psycholinguist who became its caretaker
when Fromkin died in 2000, showed it to me. I had thought five
thousand slips (most in English, but also in French, Italian,
German, and Spanish) would have occupied more space. But
the collection is remarkably compact, filling four narrow metal
trays that look like big recipe boxes.

Each slip that Fromkin collected is written in pencil on an
index card in the scientific phonetic alphabet that linguists use;
each card is numbered, and they're arranged by the date when
Fromkin heard them. Schutze pulled out a few cards and fanned
them between his fingers. In the late 1980s, this collection was
moved to a searchable database and is available on the Web site
of the Max Planck Institute for Psycholinguistics.* As Meringer

---

*Most recently it was located at http://www.mpi.nl/services/mpi-archive/
fromkins/db/folder.

had done, Fromkin attached names to some samples. Jimmy Carter is there ("that is expectable"); so are Noam Chomsky ("are part, simply part of his innate intellectual equipment") and Joe Garagiola ("he knew every crook and nanny"), as well as random stewardesses, gas station attendants, students, district attorneys, cheerleaders, the head of the UCLA medical school, copious colleagues, her husband, and generous appearances of her own blundering self.

One of her favorite slips was "Rosa always date shranks." Her friend Anne Cutler, a psycholinguist, called it "perhaps the most famous verb-inflection error of all." At first glance, English has only one way to mark the past tense of verbs, as the slip "she wash upped the dishes" shows. But they also become the past tense through a vowel change ("sing-sang"). How are the two related? The slip "date shranks" suggests that underlying both "-ed" and the vowel change is a sort of past-tense essence that's as real as it is mysteriously shy. The speaker of "date shranks" meant to attach this past tense essence onto "date" (to make it "dated") but blundered and moved it to "shrinks." Somewhere along the line, "shrinks" as a noun is mistaken for "shrinks," the verb. And that's where the past-tense essence floats to the surface, making "shranks."

Part of the success of slip science came from the fact that collecting slips gave linguists something to do. Like many who get pleasure from puzzling over very small, oft-overlooked corners of the world, linguists can be socially awkward, especially if they have to spend time among others who don't share their fascination. Collecting, an all-weather, all-season activity, was (and is) a convenient social mask. "It can give the collector a feeling of doing some useful work while on holiday, at a dinner party, or watching a television interview," Anne Cutler once wrote. The well-mannered Archibald Hill bemoaned that he was too sensitive to interrupt conversations to collect slips. As a result, he said he never accumulated the extensive collection he longed for.

Merrill Garrett, another early slip researcher, told me that it is difficult to stop collecting slips once you're accustomed to listening for them and writing them down. When your ears are attuned to slips, it's hard not to listen that way all the time. Garrett used to set a time period during which he'd listen assiduously. People remember that he was always flipping open his notebook to write down something someone said. He doesn't study slips exclusively anymore, but he still listens for them.

Slip science was also successful because of the valuable insights that scrutinizing a slip led to. One of Garrett's favorite slips of the tongue is "the skreeky gwease gets the wheel." This slip has two parts. One is a sound exchange, the other is a word exchange. Which one happens first?

If you try the sound exchange before the word exchange, you couldn't get the slip that Garrett heard. You'd get something like, "the sweeky kweel gets the grease." On the other hand, if you posit the word exchange before the sound exchange, you get the right answer. That is, the word exchange ("wheel" for "grease") gets you "the squeaky grease gets the wheel." Then the exchange of sounds between "squeaky" and "grease" gets you "skreeky gwease." The implication? That words are selected in the brain as soundless frames and placed in slots in the sentence, before the individual sounds of those words are located and imported into those frames. That is, language processing works at a word level before it works at a sound level. Such suppositions were grounded in evidence from slips long before other experimental methods were invented.

Just as slips in English follow the underlying structure of the English language, slips in other languages fall in line with the rules of those languages. In Arabic, for instance, slips never occur in combinations of sounds that a native speaker couldn't—or wouldn't—say. And when an Arabic speaker selects the wrong word, he reaches for a noun when he means to say a noun, and he reaches for a verb when he means to use a verb. These patterns reflect basic properties of human language that are shared among all languages.

Slips also take a specific language's shape. In English and other Germanic languages, words are made up out of pieces of meaning that are connected contiguously. The word "destabilizing" is composed of four of the smallest possible units of word meaning (called "morphemes"), "de-," "stable," "-ize" and "-ing." In Arabic, however, the morphemes that make up words do not appear continuously. There's a root of the word, its stem, which is a sequence of consonants with spaces between them. The stem for all things related to writing is k-t-b. To make nouns, verbs, and other words, you add other morphemes, which appear as a sequence of vowels that slot between the consonants. Thus, to make the verb "to write," you add the morpheme a-a-a to the morpheme k-t-b. The resulting word is *kataba*. Other vowel patterns produce other words. "Book" is *kitab*. "Library" is *maktaba*.

Slips of the tongue in Arabic follow this word structure. In some slips two words exchange their consonants, leaving the vowels in place. Here's one example, which I've taken from Hassan Abd-El-Jawad and Issam Abu-Salim, two Arab linguists. They had a Jordanian speaker try to say *sakta qalbiyya* (heart attack), but it came out as *qalba saktiyya* (which doesn't mean anything). In other words, the vowel morphemes (a-a, a-i-a) stayed put, while s-k-t and q-l-b danced around them. There's no English analog to this—you might exchange vowels between words, but those vowels aren't morphemes, as in Arabic.

Getting words in order in time is also an issue for those using sign language, who can say, "Seymour sliced the knife with the salami" or "a Tanadian from Toronto." In the 1970s, slips of the hand gave researchers Edward Klima and Ursula Bellugi evidence that signed languages were, in fact, languages and not, as some supposed, mere mimicry or a word-to-word translation of spoken languages.

As with the features of spoken languages, slips of the hand showed how signs can be broken down into smaller segments that can be combined and repeated in near-infinite sequences. The equivalent of features in sign languages are hand shapes, where the sign is made on the body, and how the sign moves. Klima and Bellugi collected 131 slips of the hand, most of which consisted of an incorrect hand shape. For instance, in ASL one signs "be" with a flat hand slicing out away from the face, but a typical error replaced the full hand with only two fingers in a victory sign. These were "knows better" errors, not made by children or new learners but by otherwise fluent signers of the language.

Slips of the tongue—from well-known ones like "the skreeky gwease gets the wheel" and "Rosa always date shranks" to thousands of others—became so widely accepted in discussions about language that it is virtually impossible to have an empirical or theoretical discussion about language or speech without addressing Fromkin and mentioning Meringer, even if to dispute in passing the details of their analyses. Willem Levelt's exhaustive 1989 work, *Speaking,* discusses speech errors on nearly every page. Using slips, researchers have devised at least seven different models of how speakers find words in memory and say them. Slip science showed how words and sounds are organized in the brain and how they interact; it even opened ways of studying other activities, such as musical performances.* A collection of speech errors at MIT contains 6,000 English slips; there are 900 in Dutch at Utrecht University in the Netherlands, 4,000 at the University of Toronto, 7,200 at the University of California, San Diego, 6,000 at Technical University in Braunschweig, Germany, 3,612 at the University of Oviedo in Spain, and 2,400 at the University of Lyon. Another mark of the popularity of slips is in how many languages the phenomenon has been observed. Though slip research began in German and English, linguists have looked at slips in Greek, Latin, Arabic, Croatian, Spanish, Japanese, Dutch, Hindi, Finnish, Korean, Breton, Chinese, Choctaw, Hungarian, Portuguese, Swedish, Thai, Welsh, and American Sign Language.

---

*Pianists, even highly skilled ones in rehearsed musical performances, often play the wrong note. In one study of expert piano performance, by Caroline Palmer, a cognitive scientist at McGill University, when pianists played familiar, memorized musical pieces, they played the note too early. When they sight-read but added emotional or stylistic inflections, they played notes too late. Like slips of the tongue, slips of the keyboard occur within musical phrases or at their boundaries, which suggests that musicians plan and execute their playing in discrete lengths. Also, if the melody is controlled with two separate hands, then the musicians typically had more errors on the low notes, or those played with the left hand—Western piano music gives a musical advantage to the outer fingers of the right hand.

· · · ·

While the enthusiasm for slips has never waned, the science of slips eventually began to slow, because of a single problem. In general, we utter more slips than we notice—as nearly as anyone can estimate, people make about one or two slips every 1,000 words. If we assume that someone giving a lecture says about 150 words per minute, this means a lecturer might slip once or twice every seven minutes. (Greater time spans will separate slips in conversations, which unfold more slowly.) However, people report noticing about one slip a week. Moreover, people tend to hear some sorts of slips more than others. In one experiment, Rosa Ferber, a Swiss linguist, found that listeners detected only one-third of slips she gave them; of these, one-half were perceived incorrectly. Another test by the Australians Jan Tent and John Clark showed that people tended to mishear slips involving individual sounds, but they caught ones involving syllables, parts of words, and whole words.

Was it possible that these discrepancies influenced the science of slips as well? After all, people built theories using slips that they had heard and written down. This implied that celebrated collections of slips of the tongue like Meringer's and Fromkin's, built by listening to real-life conversations, contained more of some types of slips than others. Thus, to use Goffman's terms, they weren't comprehensive lists of technical faults. Rather, they were incomplete lists of perceptible faults. This has hampered efforts to compare the frequency of exchanges (such as Reverend Spooner's) to that of other types of sound slips. As a result, most linguists qualify their comparisons or don't make them at all.

Listeners can be prone to mishearing certain sounds, even if they're spoken correctly, what are called "slips of the ear." People tend to mishear consonants more frequently than vowels, and the misheard sound or syllable is usually unstressed and comes in the middle of a word. For this reason it's easy for people to mishear "It's about time Robert May was here" as "It's about time to drop my brassiere." One type of slip of the ear has been labeled the "mondegreen," a term coined in 1954 by Sylvia Wright, an American writer, to describe her childhood mishearing of the line of poetry "and laid him on the green" as "and Lady Mondegreen." Song lyrics often become mondegreens (I never fail to hear the line from Handel's *Messiah* "for we, like sheep, have gone astray" as the more alarming "for we like sheep"), and the bumper sticker "visualize whirled peas" depends on a deliberately misheard "visualize world peace."

For linguists, relying on casual slip collecting turned out to be problematic. One could listen to taped conversations, but as Anne Cutler puts it, "It means living your life twice." In the 1980s, she invented a more efficient method: keep a microcassette recorder on all the time. Then, when you hear a slip, immediately stop the tape and pop in a new tape. With this method, you would always know that the slip occurred close to the end of the recording.

This method didn't eliminate some other confounding factors, such as the frequency of a word. Some words (like "some" and "words") show up fairly frequently in normal English usage; other words (such as "dehisce" and "merisma") hardly show up at all. Which words more frequently go awry? Joseph Stemberger, a linguist who collected slips from his children for years but now studies slips exclusively in a laboratory, showed that the more infrequent the word, the more prone you are to slip with it. Why? It was basically a matter of practice—the neural connections for more frequently spoken words were more durable.

The word-frequency problem was solved in the 1970s by Bernard Baars, a cognitive scientist, who devised a way to make people slip in laboratories. Rather than waiting for slips to occur, he would set up experiments with lists of words, types of sounds, and various sorts of distractions. The setup worked like this: a person sat in front of a computer that flashed words (or sometimes sentences) about a second apart. The person was told she was being tested on her memory of the pairs, so she should read them silently. In some cases, a buzzer sounded, prompting the person to read the pair out loud. The person did so correctly—unless some of the preselected pairs biased her toward certain patterns. If the pairs were "bill deal," "bark dog," and "bang doll," then the prediction was that when she reached "darn bore," she would say "barn door." This happened 10 to 20 percent of the time. If the pair was "Do I have to put my seatbelt on?" and "Put on your seatbelt," the person would tend to make what is known as a "phrasal blend," such as "Do I have to put on my seatbelt on?"

In other experiments, the buzzer accompanied other instructions, which produced other types of slips. For instance, asking the subject to reverse the order of words or to repeat a reversed order would lead to spoonerisms, blends, and word substitutions. This method was indeed reliable enough—speakers would slip up about 10 percent of the time—which eliminated the need to wait for people to blunder, thus allowing Baars to test a hypothesis about the origins of slips of the tongue. He called it the "competing plans hypothesis." The lab situation created slips, he posited, because speakers had to navigate conflicting goals. In some situations the speaker had to be fast—

but she also had to be accurate. In other situations, she had to pronounce what was in front of her—yet she had also been prepared to say some sounds, not others. The two mental plans competed for cognitive resources that could be taxed only so far. When the competition resolved itself, a slip plopped out. Most often the resolution favored an automatic or habitual process. This explains in part why slips of the tongue hew to the language's basic shape. And recalling Spooner, it also explains why transpositions of sounds tend to create actual words—when the words are real, the speaker lets them pass, but when they aren't real, the speaker notices what he is about to say, then repairs.

The competing plans hypothesis was a clear step forward. It was also an opportunity to reappraise Sigmund Freud's ideas about *Fehlleistung*, or "faulty performances." Hadn't he posited that a slip resulted from a repression? Wasn't a repression simply a competing plan? Baars wondered if the repression was simply another competing goal. To test this formulation, he rigged a situation in which people who admitted to eating problems would have to make food-related spoonerisms. The speakers were primed with nonsense word pairs, like "rork poast," "froocy joot," or "shanilla vake." To make the experimental subjects even more food-conscious, he placed a bowl of candy on the table. If Freud had been right, Baars hypothesized, the food-sensitive subjects should have made more food-related spoonerisms than people who had no eating issues. That is, if emotionally laden and repressive thoughts were a kind of competing plan, then people would tend to make spoonerisms that communicated this repression. In the end, the correlation between their admitted eating problems and their food-related slips was too weak to establish Freud's hypothesis incontrovertibly.

Yet in one sense, Freud was right: a plan to say something could be knocked off course by a rival plan. He'd looked for gaps between what we know and what we actually do. Even Freud's critic Sebastiano Timpanaro was willing to accede the existence of true Freudian slips that arose because of some intruding emotion—for instance, when a Viennese politician said that people should follow the emperor's orders spinelessly *(rückgratlos)*, not unreservedly *(rückhaltlos)*. It may be that because Freud minimized alternative explanations for slips, he delayed a more comprehensive consideration of their meaning for some sixty years.

Here is a related experiment that you can do yourself that shows how Baars's method worked. It also underlies another theory about the cause of slips. Find a person and ask her to repeat the word "poke" a few times. (Don't tell her what you're doing.) Seven is a good number of repetitions. Then ask what she calls the white of an egg. Almost inevitably the person will reply "yolk." (Likewise, she'll slap her forehead when she realizes what she's said.) What happens here is that you've "primed" her perceptual system in a particular way, overstimulating the neural connections that map onto the "oke" sound. Her brain reached for the overstimulated version because it was the most immediately available one.

This priming is fundamental to a theory about what causes slips of the tongue, called "spreading activation theory." It was developed by Gary Dell, a cognitive scientist at the University of Illinois Urbana-Champaign. In his model, associations between words, sounds, and meanings are triggered electrically in the brain when the units are selected to be spoken. Because the units are arranged in a weblike fashion, these electrical activations sometimes overlap, stimulating the wrong word or sequence of sounds as much as the correct ones. This creates momentary confusion about which is the strongest activation. This occurs because activation "spreads." It goes top down, from sentences to words to sounds, as well as bottom up, from sounds to words to sentences. The theory of spreading activation predicts the following errors, which Rudolf Meringer would have called "contextual" errors, because interfering sounds appear around the error:

Sim swimmers sink
Swum simmers sink
Some simmers ink
Some swummer sink
Some swinkers sink
Some sinkers swim
Some simmers swim
Some swimmers drown

Dell's model has more facets than I can present here, but it does explain why faster talkers produce more slips. It's not because more words equal more opportunities to err. Rather, more talking keeps certain electrical activations from fading. This is the interference apt to spread and get in the way. Dell's model also predicts, not surprisingly, that slower talkers make fewer errors. When they do err, their errors will more likely be the future-looking anticipations. This model is powerful in other ways, too. It accounts for noncontextual errors, those where the interference is not visible in the utterance. If you were to ask someone to close the door, your brain will have registered (or "activated") that the door is open. This activation might lead to the error, "Could you open, I mean, close the door." The spreading activation model also accounts for a wide range of speech errors as well as their patterns: the bias for spoonerisms to produce real words, their tendency to involve the first sounds and syllables of words, their tendency to come from the same part of speech. This is hardly the last word on explaining slips of the tongue, and Dell is apparently now extending his model beyond normal speakers to people with language disorders.

Ultimately, however, language is only one sort of behavior that needs to be performed in a sequence, though errors in language are unique because they are less expensive than errors that occur in other realms. For example, according to the Institute of Medicine, between 44,000 and 98,000 people a year die in the United States from medical errors. More than seven thousand of these die because someone gave them the wrong drug or dosage, or because two drugs had an adverse interaction. In the 1970s, NASA research showed that crews were responsible for two-thirds of air crashes. During the Gulf War, in which highly technologized battles were waged with long-range weapons, "friendly fire" caused 23 percent of American casualties: we were dropping our bombs on ourselves.* From warfare to nuclear power plants to robotic surgery, minimizing the cost of errors by redesigning systems to be redundant and flexible

---

*When asked about radio identification tags on vehicles that send a "don't shoot" command to targeting systems, Defense Secretary Donald Rumsfeld warned against a technological panacea. "There have been friendly fire incidents in every war in the history of mankind," he said. "Human beings are human beings, and things are going to happen."

when errors occur has sparked research in the psychology of error.

One basic idea is that "control" consists of both voluntary and involuntary elements. In the classic example by James Reason, an expert on the psychology of error, a person comes out of a subway turnstile and takes out a wallet to pay, though no money is required. While speech errors reveal the invisible seams of language, slips of action show units of action—how they're stored in the brain and how the brain uses them. Taking out a wallet when payment is required forms one unit. That it's done unconsciously is a sign that such a unit automatically exists in your head. These units can also be temporarily deleted, as in the example of the person who goes into the room to fetch a book, takes off her rings, then comes out of the room without the book. There are also exchanges of behavior, such as offering the cat a can of pudding instead of a can of cat food.

Most human action can be broken down into sequences of deliberate action and automatic action. Lifting a foot, for instance, is more conscious than putting it down; walking through the turnstile may be more conscious than paying the fee. That we shift back and forth between conscious control and unconscious instinct or habit in many activities sheds light on the psychology of action. We're more familiar with the intentional part of the cycle, because the habitual is taken for granted and off the map. As Reason notes, whenever conscious cognitive plans go awry, they're usually taken over by automatic plans. Both slips of action or slips of the tongue result in something that is familiar and predictable and takes the shape of what we already know.

What we call "intentional activity" is, itself, made up of actions that have been learned and can be repeated—they are not new behaviors that come from nowhere. It also means that what we see as an "error" can merely be the appearance of a competent behavior in the wrong context. This could provide insight into a range of everyday situations, from dialing the wrong number to traffic accidents to picking the wrong item off the supermarket shelves. It also explains why slips of the tongue are constrained by a language's grammar and sound system. These make up a sort of safety net to which your cognitive system automatically reverts in times of trouble.

Admittedly, this doesn't leave much room for slips as creative acts—after all, no one would call walking out of the room without the keys an unintentional innovation in behavior. In the early days of the slip renaissance, slips of the tongue were celebrated, sometimes even fetishized—if you were a linguist or around linguists enough, you didn't feel embarrassed about saying them, because you knew that your slip of the tongue, a singular, irreproducible instance, represented a transmission from the place where language dwelled and a connection to its creative forces. (You also knew that it would be written down and kept forever.) How disappointing it must have been for linguists to see slips of the tongue lumped in with errors of the mundane and dangerous sort.

As a result, linguists tend not to discuss nonlanguage errors. Nevertheless, they are studying slips of the tongue in more sophisticated ways that are sensitive to factors that Meringer or Fromkin hadn't considered. One such factor is the individual's experiences with language. This is not Freud's sense of experience—linguists still don't believe that repressed feelings, traumatic experiences, or neuroses are the central or universal cause of slips. They do, however, recognize that a person takes idiosyncratic paths through life, paths that can shape how they blunder and who hears them do it.

# 9

## *Fun with Slips*

Arnold Zwicky, a linguist at Stanford University, has spent the last thirty years researching spelling errors, double entendres, spoonerisms, "schoolboy howlers of the malaprop variety," mixed metaphors (such as "the Internal Revenue Service appears to be totally impaled in the quicksands of absolute inertia"), and a whole menagerie of linguistic deviations and innovations. Zwicky is such a slip geek that he has expanded the accepted scientific labels far beyond the primitive categories of "knows better" and "doesn't know better," the intentional and the voluntary, the true and the false. Others use mistakes as props in their intellectual vaudeville acts. Zwicky turns them into performances of connoisseurship more akin to wine tasting than linguistics: he appears to be able to sniff the bouquet of a verbal blunder and tell you whether it was spoken in the morning or the evening. To him there's as much difference between the "Blue Bonnet plague" (or bubonic plague) and "the pastor cut the shermon sort" as between a merlot and a chardonnay.

Zwicky is a genial, white-haired man in his midsixties who, on the day I meet him in his office, is wearing a T-shirt with a pocket out of which peeks the small, inevitable notebook of the inveterate slip collector. Somewhere in his office is a box of similar notebooks, the precious reward of thirty years of listening like, as he calls it, "a Martian." (By which he means, you assume nothing about what you hear.) People who work with him know that if Zwicky grabs for his notebook midconversation, you've said something interesting.

His fascination with slips of the tongue began in the early 1970s, when he sat in on a course taught by Vicki Fromkin. (He appears seven times in her slip collection, six times making a slip and once when someone observes that "Zwicky has gotten skwinny.") It occurred to him that slips might be useful for teaching linguistics, to illustrate the abstruse technical concepts of linguistics (imagine trying to enliven phonological features without "glear plue sky" or illustrate the abstract past tense without "Rosa always date shranks")—and to invest serious analysis with a bit of fun. Fromkin taught him how to take dual notes at lectures: on one pad you write the slips; on the other you write notes about the lecture. Zwicky doesn't have a reputation for making many speech errors, but after listening to him give a talk once, Fromkin told him she'd recorded him making one slip a minute. (The average may be closer to one every seven minutes.) "The other people in those audiences heard maybe one an hour," Zwicky told me. "A damn good thing, too."

In 1980, he published *Mistakes,* a slim but exhaustive workbook (intended for students) that listed and discussed the gamut of things called "errors." On one end were the true accidents, like "a bright flire," "loosely flew" or the "tropic of cancercorn";

at the other, the inventions and creations of writers like Lewis Carroll ("gyre and gimble") and James Joyce ("museyroom," "bisexcycle"); in between was the jargon of subcultures and the deliberate misspelling of words from dialects ("I kin git yew"). Such distinctions can seem unnecessarily detailed. After all, what do intentions matter if the end product is annoying, offensive, or deviant? For Zwicky, it's to account for what our brains contain: words from speaking and reading; social conventions; formal education; unpleasant or happy experiences speaking or writing; and personal preference and talent. Too often, he thinks, people fault those who make errors for not having enough discipline, rules, or knowledge. But suppose that we don't assume deficits; instead, assume that someone knows rules and words but applies the inappropriate ones. The question becomes, what is the speaker doing in that instance? And why? How much does linguistic performance depend upon intelligence and memory— and on community and experience, too? After all, language takes brains communing, not isolated brains.

Zwicky has also written about the language of menus, the language of police blotters, and the names of gay male porn stars, the ordinary material of everyday language that is important to him as a working-class kid who grew up in eastern Pennsylvania, then went to Princeton and MIT. His intention is "to celebrate the speech and behavior of ordinary people, including an assortment of otherwise marginal groups, such as the rural working class," he says.

The slips that vary among individuals perhaps the most are word errors—or, as word slips have come to be called, "malapropisms." The word "malaprop" was inspired by the wildly

word-misusing character, Mrs. Malaprop, in Richard Brins-
ley Sheridan's 1775 romantic comedy, *The Rivals*.* Sheridan
crowned his character with the French term, *mal à propos,* or
"inappropriate." And the play's comedy is not just that Mrs.
Malaprop uses words incorrectly as she blocks a love affair
between the hero and heroine; it's that she claims to be a verbal
expert. Her name is the play's signal that her verbal preten-
tiousness is going to be skewered.

If you go to a university library for a copy of *The Rivals,*
you're likely to find that generations of students have already
underlined some of her butcheries, which takes away your
pleasure in finding them yourself. "Oh!" Mrs. Malaprop
exclaims at one point. "It gives me the hydrostatics to such a
degree. I thought she had persisted from corresponding with
him." At one point she intercepts—and has read aloud—a letter in which Captain Jack Absolute, the play's hero, mocks her
use of language. As he does not have the word "malapropism"
to use, he charges her instead with "deck[ing] her dull chat with
hard words which she don't understand."

Understandably, Mrs. Malaprop is incensed—and sent into
a fit of *mal à propos* speech: "There, sir! an attack upon my language! What do you think of that?—an aspersion upon my parts
of speech! Was ever such a brute! Sure, if I reprehend anything
in this world, it is the use of my oracular tongue, and a nice
derangement of epitaphs!"†

A couple of years ago, I saw a production of *The Rivals* in

---

*The *OED* lists "malaproipism" as another form of "malaprop" or "malapropism" that evidently never caught on.

†Characters who comment on her malapropisms are also mistreated in
the play—Captain Absolute is raked over Mrs. Malaprop's coals when she
finds out he's made fun of her language. Pity Mr. Malaprop.

New York City, where the role of Mrs. Malaprop was played by Dana Ivey, an accomplished actress who specializes in playing power matrons on stage and screen. Just as college student underlining had removed some of the surprise of the malapropisms, so did the live performance. Each time Ivey malapropped, the audience laughed, and each time I recognized something odd about the laughter but couldn't identify it. Then I noticed that the laughter followed on Mrs. Malaprop's line far too soon for the audience to have known that the word was ill-chosen. Imagine telling a joke and having your listener begin laughing before the punch line's out of your mouth, as if they knew already where the joke would be. Listening more closely, I realized that Ivey was slightly overenunciating each malapropism—effectively signaling to the audience that a humorous moment was coming. The actress's portrayal of the character was appropriately dragonlike, yet vulnerable. But the difficulty of deliberately saying an incorrect word adds another layer to an understanding of verbal blundering.

Sheridan's play is an artifact of a historical period when people thought differently about verbal blunders than they do now. In Sheridan's day, Mrs. Malaprop was more than simply a figure of linguistic derision; she also embodied anxieties about manners, language, and social class. Such anxieties materialized on American and British stages in characters like Jemima Blockhead, in a play titled *The Blockheads,* or Mrs. Sententious, who appeared in *The Better Sort.** All three of these characters flaunted their high social status yet couldn't fulfill its linguistic

---

*The Blockheads,* from 1776, is usually attributed to Mercy Warren; *The Better Sort: Or the Girl of Spirit* was written by William Hill Brown and first performed in 1789.

expectations. Not that they noticed, however—if performing at a high level outstripped their abilities, they were incapable of monitoring their own performances. In his history of American eloquence, historian Kenneth Cmiel writes that Blockhead, Malaprop, and Sententious were humorous (not tragic) characters because they thought they expressed themselves as others in their community did, but could not. As Cmiel puts it, "They did not strike the pose of restraint necessary in a republican world." By comparison, Spooner and Freud questioned the relevance of restraint in an increasingly complex world.

As the study of verbal blunders became more sophisticated over the twentieth century, researchers wanted to know how intention and intelligence figured into a malapropism, whether it was a one-time occurrence or a repeated performance. Patterns in malapropisms also held the power to tell about language's hidden structures, as two psychology graduate students at the University of Texas, Anne Cutler and David Fay, found in the early 1970s. Fay, who had been inspired by Franklin to begin collecting slips, discovered Meringer and Mayer's book, *Misspeaking and Misreading*. Fay couldn't read German, so Cutler, who could, translated for him. She not only became a leading expert on Meringer, she and Fay began to do what other scientists were doing: collecting slips.

They listened for instances where someone said "equivocal" when they meant to say "equivalent," or "tambourines" when they meant to say "trampolines." Fay (now at Verizon Laboratories) and Cutler (now director of the Max Planck Institute for Psycholinguistics) found that 99 percent of the time, the words a speaker meant to say (the target) belonged to the same grammatical category as the inadvertent mistake. If you meant to say a noun, the mistake was almost always a noun, and likewise for other parts of speech. Lawn, line. Week, work. Accurate, adequate. Map, make. Gaudy, gory. Among other things, this means that a sentence in which a malapropism occurs doesn't suddenly become ungrammatical. (Nonsensical, certainly: "That's a gory piece of jewelry.") Fay and Cutler also found that 87 percent of target-mistake pairs had the same number of syllables and 98 percent shared a stress pattern, so that the stress would fall on the second syllable of both words, for example.

For the sake of simplicity, Fay and Cutler ignored the pairs that were related only in meaning. For instance, you might say "black" when you mean "white," or "write" when you mean "read." Good, bad. Nearly, barely. Specific, general. Saying "she got hot under the belt" when you meant "she got hot under the collar." These types of errors are fairly obvious when they occur, so one might be tempted to think they are the more frequent ones. In fact, just as there is a bias for sound exchanges to produce actual words, there is a tendency for malapropisms to be related in meaning to the target word.* Vicki Fromkin wondered if there was a semantic reason for saying "art of the flute" instead of "art of the fugue" and not, say, "art of the flue." ("Flute" and "fugue" coming from the world of music, and "flue" from the world of chimneys.)

Later, Wilhelm Hotopf took a closer look at the malaprisms that Fay and Cutler had ignored, the meaning-related ones. (These were the second-most numerous in Meringer's collection.) He saw that he could divide a small collection of 224 malapropisms into three groups. About 31 percent were

---

*Not by much, Fay and Cutler claimed. Semantic malapropisms made up only 54 percent of their collection; the remaining 46 percent were related by sound.

complements, antonyms, or converses, in which people said "early" (not "late") and "husband" (not "wife"). The greatest number, more than 44 percent, were "cohyponyms." That is, they weren't opposites but belonged to the same category, such as saying "breakfast" instead of "lunch" or "red" instead of "black."* The rest were faux hyponyms (such as Monday-February or Asia-Japan). None of the pairs were synonyms (as in "wife" for "spouse"), and most were adverbs and adjectives; there were very few verbs. (However, Vicki Fromkin's collection contains many verb errors, such as "a subject can be learned to change" or "different strategies that left to the same result.") These are the errors we make when we call one friend, coworker, or family member by another's name. I'm fairly certain that my mother doesn't secretly prefer my brother over me. Then why does she switch our names? Because her constant use of both of them has activated them to the same level in her brain, which makes them both available for selection. The words, not the brothers, are rivals.

Zwicky took the study of malapropisms one step further. Rather than deal with pure "knows better" errors as Fay and Cutler had, he took up what he called "classical malapropisms": words that people used incorrectly but believed to be correct. He noted the guest who admired someone's "handsome soup latrine" because he or she had misheard the word "tureen."

---

*A hyponym is a relationship between two words in which the meaning of the first is included in that of the second. Any dog or any cat is also an animal; therefore the words "dog" and "cat" are hyponyms and are cohyponyms of "animals."

Another person said "cholester oil" for "cholesterol" through out a conversation, even when she was asked directly for the name of the substance. What Fay, Cutler, and Hotopf looked at were one-time accidents; Zwicky dug around in errors that occurred over and over. It's often thought that malapropisms are made by people who (like Mrs. Malaprop) are overreaching their station in life. Though many malaproppers err with long words with Greek or Latin roots—the hard words, they're often called—not all of their mistakes are long, multisyllabic Latinate words. Sports announcers, not necessarily known for their social climbing, often reach for a vivid word and say "arduous" for "ardent" or "periphery" for "paraphernalia." A full quarter of the classical malapropisms that Zwicky has collected involve a vocabulary that's decidedly untechnical, as in "it warms the coggles of my heart" or "the queen's eclectic blue eyes."

These classical malapropisms are a sort of ossified slip of the tongue. A word is mispronounced or misheard once. Then an individual continues to use the wrong form, insisting it's correct and often inventing little stories—what linguists call "folk etymologies"—to justify them. One reason why classical malapropisms persist in a person's vocabulary is that one can conceive how, even in the incorrect form, the mischosen word makes sense. Take, for example, the word "lambash," which is what came out when someone tried to say "lambaste." There is a relationship between the sounds and meanings of the two words. In an odd way, "bash" seems more appropriate than "baste."

Zwicky calls "lambash" a type of classical malapropism known as an "eggcorn." "Exercise regiment" is an eggcorn of "exercise regimen"; "heartrendering" is an eggcorn of "heart-rending." A few eggcorns become fixed as a persistent conundrum of usage, such as "tow the line" (instead of "toe the line") or "for all intensive purposes" (instead of "for all intents and purposes"). More circulate as in-jokes in families or groups of friends (in my family we say "phonemuffs" instead of "earphones" because that's what my brother asked for when he was six or seven). But most eggcorns remain individual idiosyncrasies—your eggcorns will be unlike mine. What distinguishes eggcorns from other sorts of malapropisms is that they often make a kind of sense—though the eggcorn isn't the right word, strictly speaking, it sounds as if it could be right. An eggcorn isn't a spelling error ("definitly"), a hearing error ("quaffed" for "coiffed"), or what's known as an "idiom blend," as in "out on a lurch" (which blends "left in the lurch" and "out on a limb"). But something like "pus jewel" (for "pustule")—which is an eggcorn—possesses a nearly poetic resonance.

A group of linguists, Zwicky among them, who post to a Web log called Language Log (www.languagelog.com) appropriated the word "eggcorn" to name this particular type of malapropism. ("Eggcorn" itself is a twist on "acorn" when someone misheard "acorn" as "eggcorn," then repeated it, adopted it, spread it, and when they were questioned about their misuse might have replied, "Oh, well, it looks like an egg, and it sort of looks like a corn kernel, and both eggs and kernels are seeds, in a way, which is what the eggcorn is.") Eggcorn gems have been collected at http://eggcorns.lascribe.net, such as the line from the Richmond, Virginia, *Times-Dispatch* that says, "Meanwhile Richard Parker Bowles, brother of Camilla's ex-husband, Andrew, said that from the beginning Camilla approved of Charles marrying Diana while she remained his power mower." There was the San Francisco theater review that stated "Bianca Marroquin, a real pre-Madonna, boasts an almost innocent tawdriness and brings a refreshing gamine quality to Roxie Hart's need for fame." (The first should have been "paramour" and the second "primadonna.")

Every social group seems to make classical malapropisms, says Zwicky, and the gems are repeated over and over, with speakers insisting their word choice is correct. "They're astounded to discover that most English-speaking people don't have the same history of the word," Zwicky says. It may look as if we all try to follow the same standards of English and believe we belong to the same community of English speakers. However, the persistent life of eggcorns is evidence that people are connected to the linguistic mainstream more tenuously than they may think. Social feedback about language correctness is important. But what if it's intermittent? What if the feedback givers are hesitant or, worse, wrong?

Slips are often collected as if they were butterflies, singular instances of a colorful creature. "Each slip is a universe," wrote linguist Annette Hohenberger, "and deserves being admired for its intricacy and beauty."

Yet for every slip you make, you will have said approximately 999 other words, and for every split second in which you utter a speech error, you will have talked for hours, faultlessly (or mostly so). This makes up part of the language ecology in which those single slips live. You also have a set of experiences with other speakers, formal education, and the written language that is particular to you. And you will possess varying sensitivities toward speaking and listening, as well as an internal monitor with varying thresholds for catching errors. When verbal blunders are considered only in a single flash or slice of time, we lose sight of the life of the speaker, isolating him from what else may have influenced him. On the other hand, we don't want to risk imputing to a speaker a life in which he always forgets words, listens carelessly, reads too little, or misjudges his surroundings. I like the classical malapropism because it situates the verbal blunderer properly in time, in both the moment and the lifetime. It's also more accurate to consider that you're more than an utterance generator that trips over itself on occasion; you're a person who learns words from other people, who themselves possess fallible ears and tongues. So you may want to think twice before trying to root out and correct your eggcorns and mondegreens. You may be erasing a part of what makes you who you are.

At first glance, the work of Jeri Jaeger, a linguist at the University of Buffalo, doesn't resemble Zwicky's work very much. But over the course of her twenty-year research project collecting children's slips of the tongue, she saw how slips reflected individual paths of language development and even personal preferences and styles. In 2004, she published *Kids' Slips*, a 750-page tome that resulted from an innocent dinner conversation with a colleague who asked what she was working on. Speech errors from kids, Jaeger replied. He was surprised. "It's a well-known fact that children do not make slips of the tongue until they are seven years old," he said. They don't have mature motor control, memory, or language firmly established in either brain hemisphere, he explained. This unstable brain lateralization meant that it was impossible for kids to slip like adults did, in the sense of an inadvertent, involuntary accident by an otherwise expert speaker. Jaeger had already been collecting slips from her eldest daughter, Anna, so when she got home, she sent her colleague one hundred of Anna's slips. She demonstrated that as early as eighteen months, children make slips much like adults do, in the sense that they inadvertently blunder with a sound or word they know. He replied that he'd have to revise his own ideas not only about slips but about brain lateralization, too.*

Linguistics may be unique among scientific endeavors because it's so homey—eating dinner or watching TV are perfect venues for informal linguistic analysis, and observing the abilities of children is easy and fascinating. Over twenty years, Jaeger amassed considerable evidence comparing children's slips to adult slips—1,383 speech errors of all types from the children, 716 from adults—collecting many of her riches from her own children. One of her entries lists a code name for the speaker, the child's age, a description of the context ("while we were looking for a parking spot," "explaining why he should be first in the bathtub"), the slip itself, and the intended utterance. To really pull this off, Jaeger used her intimate knowledge as a mother to distinguish one-time inadvertent errors from what a child gets wrong over and over because they haven't learned it. Once Alice said, "She already showed me tomorrow!" When corrected, she said "yesterday" instead. This wasn't a slip, Jaeger explains, because Alice didn't know the meanings of the two words yet and was using one or the other randomly. Another time, Anna said, "And now I will appear my assistant, right

---

*Jaeger's work put another nail in the coffin on Freudian explanations for slips. As late as the 1980s, some Freudians still maintained that children were too young to suffer the emotional repressions that caused slips of the tongue.

under this table!" Her misuse of "appear" wasn't a slip; children her age (she was five and a half at the time) often overextend what verbs mean.

Anna is now a vivacious twenty-five-year old who is studying acting at a prestigious graduate program in the Northeast. If you saw her onstage, you would never guess the role she played in her mother's work. When she was one year, four months old, she made her first slip of the tongue. She had a counting phrase—"one two three, one two three, one two three"—that she said all the time. On one particular day, she collapsed "two" and "three" into the same word. She said "one, tuwee." Delighted, Jaeger wrote Anna's slip down. Three months later, Anna was making slips more frequently, ones like "beek-a-poo."

Anna is a character in her mother's academic articles. One of her slips, "not by the chair of my hinny hin hin!" serves as a title of one and her photo appears on the cover of *Kid's Slips*. Anna remembers inviting her friends over to play so her mother could listen to them talk. With their parents' permission, Jaeger might jot down their slips. She also listened for slips anywhere she found children (and willing parents): in supermarket check-out lines, in preschools, and, of course, at her dinner table.

Scientist parents have long observed their children's behavior, producing what became known as "diary studies." Hippolyte Taine wrote the earliest baby biography in 1877, observing his daughter, whom he calls a "little girl whose development was ordinary, neither precocious nor slow." The diary study became a famous research method—albeit a problematic one, if scientific objectivity was trumped by a parent's love. Rudolf Meringer included his own children's slips in *Scenes from Out of the Life of Language*, the English title of his 1908 book published in German. Werner Leopold's observations of his daughter, Hildegard, take up four volumes. In the early 1980s, Joseph Stemberger kept diaries of his two daughters, Gwendolyn and Morgan, from the age of one onward, logging their new words and mapping their slips. In the annals of science, most subjects are anonymous. Not Gwendolyn and Morgan. They're now known in university classrooms around the world because their father wrote down when they said "tweemtweez" (or "cream cheese") and "twap pweyin" ("stop playing").* But none of these projects analyzed slips as prolifically or as thoroughly as Jaeger, who ultimately coded fifty different kinds.

One way to study how children learn language is to note what children say, when they say it, and for what purposes, then track the changes over time. But linguists have been interested in a bigger picture of things, one that's hard to build if you wait for each word to dribble out. If a linguist wanted to know how the words you know—your "mental lexicon"—are organized in your brain, she wouldn't wait for you to tell her all the words you know. She would design tests, games, and other probes to catch glimpses of that weblike structure in your head. Slips of the tongue have been impromptu experiments to study adult language. Until Jaeger came along, slips hadn't been used to look at how children become the linguistic experts they will be as adults.

Scientists disagree about how many stages are involved in child language learning; estimates range from three to five. But regardless of how many stages there are, listening to a child's slips of the tongue is a good way to place the child relative to the other stages. That's because children don't make true slips

---

*Or in the phonetic notation, "t$^h$wiimt$^h$wiiz" and "t$^h$wap p$^h$weyin."

of the tongue with a sound, word, or other linguistic unit that they haven't learned or acquired. In the earliest stage, children learn how to say individual words, though they don't yet conceive of words as strings of sounds. Next, they learn how to say two-word sentences, acquiring the most basic grammar—distinguishing nouns from verbs, for instance, and arranging them in the sentence so that some action and some object or person are related. At the same time, they learn that words can be broken into sounds. Somewhere in there they string words together, often with simple grammatical terms, though they leave others out. Finally, at the stage in which their grammatical abilities take full adultlike shape, around the age of three or four, they learn longer sentences with words arranged in more complex, hierarchical patterns. (Even so, children by that age will not yet have learned to say "uh" and "um" like adults—they introduce sentences with pause fillers but place them inside sentences rarely.)

Kids' slips are shaped by these stages. Jaeger points to her conversation with her then two-and-a-half-year-old daughter, Alice, about her bottle. "My stick . . . My bottle sticky. My apple juice. My sticky bottle," Alice said. Not only does it count as a slip, because the first "sticky" anticipates the second one, it also indicates that Alice, who was trying to figure out word order, was in the second stage of language development. Because such slips are one-time events, a parent doesn't need to correct them.


From her collection of slips, Jaeger has drawn the best profile to date of the beginning of our lives in verbal blundering. The slips that children make involve the same linguistic units and the same grammatical constraints (that is, nouns swap with nouns, verbs with verbs) as adult slips. Like adults, children swap or substitute sounds or syllables from the beginnings of words and sounds that tend to come from the syllables that carry the stress. Only one sound error was unique to the kids, and it was extremely rare. Alice once said something that sounded like "coff timee" instead of "coffee time"—that is, the "ee" sound of coffee had jumped to the end of the second word. In Jaeger's analysis, children learn one "ee" sound in words like "blankie" and "kittie" and another meaning of "ee" in words like "slimy" and "messy." When Alice made this error, she was figuring out if the "ee" of "coffee" was one of those two suffixes. Thus, because adults know which words have the "blankie" and "messy" endings, they don't make errors which move a vowel that isn't a suffix.

On the other hand, adults had two kinds of slips that the kids didn't. One such error involved the stress on words. For instance, someone said "talks between us and Japanese negotiAtors" (instead of "Japanese neGOtiators"), or someone who says "reFERence" instead of "REFerence." Jaeger hypothesizes that adults make these errors more often because of the Latinate words one encounters only in school. Another adult-only error was word substitutions between words that are related in spelling, as when someone replaces "AOL" with "HBO" or says "K-Mart" instead of "X-Files." Because Jaeger's children hadn't been to school yet, they wouldn't make any spelling mistakes.

One curious observation was the children's high number of errors in which sounds within words moved around, as in "I want my blaceret" or "shunsine." (Recall that adult sound slips tend to come from the beginnings of words.) Because one-year-olds make more within-word errors than two-year-olds, who make more of these errors than adults, this means that young children have a rougher mental plan for how words sound. With kids it's almost as if the sounds swim around inside the words, which leads to more within-word errors.

At the age of three, children's slips become most adultlike. They have the sounds of their language, the ability to produce sentences (not merely two- and three-word utterances), and the complexities of words.

Yet it's a paradoxical age, three years old. Children at that age also slip most unlike adults—for instance, twice as many of their errors involve vowels and consonants. Joseph Stemberger found children at this age making more perseverations ("I brushed the brush") than anticipations ("I catted the cat."). Children also catch fewer errors of the "catted the cat" type, which suggested that their internal speech monitors—their blunder checkers—aren't fully developed.

They make more errors with function words (prepositions, articles) than adults, for whom these are automatic. Misplacing words in the grammar of a sentence peaks at three years old, when they are learning new structures for sentences. By five years old, they have more practice manipulating sentences, so they misplace the word in a sentence less often.


As Jaeger and Stemberger will tell you, collecting slips from your own kids at home is a challenge. On one hand, you don't want to make your kids self-conscious—or worse, so tentative that they talk less. On the other hand, kids are such a good source of data. And you have to write it down. You'll forget it if you don't. Stemberger says he simply kept a notebook open whenever he was around his daughters. Jaeger practiced more surreptitiously, sneaking away from the kitchen table to write down a slip—leaving her then-husband to tease the children: "Somebody made a speech error!! Who made the speech error?"

The parent in the scientist wants to respect the kids, but the scientist in the parent doesn't want critics to claim that the data source was sullied or that the children made slips to please their parents. Jaeger still remembers when her son, Bobby, made his first speech error, at one year, seven months. Waving good-bye to his grandmother, he said, "kye . . . car, bye." "Of course I got extremely excited over Bobby's first speech error, like some parents get excited about baby's first steps," she said.

She also recalled the time that her husband was teasing Bobby (then almost six years old) about speech errors. "What's a speech error?" the father asked.

"You know!" Bobby said. "Can I do one, please, Mom?"

Oh great, Jaeger thought. Could he really produce a slip on his own? Maybe I've corrupted my data, she worried. She told him to tell her his slip.

"Cake coffee," Bobby said, putting the stress on the second word, "COFFee."

*Cake COFFee?!?!* Jaeger wondered.

"Cake COFFee," he repeated. "That's one, 'cuz it's supposed to be COFFee cake."

Jaeger breathed a sigh of relief, because Bobby had blown his error—he'd gotten the stress pattern wrong. The normal stress of compound words is on the first syllable ("COFFee cake," "BASEball"), and even when the words change places, the stress remains. To pull it off, Bobby should have said "CAKE coffee," but he didn't. Did Bobby get a long lecture on English stress? I asked Jaeger.

"No," Jaeger replied. "I was overjoyed."

Why?

"It meant he couldn't consciously make a slip," she explained. "Even if he had some understanding about compound stress, which would be nuts for a four-year-old, he would have no way of knowing how compound stress would look in a reversed word."

The larger point is that all the knowledge in the world about slips and how they work doesn't prevent them from occurring. "I know everything there is to know about speech errors, and I still make them in great abundance," Jaeger said.

Jaeger doesn't speculate too much about what slips say about her kids, though she acknowledges that they slipped and corrected themselves in ways that reflected their personalities. Lively, talkative Anna developed linguistic skills very early. In technical parlance, she was the "expressive" one. Because she began speaking in two-word utterances at a very young age, her early slips involved more grammar than is typical in fifteen-month-olds. Meanwhile, Jaeger described her two youngest, Alice and Bobby, as more precise people. They are more "referential." This, too, is reflected in their slips, making errors with individual sounds as they acquired them; they also made slips with individual sounds first, then added word slips and grammatical errors. They also tried to cover up their slips, saving face by explaining why they said something. Once Bobby, almost five years old, told his mother that his imaginary "off" switch was located on his back. "Press stak!" he instructed.

"Stak?" his mother asked.

"I said 'Stop!' " he said, denying his earlier blunder.

What also emerges from Jaeger's study is how children learn

to repair what they say. Aware of the correct forms at a very early age, children do their best to be correct. They acquire sounds and single words first; they correct those first. This leads to what sound like word repetitions. As their vocabulary grows, they correct word choices gone awry. And when they acquire two-word sentences and then more complex grammar, they correct those, too, all because they've acquired that most human of desires: to be recognized, comprehended, understood. Someone may have told them to correct their mistake. But they also do it spontaneously, on their own.

Of Jaeger's three children, Bobby was the only one who reportedly learned and used the term "speech error." At five years old, he was explaining why he should be the first child to take a bath. "Because I was last nast night," he said, then he laughed. "I made a speech error."


If Erving Goffman were alive (he died in 1982), he would remind us that error isn't solely a linguistic phenomenon. It is sociological as well. We might add that it is something personal also. Both Arnold Zwicky and Jeri Jaeger have illuminated this. To truly grasp how and when error occurs, you have to look beyond the error itself to the standards that sift the correct from the incorrect, the normal from the abnormal. Are they personal standards, which may be erroneous themselves? You also have to understand the standard you are measuring against. Are they standards that a speaker (such as a child) can't possibly meet?

Goffman argued that lists of errors tell you little about the context in which the errors are perceived and dubbed "errors." So merely collecting them can be somewhat misleading. "The way to obtain a corpus of errors is not to start with an intuition as to what a quintessential error is and then seek for some prime examples," Goffman wrote. Rather, the more accurate strategy is "to force oneself to collect what gets treated as an error, whatever that might be."

What gets treated as an error is the result of a mismatch of norms and expectations between speakers and listeners. At home or among friends, such divergences may not have great repercussions, but in the political arena they can be great. As Kermit Schafer knew, broadcast audiences are offended by faults, and if not personally, then for the other guy, who might be. Add to this how politicians manage their listeners' expectations, and changes in how listeners actually hear political speakers, and you get the most recent installment in the story of verbal blunders: the talking of George W. Bush.

# 10

## *President Blunder*

I n contemporary America there is no more visible verbal blunderer than George W. Bush, forty-third president of the United States. Commentators have remarked upon his tortured syntax, tortured meaning, scrambled syntax, tangled tongues, linguistic loopholes, mangled syntax, mangled English, outright gibberish, verbal goulash syndrome, verbal howlers, flubs, gaffes, bloopers, sins of syntax, misnomers, verbal knots, and verbal clangers, and an occasional column in the political Web magazine *Slate* has been dedicated to the "Bushism." Compared to the Reverend Spooner's, Bush's blundering is less apocryphal and more a matter of perspective. When Bush served as governor of Texas from 1995 to 2000, people didn't think of him as a verbal blunderer. And even during his first presidential candidacy, his early verbal gaffes on foreign policy raised eyebrows, but he didn't emerge as a figure of full-blown verbal comedy until Dan Quayle, former vice president under George H. W. Bush, left the race on September 27, 1999. According to a LexisNexis search, national newspapers and magazines noted Bush's language gaffes but didn't explicitly label him a verbal blunderer until Quayle was out of the picture.

Once labeled by the *Washington Post* as the "human punch line," for years Dan Quayle and his phenomenal gaffes over-shadowed any contributions he made and reduced the respect he otherwise would have garnered. Whether or not his missteps were real linguistic accidents, they were treated as "doesn't know better" errors. A near-chronic lapser, Quayle appeared to have few resources at his fingertips, linguistic or intellectual. He also misused the ones he might legitimately claim, such as correct spelling.* His reputation ever since has hardly been as cheerfully clubby as the legend built at Oxford around Spooner.

When the former vice president quit the presidential race, the media filled the resulting vacuum by promoting George W. Bush to the role of linguistic punching bag. Later Bush would be criticized for his tough-guy talk ("Either you are with us or you are with the terrorists"), his affected regional pro-nunciations ("nookyular"), his penchant for stating the obvious ("I'm the decider, and I decide what is best"), and his reliance on stock phrases ("spreading freedom"). But he attracted the most derision for soundbite-able errors that were widely quoted and collected.

In those days, the verbal blunders called "Bushisms" were recognizable "knows better" speech errors. Grammatical fum-

---

*The incident for which Quayle may be most remembered occurred in June 1992, when Quayle participated in a mock spelling bee at an elementary school in South Trenton, New Jersey. When twelve-year-old William Figueroa, spelled "p-o-t-a-t-o," Quayle corrected him and spelled it "p-o-t-a-t-o-e." Figueroa gained brief notoriety as the "potato kid." Quayle's infamy has been longer lived.

bles led to incoherence (such as the famous "I know it's hard to put food on your family"). In early interviews, he called Kosovars "Kosovians" and Greeks "Grecians." There's also the syntactic maze, as when he defended an appearance at fundamentalist Christian Bob Jones University in 2000: "I did denounce it," he said. "I de—I denounced it. I denounced interracial dating. I denounced anti-Catholic bigacy—bigotry. . . . No, I—I—I spoke out against interracial dating. I mean, I support—the policy of interracial dating." Some of his flubs were quasi-spoonerisms, such as "terriers and barriffs." Others were malapropisms, like "misunderestimate" and "subliminable." Intending to say "infallibility," Bush said "fallacy," and intending to say "malfeasance," he said "malfeance." Some of the blunders erupt only once, which indicates their "knows better" status—that is, Bush does know the words but in a single instance accidentally speaks the wrong form. What also indicates that these early Bushisms were "knows better" errors is that Bush often repairs or corrects himself, if not always smoothly or successfully. Thus "misunderestimated" didn't exit his lips smoothly—but was interrupted, after nearly each syllable, sometimes with a pause, sometimes with a repeated syllable, or with "uh," all of it the sign that his internal blunder monitor was, in fact, working. (In his next sentence, however, he chose "misunderestimated" again and pronounced it fluently.)

Bushisms aren't interesting because we need more evidence about how the brain works. They catch our eyes and ears because of the person who makes them and because they say something about us.

. . .

In the early 1990s, *Slate* editor Jacob Weisberg coined the term "Bushism" to help pummel the speaking of Bush *père,* whose sentences rambled like broken-down fences.* One writer speculated that he suffered from some sort of aphasia.† A decade later, his son would be pop-diagnosed as "dyslexic" for the same sort of language behavior. Such amateur diagnoses of deviant language change with the political winds. In the 1950s, Kermit Schafer ignored Eisenhower's gaffes, but early in George W. Bush's first term, humorous books, CDs, DVDs, and Web sites filled with Bushisms were best-selling hits; in addition to his column, Weisberg collected Bush *fils*'s blunders in several best-selling books. The president was perceived not only to be inarticulate but also unable to control his language, a flaw unbecoming in a man with two Ivy League degrees. Whereas the blooper showed a momentary divergence between the media persona and the real person, the Bushism demonstrated that the persona and the real person were hopelessly divorced from the outset. It also marked the sad conflation of the political world with the entertainment world: a politician who couldn't remember his lines.

---

*Writing for *The New Republic,* Jesse Furman starts his piece about Bush's language with this tangle: "Is it too early in—well, thanks for those kind words. But is it too early to ask the commissioners—are you beginning—of course, the commission's been, what, in effect seventy days or something like that, seventy-seven days—traveled to many states, which I think is very important, because I think it's important that when the report comes in, it has a national concept to it, that it isn't regional in any sense."

†Furman quotes neurological experts who warn him that not everyone with aphasic symptoms—frequent grammatical errors, tip-of-the-tongue experiences, and malapropisms—is aphasic. Throwing these warnings aside, Furman, a journalist, apparently felt no embarrassment offering his own diagnosis that Bush's speech revealed a pathological disturbance.

Bush's political opponents tended to hear his blunders as a sign that he was unfit to serve as commander in chief, that they betrayed minimal expectations of public speaking in a leader. They felt that an articulate leader mattered because they felt they deserved someone who could communicate a vision and call upon a repertoire of images and ideas that they shared with him. It certainly didn't help that the Texas accent he uses fits a Northern stereotype of Southerners as backwater hicks.

Bush partisans tended to hear his verbal blunders as a sign of his human fallibility, modesty, and authenticity. A thick-tongued man whose values you can cheer is preferable to a silver-tongued man who, as in the Flannery O'Connor story, seduces you in the hayloft, then runs off with your wooden leg. Democrats made a fatal error by underestimating the power of this appeal, and by assuming that all Americans made the connection between leadership and language style.

Perhaps the strangest moment in the entire story of Bush-as-verbal-blunderer came in 2002, when two California men, Jim Wessling and John Warnock, began marketing a line of "Talking Presidents" dolls, the first of which was a doll of George W. Bush. Sales boomed when the story broke on the Drudge Report, the Washington, D.C.–based political gossip blog. By Christmastime, they'd sold twenty thousand of the figures, and their Web site, talkingpresidents.com, received six hundred thousand Web hits in a single day. A sound chip embedded in the doll was programmed with seventeen of Bush's well-known phrases, most of which were patriotic blandishments. But Wessling and Warnock were wise enough to include two Bushisms: "You're working hard to keep food on your family" and "I will not keep this nation hostile." (The full quote is "We cannot let terrorists and rogue nations hold this nation hostile or hold our allies hostile.") Though Warnock and Wessling considered themselves devout Republicans who called Bush "one of America's true heroes," the blunders were essential to their political homage, celebrated as part of the cloth from which he was cut. During the 2000 campaign, some Bush campaign staffers wore T-shirts they designed that read, "Major league asshole dyslexic rats for Bush-Cheney. Not a subliminable message. Not paid for by Bush/Cheney 2000." A video during the Republican National Convention offered Bush chuckling at his gaffes, and in an appearance at Yale's graduation in May 2001, Bush joked about his speech style: "My critics don't realize I don't make verbal gaffes," Bush told the graduating class, as reported in the *New York Times.* "I'm speaking in the perfect forms and rhythms of ancient haiku."

Perhaps the most important stretch of Bush's language biography began when an advance version of a Bush profile, written by journalist Gail Sheehy for *Vanity Fair,* "The Accidental Candidate," appeared. In her story, Sheehy made the shocking claim that Bush, a class clown who'd compensated for academic weaknesses with social charisma and leadership, had dyslexia. As proof she offered that his brother, Neil, was a confirmed dyslexic. Sheehy also found meaning in the fact that Barbara Bush had actively promoted literacy, a cause one might take up if one had personal experience of a child with reading difficulties. Over the next two months, a firestorm of criticism and name-calling (not only of Bush but of Sheehy and her journalistic credibility) exploded. The Bush campaign eventually appropriated the word as an inside joke—this was the reference to dyslexia on the campaign T-shirts—but not before Bush was asked about Sheehy's story. Bush's reaction is well known because he garbled the reply. "The woman who knew that I had dyslexia—I never interviewed her," he said.

In the first eight months of Bush's presidency, the media poked good-natured fun at his talking, even making gibes about his Spanish. Yet, after September 11, 2001, criticisms of his speaking ceased, and he gained wide praise for a speech he gave on September 14, shouting into a bullhorn, "I can hear you. The rest of the world hears you. And the people who knocked these buildings down will hear all of us soon." His simple sentences somberly matched the nation's mood, and his tough talk made Americans feel as if they were in the hands of a leader. He was finally showing himself to be the uniter he had campaigned as. The September 12 mood brooked no frivolity, either. Amid the patriotic fervor of a nation in crisis, criticism of his verbal blunders abated. But as the ramp-up to the Iraq war began in 2003, the verbal criticism resumed. This time, it returned as a punch line for late-night comedians, a tired cliché.

One of the best trackers of such trends is the founder of www.dubyaspeak.com, a man I will call "Thomas" (he did not want his real name used), who since the 2000 Florida recount has collected Bush blunders, posting them to a Web site with the help of a "very informal group of irregulars." They verify each blunder against White House transcripts, wire service reports, and audio and video clips. Each blunder is annotated with a sarcastic or quizzical comment, then categorized. With Bush's statement, "September the 11th changed me. I remember the day I was in the—at Ground Zero, on September the 4th, 2001. It's a day I will never forget," Thomas observes: "The day . . . maybe not, but the date is an entirely different matter."

The criticism Thomas has received about the site has varied. Before 9/11, people accused him of being sour that Al Gore lost the election. "People said, the way [Bush] talks is endearing, it's merely a personality trait. [They said] you're taking every single thing out of context and blowing it out of proportion," he said. After 9/11, his patriotism was questioned. Other anti-Bush sites shut down after 9/11, but Thomas never considered closing his.

If Bush's coronation as a verbal blunderer was partly an artifact of how closely people scrutinized his speech, then once the scrutinizers were distracted or found other facts, the artifact began to decay. A trial balloon for a full rhetorical rehabilitation came in the spring of 2005, when John McKinnon, a reporter for the *Wall Street Journal,* wrote about Bush's newfound confidence. McKinnon got Jacob Weisberg to admit that Bushisms were harder and harder to find. Even Thomas agreed about the improvement. "He's more relaxed now than he has been in the past," he said, "and he's more confident in speeches, and that's resulted in not as many obvious mistakes as in the past."

But Bush hasn't become a better speaker. It's just that listeners' expectations have changed. Bush's public language has also become more formulaic, which reduces the pressure to be spontaneous and fluent. Meetings are highly scripted, to reduce the opportunities for gaffes. Critics no longer need to scrutinize Bush's speech for evidence of his character. It's all around us now, the accumulation of his mishaps and mistakes—or, if you prefer, of his steadfast leadership.

For their part, linguists were not that critical of Bush. In a 2002 commentary for the NPR show *Fresh Air,* Geoff Nunberg distinguished "thinkos" from "typos" and said it's hard to tell them apart. (A "thinko" corresponds to what I've been calling a "doesn't know better" error; a "typo" is a "knows better" one.)

Nunberg argued that Bush's pronunciation of "nuclear" was a "typo par excellence" but in the end was probably just "a bit of borrowed Pentagon swagger." As for the Bushisms, linguists knew better than to think them abnormal. "What happens with Bush is that some people are listening for mistakes," Arnold Zwicky told me. "I haven't done any comparison with Bush as opposed to someone else, but I wouldn't expect it would be hugely different from any random person."

Invisible factors alerted the American public to listen more sensitively and completely to Bush's linguistic faults. For one thing, Americans seem to hold ideals about how their presidents should speak—witness the presidents in the movies, for instance, who bestow the charisma of the actor on the actual office. Not only are these ideals at odds with how real presidents have spoken, but for less than half of the country's existence have Americans been in a position to actually hear their president speaking. Given how highly we regard the Founding Fathers, it may surprise people to learn that in June 1776, when representatives of thirteen American colonies met at the Continental Congress to discuss what criticisms they should send to King George, they gave the job of writing a declaration of independence to a verbal bungler with a lisp from Virginia who, though he was intellectually prodigious (he could read Latin, Greek, French, Spanish, Italian, and Old English, he didn't read newspapers, opting instead for classical historians like Thucydides and Tacitus, and he began reading Plato's *Republic* when he was seventy-one years old—in the ancient Greek of the original), was an anxious public speaker and an apprehensive talker: Thomas Jefferson.

Jefferson, who eventually served as the new nation's third president, wrote a letter to a friend when he was nineteen years old describing his encounter with the woman he loved. He'd prepared comments "in as moving language as I know how," but he flubbed his romantic lines. "But, good God!" Jefferson wrote. "When I had an opportunity of venting [my thoughts], a few broken sentences, uttered in great disorder, and interrupted with pauses of uncommon length, were the too visible marks of my strange confusion." The young woman, Rebecca Burwell, eventually spurned Jefferson for another man. Because he blundered? The historical record doesn't say.

John Adams, the second president of the United States, father of John Quincy Adams ("Old Man Eloquent" himself), recalled that during the time he and Jefferson spent together as members of Congress, he never heard Jefferson say more than three sentences in a row. Jefferson's biographers noted that in conversation, his voice could be pleasant and modulated. Given how widely read and well traveled he was, he lacked nothing to talk about. There is no evidence that he did not meet the eighteenth-century expectation that intelligent people could hold excellent conversations. But when he got up to speak in public, his voice "sank in his throat" and turned "guttural and inarticulate," as his eulogist, William Wirt, described it. As president, he delivered both of his inaugural addresses in a whisper. He was so uncomfortable with public speaking that he wrote out his State of the Union addresses and sent them to Congress, where they were read by a clerk. No American president delivered a State of the Union address directly to Congress until Woodrow Wilson.

Writing in 1922, the historian Carl Becker described Jefferson's quality of starting and stopping his sentences, in perpetual revision as he spoke. Becker suggested that Jefferson was too intelligent to be a good speaker. "One who in imagination hears the pitch and cadence and rhythm of the thing he wishes to say before he says it," he wrote, "often makes a sad business of public speaking because, painfully aware of the imperfect felicity of what has been uttered, he forgets what he ought to say next. He instinctively wishes to cross out what he has recently said, and say it over again in a different way—and this is what he often does, to the confusion of the audience." George Mahl might say that Jefferson was a chronic sentence-changer, not someone who said "um."

Not all Jefferson historians have been comfortable with these assessments, which are foreign to Jefferson's enduring image; the historian Daniel Ross Chandler, for example, called them "unfortunate and regrettable," and cited Jefferson's ideas for their intellectual merit, his long history of public service, and his private charm. It's true that even if Americans knew about Jefferson's speaking style, his reputation as a Founding Father and Enlightenment polymath would likely not suffer. Jefferson, who spoke well before the era of the mechanical reproduction of the human voice, is spared the judgment that we reserve for public figures whose speeches are engraved in analog or digital form.

We have surprisingly little access to the actual sound of the voices of the people who serve as models of presidential eloquence—and whom we hold up to judge modern presidents such as Bush, who was regularly critiqued as sounding "unpresidential." But what does a president, or any other politician, sound like to the popular American ear? We know more about the history of political speaking than the history of political listening. Such a history might show how blunders produced emotional effects and political situations that were desirable; how twangs, drawls, and dialects provided entrée to power, not exclusion from it; and how garbled syntax and obfuscation have given people power they might not otherwise have had.*

Curiously, Jefferson's spoken ineloquence at the Continental Congress had a positive outcome for the nascent nation: to compensate for his discomfort with the spoken word, the Virginian developed writing skills recognized by other colonial leaders. Because Jefferson had participated little in the spontaneous speech making, and because Benjamin Franklin, another potential author, was ill, Jefferson was chosen to draft a declaration of independence. (He also had some ideas about the natural rights of the people.) He was also asked to read his completed draft aloud to the assembled colonial representatives. It isn't clear whether he did this himself or had someone else do it. We do know that on June 28, 1776, the Declaration of Independence was read aloud, and that the actual copy that was read has disappeared. We also know that Jefferson wanted the Declaration to be enunciated in a particular way, and he added marks to the text that looked like single and double quotation marks floating above the sentences between words. Revolutionary-era printers, mistaking these marks for quotation marks, included them in some early printed versions of the Declaration.

---

*One thinks of Senator Charles Sumner's 1856 speech, "The Crime Against Kansas," an antislavery speech that was also a personal attack against the South Carolina senator Andrew P. Butler. Because Butler had recently suffered a stroke, Sumner's accusation that Butler had spoken "with incoherent phrases, discharged the loose expectoration of his speech" was particularly offensive. The beating of Sumner by Representative Preston Brooks on the Senate floor—and the cheering of the beating among Southerners—is noted as the first sign of violent civil war.

Historians later realized these were oratorical notations, probably Jefferson's reminders to himself. Some believed that they were stress marks for certain words and phrases. But in 1993, Stanford literary critic Jay Fliegelman argued that these marks indicated pauses. In other words, Jefferson had scored the document with prompts to help him achieve a natural-sounding spoken performance.

To explain the factors that attuned listeners to Bush's speaking, we should also trace the evolution of our taste for knowing a president's exact words and why we place so much power in the verbatim. Calvin Coolidge was the first president with a policy against being quoted verbatim, probably because he realized that the mass media, which was becoming increasingly important, would all too faithfully broadcast his blunders. He met weekly with members of the press to explain government policies and political developments but kept his exact words private. The reporters weren't allowed to quote Coolidge directly (they often quoted him but didn't attribute the quotes to him) or even write down his exact words. Coolidge didn't feel his privacy was at stake; it was the weight that he knew could be given to presidential diction. In one exchange recorded by a White House stenographer, Coolidge barked at a reporter he saw sneaking shorthand notes.*

*It's a notable irony that a president chewing out a reporter for transcribing exact words was apparently captured verbatim. George W. Bush is followed by a small army of court reporters who transcribe his every word; some of them work for the White House, others for media organizations, and yet others are freelancers. Journalists on daily deadlines check their quotes against these transcripts, not against their own notes or recordings, even though the transcripts have been "cleaned up" according to what court reporters are trained to do.

"Are you taking down in shorthand what I say?"

"Yes, sir," the reporter replied.

"Now I don't think that is right," Coolidge said. "I don't think that is the proper thing to do. Who do you represent?"

"David Lawrence," the reporter replied.

"Well, I wish you would tell Mr. Lawrence that I don't think it is the right thing to do . . . I don't object to you taking notes as to what I say, but I don't quite throw my communications to the conference into anything like finished style or anything that perhaps would naturally be associated with a presidential utterance," Coolidge said.

If he expected to be quoted verbatim, he would "want to give considerable thought to and perhaps throw a little different form of language."

Coolidge would go on to be the first U.S. president whose words were broadcast on the radio—on December 6, 1923, millions of people tuned in to listen to him speak. Some historians have said that he was soundly reelected the following year as a result. Later, Franklin Delano Roosevelt, frustrated with being misquoted by reporters, installed the first recording system in the Oval Office. Harry Truman explicitly forbade verbatim quoting by journalists.

Yet the end of the twentieth century brought a growing taste for the vérité, perhaps to counter the feeling that mass media offerings were scripted, simulated, and inauthentic. Reality television shows like *Big Brother, The Real World,* and *Survivor* became popular with audiences and networks alike as people discovered the appeal of unscripted reality (albeit a heavily edited one). It was also a time when Americans were reading more transcripts: in 1974, they could read hundreds of pages of Nixon's White House tapes, which flattered the president as little as his 1960 television debate with John Kennedy did. The flurry of verbatim depositions from Kenneth Starr, published as the *Starr Report,* was also a best seller, as much because of its shocking, titillating contents as for its verbatim presentation. The vérité style puts the stamp of truth on things because it seems unmediated by human judgments. It is the closest that written language can come to photography. Yet a vérité quote, just like a photograph, is the product of choices by people about what to include or exclude. The "natural" depends on how invisible the choices are kept.

Journalists, who bring the words of powerful people to the rest of us, have a peculiar relationship to vérité quoting. Normally they are required to present solely facts, a principle that becomes difficult to implement or defend when representing speaking. Vérité quotes aren't often readable. Moreover, they can make people look more stupid or low class than they actually are. Yet journalists' palette of literary techniques has always included the verbatim quote. A recent profile in the *New York Times* of painter Cy Twombly captured his feelings about his past with beautiful swiftness. " 'I loved basic,' he said of his army training. 'It was so regulated.' But then the army sent him to cryptography school, which he said put him under severe strain. 'It's very exacting,' he said. 'I'm not—it's very, very—they—you know.' "

As a novice reporter, former *New York Times* columnist Anthony Lewis was told not to quote verbatim. "I was told when I started," he wrote in an e-mail, "not to use 'ers' and 'ums' or words that reflected a particular accent in a demeaning way." The *Washington Post*'s David Broder agreed that in most cases, verbatim quoting was to be avoided. "Leaving the 'ums' and 'uhs' isn't useful to the reader, because we all do that when we speak," Broder said. He also explained that before microcassette recorders and minidisc players, reporters who attended the same event would typically gather afterward, comparing notes and agreeing on a version of what was said. Now the technology allows reporters to work autonomously; they check their notes against their recordings—or, often, against the official transcripts, which are themselves cleaned up.

Yet, in 2000, unforeseen factors made the vérité quote fashionable again. In the January 31, 2000, *New Yorker*, Nicholas Lemann published a profile of George W. Bush that reproduced large chunks of Bush's speaking, apparently verbatim. Lemann also focused on the quality of Bush's voice. "His voice isn't a fabulous instrument, either: the range of tone and volume is too flat; it lacks richness and roundness," he wrote. Lemann's attention to linguistic detail was the result of having limited time to interview the presidential candidates, whose language was unusually rehearsed and managed that year. Any spontaneous behavior, no matter how small, took on amplified importance—particularly the blurts and blunders. Whenever access to a candidate was curtailed or when the candidate resisted a journalist's probing, the verbatim quotes would serve for a greater proportion of the raw material of portraiture.

Bush supporters complain that vérité portrayals of their candidate suffered at the hands of reporters with a liberal bias. In 1999 and 2000, however, it was a tool for evaluating all politicians. Lemann performed the same analysis of Gore, quoting huge amounts of the candidate talking. And in March 2000, the *New York Times*'s Katharine Q. Seelye quoted Al Gore as saying "Uh, I, I, my message is for the, the voters of the country. Uh, I ask for their support. I'm not taking a single vote for, for granted.' " Gore had been responding to a question that caught him off guard, which Seelye said she wanted to capture. "I was trying to convey that he wasn't prepared to say anything that he hadn't scripted," she said.

Along with his actual blunders and the apparent vogue for vérité style of quoting, George W. Bush was also crowned as a verbal blunderer because he was a canary in the linguistic coal mine. Just as Mrs. Malaprop was a sign of her times, so was George Bush. The rise of Bush-as-blunderer occurred in a context in which, according to the U.S. Census, in 2000, one out of five Americans spoke a language other than English at home. By 2010, the number may rise to one out of four. Half of these will speak Spanish. More than two dozen states and numerous cities have passed either English-only or antibilingual education laws, while the Equal Opportunity Employment Commission has investigated increasing numbers of workplace language discrimination cases, all of which point to simmering anxieties over the connections among language, citizenship, patriotism, and belonging.

The anxiety also includes questions about literacy and language standards. Is there a standard language anymore? E-mail, instant messaging, text messaging, and cell phone communications have created forms of language that often offend traditional sensibilities, particularly because these devices are adopted by the young. To challenge adult culture, the young create vocabularies and grammars that are as different as possible from adult usages. Educators constantly bemoan the lack of spelling and reading skills. Meanwhile, anxieties about language diversity and the standard language are also converging. The United States has never had an official language, though census figures and fears about immigration continually energize the movement to pass a federal law.

Dialects, jargon, and slang continue to proliferate in ways that affect communities and families, whether they speak only English or other languages, too. For every punctuation vigilante who bemoans the imminent demise of Western civilization because the apostrophe gets misused at the supermarket ("Orange's for sale!"), a Mexican-born father is telling his daughter to speak pure Spanish, not to mix in English words, while Chinese parents are waking up their sons on Saturday mornings to go to Chinese school to learn how to read and write Chinese characters. Not all immigrants decide to retain their mother tongue, but the point is that the gatekeepers of standard English aren't the only ones worried about linguistic purity. This is the story of language in America, a place where language loyalties have always been tested.

The case of Bush is a perfect example of what happens when the norms and expectations of speakers and listeners diverge. In recent years, a broader set of social and cultural factors (an accelerated news cycle that increases the scrutiny on the president's every word, our increasing access to presidents as talkers as well as orators) changed public expectations. This was exacerbated by the fact that once the public's opinion is fixed, one's reputation as a speaker is hard to change. Clinton's speaking was also overparsed for evidence of slipperiness, and no matter what Al Gore does, he is doomed to play Adlai Stevenson to W.'s Ike, promising liberation to imaginary eggheads. One is left to wonder how the real person behind the persona feels about his public reputation, how he attempts to manage it, and if he pays attention to it at all.

To build up, preserve, undermine, or even question the linguistic legacy of Bush can hardly be done without being accused of having a political agenda. Yet in a nonpartisan sense, evaluating his linguistic performances in light of the political agendas of both Right and Left highlights social attitudes about language that are directly relevant to questions about power, who has it, and who doesn't.

On one hand, criticizing how smart or competent or moral a person is because he or she doesn't speak like you do (or as you expect them to) smears a larger set of people than you'd think, including nonnative speakers of English, stutterers, people with diseases that impact their motor control, and the elderly. Liberals shouldn't talk about speaking this way—it contradicts how they work to include everybody and make sure that everyone has equal opportunity. Also, long after public figures who have been criticized for their linguistic abilities are gone from the public stage, people who speak differently will still be around. We ourselves may even be among them, hoping we don't get smeared for the way we talk, too.

On the other hand, anyone who believes in upholding any sort of standard should neither accept nor reward public figures who speak in a way that doesn't match their listeners' expectations, whose speaking is full of errors, and who flaunt those errors. If you make excuses for such people, you send the wrong message to those who have the responsibility of enforcing the right and wrong of language, such as teachers. And if you routinely prize what's authentic over what's excellent (as political supporters of Bush seem to have done), you risk suggesting that some people can't rise to the standards set out for them. If we jettison those standards, we risk throwing out a good part of who we are—or at least whom we strive to be.

# 11

## *The Future of Verbal Blunders*

In the future, you can avoid making verbal blunders just as your ancestors did: by not speaking at all. Which is to say, until someone invents a pill that makes people say only what they intend to, the average, normal speaker of English will continue to make as many as seven to twenty-two slips of the tongue a day* and will have about two to four moments each day where finding the right word or name takes embarrassingly too much time.

Such pesky intransigence will be true for disfluencies, too. Unless someone comes up with a machine that freezes time so you can stop to plan what to say, yet make your listener hear you as uninterrupted and smooth, about 5 to 8 percent of the words that normal speakers say every day—from about 325 to 1,800 of them—will involve an "uh," "um," some other pause filler; a repeated sound, syllable, or word; a restarted sen-

---

*Based on one slip per thousand words, and a range of words spoken per day of 7,500 to 22,500.

tence; or a repair, all of which is normal for the everyday speaking that underpins our lives and our society, talk that isn't scripted or rehearsed. These blunder stats are rough estimates, of course; your own performances will vary.

It is very hard to change your natural tendency to slip and be disfluent. A person born a repeater or a deleter will likely leave this life as such. Yet you can rise above—or fall below—your blundering baseline quite readily, depending on your speaking situation and any tasks that accompany your talking. You will blunder more if you juggle eggs while talking. You will also slip more if you worry about the state of your cowlick—though your slips will not necessarily reveal your specific anxiety about your hair. However, you can probably blunder less if you reduce the number of things you have to be aware of or think about while speaking. For some people faced with formal speaking, this means rehearsing. For others, it means relaxing. Speaking in short sentences also helps. In other experiments, people speak more fluently when they're threatened with electric shocks. That's not so appealing for everyday use. Neither is shouting, another punishment with limited effectiveness. A more palatable therapy is drinking beer, which may, in large enough doses, eliminate "uhs" and "ums" entirely.

Yet consider more evidence about the meanings of disfluency. In 1995, Nicholas Christenfeld asked college students to rate speakers on a tape who filled their pauses, left the pauses silent, or who did not pause at all. The students preferred speakers with no pauses. But guess what? Ummers were rated no less eloquent than the silent pausers. Moreover, the pause fillers had less of an actual impact than listeners said they preferred. Why? Because, as Christenfeld explained, "Speakers' 'ums' were noticed only when the audience was attending to the style, and not to the content of the utterance." Left to listen as they would, some listeners notice style, others content. What seems to distinguish good speakers from bad ones was that the good ones hide their hesitation, making listeners focus on substance and content. Want people to not notice your "ums"? Be interesting.

What this research really tells us is that disfluency is utterly normal, that our rules for what counts as "good speaking" are resistant to the biological facts about it, that the rules evolve while the disfluencies remain stable, and that trying to communicate without disfluencies may be more distracting (and hence more damaging to fluency) than it's worth. It shows that everyone's baseline is uniquely their own. And it means that verbal blunders do not mean any more, in themselves, than what we attribute to them. The reality is that we talk in more situations every day where our verbal blunders pass by as unnoticed as shadows. And in the world of speaking, everyone has a shadow.

While our verbal blunders are not endangered—their numbers won't shrink in any absolute sense—it's quite possible that people's attitudes about them, the meanings they ascribe to them, and the assumption they make about verbal blunderers themselves may change subtly. In the last several years, prescripted disfluencies have begun to appear in advertisements, obviously in order to manipulate the listener's trust. Telemarketers used to leave prerecorded messages on my answering machine like "Hi! This is Bob Jones, and I'm here to tell you about a great new home equity loan!" Now the messages sound more like, "Hey, I uh, I'm sorry I missed you, but uh . . ." They still try to sell me a mortgage I don't need, but I keep listening longer than I used to. I admit, the blundering used to fake me out. Such deliberate ineloquence is nothing new: the ancient Greeks had a vast repertoire of ways to deform language in order to shock, confuse, or amuse. But doing it well is harder than it looks.

Listeners also encounter verbal blunders when a speaker doesn't rehearse a presentation to a glib polish or edit a production into a smooth-sounding stream. This can be deliberate, as when speakers who want to appear spontaneous, creative, or authentic don't monitor their speech as assiduously as they might. Other speakers want to make themselves more personable. It's not just punks; Pauline Webber has shown that doctors add words like "well," "anyway," and "now" when giving previously published remarks at medical conferences. Apparently they do this so their listeners will feel comfortable approaching them. Slips and disfluencies of everyday speaking can also be disseminated inadvertently. Media speech and fluent speech used to be synonymous, but the increased presence of video and audio on the Internet means that we'll see and hear more talk as it happens naturally.

Forms of new media have also claimed a rough-hewn, real-life style—which often involves messy speaking—in order to stand apart from mainstream commercial media. Whether this shift to the vérité is something enduring or just a passing fashion is hard to say. But it's integral to the fascination with reality television shows; the newfound popularity of the documentary film as entertainment, not simply as a teaching tool or political instrument; the blog phenomenon, a galaxy of amateur writers that threatens to surpass, in readership, the mainstream media; and the increasing popularity of do-it-yourself media culture, from YouTube to public-domain audiobooks. Because podcasters have made the homespun (or laptop-spun) aesthetic a basic tool in their toolboxes, podcasts often feature slips, disfluencies, mispronunciations, background noises, and other intrusions.

Not everyone likes the aesthetic shift. But norms about speaking may be evolving for deeper reasons that are as unmoveable as mountains. Perhaps American audiences want more variety than slick, scripted broadcaster voices; perhaps they no longer take glib fluency for honesty, substance, or charisma. Perhaps it's another instance of informality in American social life. It could also be part of the same impulse revealed in exposed conduit and pipes in buildings or open restaurant kitchens—a postmodern desire to see the backstages of life where the action really happens.

In the future, regardless of how our attitudes change about them, verbal blunders will become raw material. Instead of being ignored or thrown out, these hallmarks of natural, spontaneous speaking will inform technological enhancements and lubricate interactions between humans and machines. In Shanghai I visited a start-up software company, Saybot, which offers an online robot (or a "bot") to help the Chinese learn spoken English. People who use Saybot online won't be conscious that their errors have become useful. They will speak into their PC's microphone in response to questions or directions from the system. If they speak correctly, the system will let them continue to the next lesson or level. Saybot does this by using speech recognition software to match the learner's voice against a prerecorded acoustic waveform from a native speaker. Then it measures the learner's variation from the native norm. If the waveforms match, the student can proceed; if they don't, the system stores the mismatches in a short-term memory and allows the learner to play back each one. Human teachers correct students in the same way, but they can't do it as precisely as the software can. Saybot also aggregates the error data from all of the learners, allowing it to be analyzed by a trained linguist who can tell whether Saybot users speak Mandarin, Cantonese, or some other Chinese language, as well as the success of Saybot lesson plans, which can be tweaked to focus on pronunciation patterns that students need to practice. Verbal blunders have been used for decades as data, but they've probably never been transformed into commodities in this way.

Psychologists have recently begun to understand how verbal blunders have helped guide social interactions, involving something called the "feeling of another's knowing," or how much one person intuits about another person's thoughts or feelings. Disfluencies are among the important clues that listeners use to adjust their attention as well as their responses to other people.

At the New School for Social Research, Michael Schober, a student of Herb Clark, is applying insights about verbal blunders to the survey and the poll. If you've ever filled out a government form, you've probably encountered terms such as "family" or "house" or "ethnic background" that seemed vague. And polls feature words that can be ambiguous. Pollsters get around this by simply asking the same question of everyone the same way—and they don't offer clarifications, lest they bias their results. But Schober says they can listen to patterns in a person's speaking that might reveal a subtle request for clarification. A person who needs the meaning of a question clarified is more likely to pause longer, say "uh" or "um," and repair their sentences, Schober has found. So an interviewer trained to hear disfluencies would be attuned to an interviewee who needs extra clarification.

The principle of "feeling of another's knowing" can also be applied to interactions between humans and machines. One of the researchers at the forefront of this work is Liz Shriberg, a researcher at SRI International, where Flakey the robot once roamed. A slim, elegant woman with a quiet voice, she knows what spontaneous speaking looks like on the page, so she was reluctant to let me turn on my tape recorder—she was afraid of how her sentences would look.

Working as a technician in a speech recognition lab in the 1990s, Shriberg witnessed human speech confusing a computer. In an experiment she was managing, the human subjects spoke over the phone to an automatic system in order to make airplane reservations, giving simple commands like "Show me flights from Boston to Dallas." At first, the subjects actually talked to a "wizard," or a human posing as a machine. The wizard had no problem comprehending an "uh" or a repeated word. But when a machine replaced the wizard, speakers consistently broke it when they paused, repeated a word, or said "um."

Also, when the humans realized the machine couldn't process their normal speaking, they switched to a monotone, spoke in simple sentences, and had no pauses. "They started speaking to it like a robot," Shriberg said. Her conclusion: "If you want machines to be as smart as people, you want machines to understand speech that's natural, and natural speech has lots of disfluencies in it," she says.

But pause fillers, restarts, repeated words, and even silences plague machine ears. Automatic systems are trained on grammatically perfect written sentences, not real human speaking, with fragments, hesitations, and pause fillers. So the two (or more) parts of a restarted sentence confuse them; they also mistake "uh" for the English article "a." In general, the human brain's ability to comprehend speech is too complex to replicate. Some of Shriberg's research has focused on how to use a speaker's intonation to help the machine recognize a disfluency and what the speaker's full utterance might be. Shriberg also helped build a computer system that recognized features of a person's speech to identify him or her uniquely. The four most valuable features were what some people might find undesirable in speaking: the duration of words, any silent pauses longer than 150 milliseconds, the number of beginnings and ends of sentences (some of which may have been broken sentences and repairs), and the frequency of "uh" and "um."

If people are less disfluent with machines (as Sharon Oviatt, another researcher, showed), it's because the tasks or interactions are constrained to activities such as asking about the weather or buying tickets. But in the future, what we know about disfluencies—that they're a natural part of human speaking, that they're meaningful, that they often reliably indicate a person's mental or emotional state—will be incorporated into technologies that are broader in scope. These will be able to do more than take orders; they'll be able to transcribe conversations or, like Hal, the computer in the movie *2001: A Space Odyssey,* have wide-ranging conversations with people. The intelligence community is apparently interested in technology that will automatically transcribe spoken English as well as other languages. So is the court system, which spends millions of dollars on court reporters. Such technology will give the elderly and the disabled more robust voice-controlled appliances, vehicles, and smart homes; health care organizations may one day direct patients to robot counselors for health advice. Making machines perceive human speech isn't the only problematic issue in designing these systems—indeed, some people may never accept them, no matter what the machines can listen to. A robot therapist may be able to respond to you sensibly despite your long pauses, sobs, and stammerings, but some people may not be able to get over the fact that their HMO has dictated that robot therapy is all it will pay for.

Shriberg has been contacted by an educational company that wants to use student disfluencies to measure whether material is too hard for a student, and a toy company that wants to see if disfluencies indicate that a user is confused. Using this feedback, the machine could adjust how quickly it presents information or shift to a different level of difficulty. Such systems may also—like Flakey the robot—learn to say "uh" and "um" like people do. Right now, Shriberg says, the machines tend to barge in, interrupting people, and sound impolite. What could engineers do? They can soften the machine's start with a pause filler. Or, if the machine uses the pause filler, it could get the human to stop talking.


Machines that say "um." Pollsters who listen for disfluencies. More verbatim transcripts. Normal, unedited speaking in broadcasts. What impact, if any, might these and other developments have in the long term on attitudes about verbal blunders and the people who make them?

Jean Fox Tree predicts that neutral ideas about "uh" and "um" will someday become as mainstream as other scientific facts. "In our lifetime," she told me, "we will accept that these [pause fillers] are meaningful. Forty or fifty years from now," she added, "if not sooner, you can talk about this stuff in a high school and people are going to think it's obvious."

Once you're attuned to the great diversity of speech errors, you can find entertainment anywhere. Elizabeth Zwicky, the daughter of linguists, says that her experiences listening for slips of the tongue brightened her life, because no language environment, however boring, is without its verbal amusement. "It's like being a birdwatcher," she says. "Birdwatchers have a richer experience of birds than anybody else." And may the blunderologists we may someday become not only forgive our blunders but enjoy them.

# *AfterUm . . .**

**W**e go outdoors, to the ocean or the mountains, to encounter the untamed and untameable. It's a quality you can find closer to home, too—spoken sentences are full of wildness, right under the threshold of your attention, all around you, made by your friends, family members, and colleagues. And, yes, by you.

As I've gone to some lengths to describe in this book, it's typical to think of verbal blunders as embarrassing and marring. Even if that were an accurate view, it wouldn't be the complete story. They're also signs of the wild. I don't mean "wild" in the sense of rough and savage, but as pure and undomesticated. That's probably why they've kept my fascination for so long. They provide a striking window into what humans really are: biological organisms who have really amazing brains. Verbal

*Some portions of this afterword were previously published in *Science*, "Read My Slips," September 17, 2007, and in *The Boston Globe*, "The Beast Within," August 5, 2007.

blunders may seem like violations of the order of language. In truth, they're spontaneous eruptions of the creativity, complexity, and flexibility that gave us this order in the first place. Are they funny? Sure! But there's a lot to be learned from the wildness, too.

Why do verbal blunders occur? If it weren't for the exuberance of neurons, speech errors wouldn't happen. In order to say or sign creative, novel things, we need fast, flexible brains. But that speed and flexibility comes with a cost: so very rarely, our brains produce something creative and novel when we don't expect it. Meanwhile, speech disfluencies arise because we plan, then speak, then plan, then speak. Sometimes this cycle can't be smooth or timely, or we want to change direction. These delays, hesitations, or interruptions we vocalize, mainly for social reasons.*

Readers and reviewers of *Um . . .* often comment on how the rules for "good speaking" (at least in modern America) don't account for some of the biological facts of language. To me, this says something else about the human experience: We live in social groups that make and follow rules that constrain the part of us that's a biological organism with an amazing brain.

Contemporary human life is full of such mismatches. Human teenagers are sexually mature, yet industrialized societies keep people at that age suspended in a proto-adulthood, often regulating their sexual behavior. True, human societies often succeed because they've shaped and molded our animal impulses. Yet some adults are so blind to the arc of human sexual development that the social strictures of their time and

---

*I should also point out, we sometimes use words like "um" to be polite. Your neighbor's dog humps your leg; you say, "I didn't expect him to be so, um, friendly." This is deliberate, not a "blunder."

place become the only alternative, while other societies' strictures are unthinkable. Seeing this dynamic in the littlest of "ums" simply underscores how endless a struggle it would be to root out all these views from nutrition, health, economics, and even politics. No matter how much I explain that there's little evidence that "uhs" and "ums" actually impede communication or information processing or indicate unintelligence, a surprising number of people have been unwilling to let the notion go.

*Um* . . . tells the story of the wildness of verbal blunders—and of some of the ways that humans have tried to civilize them, to make them do social work, to fit them into stories about other people that they didn't like anyway. How do we define error and verbal mistakes? How do we perceive deviation? The subtitle, "what verbal blunders mean," was pointed at these larger questions.

Nevertheless, I suspect that some people came to the book expecting to find out what it says about them that they said "gus gazzling," or whether the preacher who said "pinched his tits" instead of "pitched his tents" should lose his job, or if they should vote for the guy who says "um." Without knowing much more about the situation or the individual, it's hard to say what each individual instance "means." But *Um* . . . will tell you what they *don't* and *couldn't* mean.

I thought I'd create a brief key of some major points in the book along these lines.

- Everyone possesses a certain style of disfluency at a certain frequency (page 86 onward)
- Mere presence or absence of disfluency isn't telling—the change from a baseline is (page 244 onward)

- Disfluency increases with cognitive load (page 92 onward)
- Disfluency doesn't indicate deception (page 67 onward)
- Disfluencies are more reliable indicators of states and not useful for traits (page 66 onward)
- When analyzing a speaker's slips, you must make sure you couldn't arrive at the same conclusion starting from a different behavior (page 37)
- Slips often occur because sounds or words in the sentence have moved (pages 41 to 51)
- Malapropisms occur because a target word sounds like, or is related in meaning, to the error (pages 207 to 209)
- Most speech errors are not perceived—only about one a week (page 193)—though people make, on average, no more than one or two every 1,000 words (page 193)

Perhaps the most important point is this: people tell stories about verbal blunders that reflect their vision of what the human self should be like. For someone who believes that the self is beset with hidden struggle, blunders point to that struggle. For someone who thinks that the self should be self-controlled, regulated, and efficient, blunders point to that failure. For someone who thinks that the self should be engaged, authentic, spontaneous, interactive, verbal blunders will be evidence of those qualities. This was true in Reverend Spooner and Sigmund Freud's time as much as in Kermit Schafer's and George W. Bush's.

Some new pieces of the linguistic story about speech errors came out after *Um . . .* was in print. If you're interested in these developments, read on. Otherwise, you might want to skip to the end of the AfterUm, where you'll find a discussion of verbal blunders and politics.

One piece of big news was the first brain study of people making spoonerisms, published in May 2007 in *Cerebral Cortex* by Thomas Münte and some colleagues at Otto von Guericke University in Germany. In their lab, they provoked spoonerisms in the classic way, by flashing a series of pairs of words on a computer screen ("bill deal," "bark dog," and "bang doll") then a final one, "darn bore." A person sitting at a computer monitor was supposed to read the first three pairs silently and was sometimes told to read the final pair. Almost immediately after the person sees "darn bore," there's a spike of brain activity. There's another spike if they're given the instruction to read "darn bore" aloud. If they happen to say "barn door," there's an even bigger spike.

As far as the team could make out, both increases in brain activity occurred in the medial frontal cortex. Damage to any part of this area can make a speaker be less spontaneous or say things involuntarily. If you physically poke this area in the brains of epileptics, they say things like "da da da" and "ta ta ta." Münte also noted that activity in this area of the brain is associated with some sort of conflict in processing and planning.

Speech errors once were one of the only tools that linguists and brain scientists possessed for peering into the brain; as studies like Münte's show, a new generation of tools and methods are confirming what speech errors had shown. These instruments may also someday help to resolve debates about slips. For instance, since Vicki Fromkin's day, linguists have accepted that speech errors like the spoonerism are pronounced with perfect fluency. That seems to be because the slippage occurs in the brain, not the tongue—it's the mental symbols that get switched around, not the motor system's commands to the tongue. But now a different view has been explored by Marianne Pouplier, a phonetician at the University of Munich.*

Pouplier tracks how speakers' tongues move inside their mouths with instruments that provide a closer picture of speaking. In one technique, called electromagnetometry, she glues sensors inside the mouth then tracks the movement; another technique is to watch tongue movement with ultrasound. Then she elicits slips by telling people to say pairs of words like "cop cop" and "top top" interspersed with "cop top." In a certain number of instances, the speakers say "top top" instead of "cop top."

But Pouplier observed how the spoonerizers' tongues weren't acting in an all-or-nothing way, substituting "t" where there should have been a "c." Rather, it looked like they were trying to say the "t" and the "c" simultaneously. Nearly 54 percent of the time a speaker's tongue would move as if it were trying to make both sounds. Pouplier still calls this an error, the tongue isn't moving to its precise target. Although the tongue mashed its movements together, only one sound was perceived by a listener. And full substitutions of the kind that linguists usually write about did occur—though only 4 percent of the time.

Critics say, each of us possesses a lot of variation in how we articulate sounds, but Pouplier's approach allows for no variation. If we set our standard too finely, we couldn't utter a single

*See "Dynamic action units slip in speech production errors" in *Cognition*, and "Articulatory perspectives on errors," in *The State of the Art in Speech Error Research,* a proceedings from an NSF-sponsored conference at MIT in 2007.

sound that wouldn't be an error.* But if Pouplier is right, that means there's more error in speech than Fromkin had ever considered, and more variability in the errors she did know something about.

They share one thing in common, though. Where Fromkin, Garrett, Anne Cutler, and others used speech errors to map how ideas became sounds (or signs), Pouplier uses slips to support a new, controversial view of how we make sounds in the first place. Linguists have usually studied abstract bundles of speech sounds (a subfield called phonology) apart from real speech sounds (a subfield called phonetics). Pouplier is forwarding a theory called "articulatory phonology," which holds that the abstract bundles may contain information about how tongues, lips, and vocal cords actually make sounds. People who work in this area study speech sounds almost entirely with instruments and don't rely on transcription (writing sounds down, as Fromkin did) at all.

Brain studies like Thomas Münte's may solve at least part of the puzzle. The location of increased brain activity right before the person in the experiment made a spoonerism is where motor commands come from. In the case of spoonerisms, there's conflict between commands. Unfortunately, his study didn't explain why correct pronunciations didn't light up the same areas of the brain. So while this brain study showed there might be conflict in articulation, it also showed how there could be conflict at the level of abstract bundles. Any definitive answer to Pouplier's challenge to the way linguists have understood speech errors will have to come from somewhere else.

*See Joseph Stemberger's paper, "Gradience and asymmetries in phonological speech errors," in *The State of the Art in Speech Error Research*.

It's long been known that children make more speech errors than adults, as I described in chapters 4 and 8. But when I was researching the book, no one could tell me if or how aging affected speech error rates. In 2006 Janet Vousden and Elizabeth Maylor at the University of Warwick in England published (in *Language and Cognitive Processes*) the first study tracking speech errors across the lifespan. They found no significant increase in total errors between young and older adults. (They weren't counting speech errors in real life but making people produce them artificially.)

However, the types of errors changed with age in interesting ways. On the whole, adults made proportionately more errors than children in which a sound segment was anticipated (frive frantic fat frogs) rather than perseverated (five frantic fat fogs).

This finding fit with a widely used model of speech errors first developed in the 1980s by cognitive scientist Gary Dell of the University of Illinois at Urbana-Champaign. He theorized that the more practice a speaker has with the sounds of a particular language, the more their errors anticipated a sound or word that they were planning to say. Adults make more of these anticipatory errors because they have more "practice" with their language. Dell explained it to me this way: "Whatever makes you more error-prone makes your errors more perseveratory, and whatever makes you less error-prone makes the fewer errors that you make more anticipatory."

It's worth reviewing Dell's model of how slips happen. (It's also discussed on pages 197 to 199 of *Um . . . .*) Working mostly from the results of speech error research, most linguists think that words and sounds are stored in a kind of network in the brain, related by variables such as how they sound, their parts of speech, and their meaning. Dell proposed that when sounds or words stored in such a network are selected, this also strengthens or "activates" neighboring units, which may be misread as the right ones. In his model, people who have practiced reduce their overall error rate but anticipatory errors make up a greater portion of them, while those made to speak faster than they prefer—even if they are practiced—make more errors overall because the stimulation of neighboring units in the network has less opportunity and time to fade. (There is also less time to activate the correct unit.)

If you're the kind of person who's interested in using speech errors as evidence about pathology, you should pay attention to this model, because it allows you to talk about "good" and "bad" error patterns. In 1994, Dell and some others compared the speech errors of an aphasic to "normal" speech errors, and found that a speech system that wasn't working well (because the speaker had aphasia, say) was "bad" if it had more errors overall, more perseveratory errors, and nonwords and nonsense strings.

By themselves, most single speech errors are limited in what they can tell you (Merrill Garrett's favorites like "the skreeky gwease gets the wheel" notwithstanding; see page 189). Errors themselves aren't good or bad, it's the patterns they make. This is the case with a lot of the verbal blunders, including speech disfluencies—only by counting and analyzing examples can you figure out these patterns, not by listening informally.

While I was working on *Um . . .* , I heard about the work of Heidi Lyn, a comparative cognitive scientist who had worked with Kanzi, a twenty-seven-year-old bonobo. While the focus on Kanzi has been whether or not what he does is linguistic, Lyn did an innovative study of Kanzi's errors and what they mean.

Let me introduce Kanzi. I wanted more than anything to visit him at the Great Ape Trust in Des Moines, Iowa, but the new facilities are behind schedule, and Kanzi wasn't accepting visitors. Raised among humans, he learned to understand spoken English and communicates by way of colorful visual symbols, called lexigrams. He learned the lexigrams indirectly, when a primate researcher, Sue Savage-Rumbaugh, was teaching his adopted mother, Matata. Matata didn't pick them up; Kanzi did. This biographical fact means that Kanzi can do so much because he's learned it, not because he's been trained. *Merely trained*, the critics imply.

But Kanzi can do things that suggest linguistic abilities. He can understand spoken English, even references to objects or people that aren't in his immediate visual view. He can communicate using a 384-symbol board covered with lexigrams, abstract shapes that refer to objects, actions, qualities, and places. And as Savage-Rumbaugh wrote in 2003, Kanzi "regulates his vocal output by producing structurally distinct sounds that are temporally associated with distinct semantic contexts." That's to say, Kanzi speaks words.

You might think this makes him a candidate for enduring the embarrassment of speech errors, but he doesn't make slips of the tongue. He does make errors when he selects lexigrams, though. From 1990 to 2001, researchers tested Kanzi and a female bonobo, Panbanisha, thousands of times, showing them a photo or lexigram or saying an English word. The bonobos then had to select the matching lexigram. The apes made 1,497 incorrect choices in those trials (choosing correctly 12,157 times), though no one thought to consider the errors as data until now.

Kanzi knows the difference between a blackberry and a hot dog. But sometimes, when researchers asked him to touch the lexigram for blackberry, he touched the lexigrams for hot dog, blueberries, or cherries instead. As is the case with human speech errors, these aren't random mistakes, but have patterns. And as with human errors, the patterns point to an order of mind that you couldn't acquire evidence of any other way. For instance, if he made a mistake when asked for "blackberry," Kanzi was more likely than chance to choose a lexigram for another fruit, much as you or I might say "red" instead of "black."

Lyn found that Kanzi and Panbanisha have arranged hundreds of lexigrams in their minds in a complex, hierarchical manner based mainly on their meaning. She coded the relationships between all 1,497 sample-error pairs along seven dimensions, including whether the lexigrams looked alike, had English words that sounded alike, or referred to objects in the same category. If the lexigram stood for "blackberry," the error was more likely than chance to sound like blackberry ("blueberries"), be an edible ("hot dog"), be a fruit ("raisin"), or be physically similar ("strawberry"). To Lyn, this higher probability indicated that the lexigram "blackberry" was a member of the same categories as the incorrect choices. Errors were also more likely to be associated with more than one category. For example, "cherries" are edibles and fruits, and the word sounds like the sample, "blackberries."

Asking a speaker who's just made a speech error what she intended to say has been a cornerstone of speech error research ever since Rudolf Meringer. But Kanzi can't tell us what he intended. (Neither could Jeri Jaeger's kids, for that matter.) On the other hand, ask a speaker how he's arranged words and sounds in his brain, and he won't know how to answer, but his speech errors will reveal everything. That much is true with Kanzi, too. The overwhelming likelihood of the semantic overlaps in Kanzi's errors indicated to Lyn how his brain stores mental representations of the lexigrams. The lexigrams aren't stored in a one-to-one association. They must be stored in a hierarchical fashion, which hadn't been demonstrated in a primate brain yet. As Lyn wrote to me in an email, "Overall, I think these findings extend our ideas of the apes' mental representation of their communicative system. The results support the idea that their representation of semantic information is much more complex than has been shown in apes to date." She closed by pointing out that there wasn't any evidence that the bonobos had grammatical categories like "noun" and "verb"— and that, to hardcore linguists, is the sign that Kanzi doesn't really have language.

My priority in *Um . . .* was to tell the linguistic story about verbal blunders, a story that had never been told before. Coming when it did, with George W. Bush providing political comedy nearly every day, the book seemed to emphasize the linguistic story too much. Readers, some reviewers, and some of my close friends accused me either of ignoring what's funny about Bushisms or letting Bush "off the hook."

Yes, the scientific story about verbal blunders can be inconvenient for political story-telling. Here's another recent example. During the 2008 U.S. presidential primary campaigns, the name of Democratic candidate and U.S. Senator, Barack Obama, was involved in an unfortunate speech error. Two broadcasters on CNN, Glenn Beck and Alina Cho, said "Osama" when "Obama" was correct, and Republican candidate Mitt Romney said

"Obama" when referring to "Osama." This inflamed Obama supporters. It's a deliberate campaign to smear their candidate!

Because you've read *Um . . .* , you know why confusing "Osama" and "Obama" is a speech error. You also know why Senator Ted Kennedy made the same slip. It's a solid gold malapropism. You commit a malapropism for two reasons: you either say a word that's related in meaning to your intended word, or you say one that's related in sound. "Osama" and "Obama" is a perfect target-error pair. They're almost exactly the same words, except for that second sound. As I noted on page 208, one striking fact about target-error pairs in malapropisms is they have the same number of syllables and the same stress pattern nearly all the time. oBAma. oSAma.

As if that weren't enough to link them, the two names are semantically related. They're foreign-sounding names, and they're names in the news. Depending on where you are on the political spectrum, both Osama bin Laden and Barack Obama might be your opponents. From both directions, whether sound or meaning, it's so remarkably easy to confuse "Obama" and "Osama," I'm surprised that it doesn't happen more frequently.

Now, it's possible that the newscasters are sitting in the back room, derisively saying "Osama" when they mean "Obama," which might have primed them to say "Osama" when they shouldn't. But not only is there no evidence that this happened, you might remember that priming for spoonerisms in the lab only works 10 to 20 percent of the time (see page 195 onward). I doubt that Teddy Kennedy was sitting offstage saying "Osama."

A writer for Condé Nast's *Portfolio*, Jeff Bercovici, asked me to comment on the Obama/Osama confusion, then wrote a post on his media blog on portfolio.com. Obama supporters responded immediately and disapprovingly. One writer couldn't fathom how such a mistake could occur in the first place, given that Obama is a "very famous U.S. senator" and "the next President of the United States." Someone else wrote about the Republican smear of Democratic candidate Adlai Stevenson in which he was systematically called "Alger" (after Alger Hiss).

In response to these comments, I posted this:

> You can tell whatever political story you like, but the plain fact is that though the slip misserves your candidate, you haven't provided any evidence of any plan, intention, or directive by any campaign to replace "Obama" with "Osama"—and I do not think any of the posters are claiming that CNN is in cahoots with Mitt Romney. (Are you?)
>
> This isn't to say that real, honest slips of the tongue don't, or won't, have historical or political consequences. And I'm not saying that propagandists don't work (and succeed) by deliberately mislabeling. But I hope the historians of the future will be smart enough to consider the linguistic story before they embrace what Richard Hofstadter called "the paranoid style in American politics" in order to tell the political story they would want to tell anyway.
>
> If you want to begin to convince me that this is a deliberate plan to smear Obama by intentionally saying "Osama," you might start by showing that all of these speakers (Beck, Romney, and Cho) make many fewer slips of the tongue in general. I haven't done this and don't plan to, but if you were to actually count their slips, you would probably find that they occur within a range consistent with people who speak a lot in high-pressure

situations. In other words, if they only screw up Obama's name and no one else's, then you might have an argument. I doubt this is the case.

This slip does your candidate a disservice, but it's not linguistically anomalous.

No matter what the outcome of this election is, new crops of speech errors uttered by or about politicians will always draw the attention of people who use them to tell a political story. That story about Barack Obama may turn out to be that deeply embedded prejudices, racism, and maybe conspiracies stood in the way of the first black president of the United States—just look at how they kept confusing his name! I hope that telling the linguistic story will keep people focused on the politics they can change, not the vagaries of the human brain, which they can't. I also hope that *Um . . .* will be around for a long time to guide people back to the linguistic story about verbal blunders. Which isn't the only story about them. But it's the best.

# Appendix A: Recommended Reading

For a full bibliography, endnotes, and errata, go to www.umthebook.com.

The classic, comprehensive view of human error is *Human Error* (1984), by James Reason. Reading Sigmund Freud's *The Psychopathology of Everyday Life* (1904) is basic, as is Sebastiano Timpanaro's rebuttal in *The Freudian Slip* (1976). Carlo Ginzburg's essay on Giovanni Morelli and Sigmund Freud, "Clues: Roots of an Evidential Paradigm," appears in a collection of his essays, *Clues, Myths, and the Historical Method* (1989). Jack Spector's essay, "The Method of Morelli and Its Relation to Freudian Psychoanalysis," published in 1969 in *Diogenes*, helped distinguish Morelli's method from Freud's adaptation. Though Meringer and Mayer's *Misspeaking and Misreading (Versprechen und Verlesen)* has never been translated into English, an essay in English by Anne Cutler and David Fay in its 1978 edition is a very good introduction to the life and times of Rudolf Meringer.

Victoria Fromkin edited a collection of early studies on slips of the tongue in *Speech Errors as Linguistic Evidence* (1973) and collected classics of the new slip science in *Errors in Linguistic Performance: Slips of the Tongue, Ear, Pen, and Hand* (1980). Another key collection of essays appears in *Slips of the Tongue and Language Production*, edited by Anne Cutler and published in 1982. The academic literature on slips of the tongue is vast. A very good overview of research to date is *Slips of the Tongue: Speech Errors in First and Second Language Production,* by Nanda Poulisse (1999). Jeri Jaeger's *Kids' Slips* is not yet a classic, but it will be. Arnold Zwicky's *Mistakes* (available at http://www.stanford.edu/~zwicky/mistakes.pdf) is appropriate for use in writing and linguistics classes.

For the discussion of Reverend Spooner, I drew from William Hayter's biography, *Spooner, a Biography* (1977), as well as a chapter from Julian Huxley's memoir, *On Living in a Revolution* (1944). R. H. Robbins' essay "The Warden's Wordplay," appeared in *The Dalhousie Review* in 1966. I also relied on John M. Potter's essay, "What Was the Matter with Doctor Spooner?" which appeared in the collection edited by Fromkin, *Errors in Linguistic Performance.*

A technical but exhaustive elaboration of a speech production model that considers both slips of the tongue and speech disfluencies is *Speaking: From Intention to Articulation,* by Willem Levelt (1989). Also technical and exhaustive is Herb Clark's *Using Language* (1996). Those interested in the early days of disfluency research should look at "Hesitation Phenomena in Spontaneous English Speech," by Howard Maclay and Charles Osgood. Frieda Goldman-Eisler's papers are collected in *Psycholinguistics: Experiments in Spontaneous Speech* (1968), and George Mahl's work is collected in *Explorations in Nonverbal and Vocal Behavior* (1987). Heather Bortfeld et al.'s paper "Disfluency Rates in Conversation: Effects of Age, Relationship, Topic, Role and Gender" appeared in *Language and Speech* in 2001; Herb Clark and Jean Fox Tree's major work on "uh" and "um," "Using 'uh' and 'um' in Spontaneous Speaking," appeared in *Cognition* in 2002. Fox Tree's article "Listeners' Uses of Um and Uh in Speech Comprehension" predates this by a year in the journal *Memory and Cognition.* Roger Brown and David McNeill's 1966 paper "The 'Tip of the Tongue' Phenomenon" in the *Journal of Verbal Learning and Verbal Behavior* is the classic there, though Alan Brown helpfully reviewed all the tip-of-the-tongue research in the *Psychological Bulletin* in 1991, and Bennett Schwartz's *Tip-of-the-Tongue States* (2002) is a lengthy and often entertaining review of tip of the tongue work. Dissertations by Elizabeth Shriberg, Robin Lickley, and Robert Eklund also provided invaluable background.

I had to omit mention of two relevant academic fields. Speech pathology, founded in the 1930s in the United States, is the focus of work on abnormal disfluency, such as stuttering, aphasias, and other language disorders. A classic work on stuttering is Marcel Wingate's 2002 *Foundations of Stuttering;* if this had been a longer work that treated pathological language I would have mentioned the seminal and controversial work of Wendell Johnson. The other field, conversational analysis, began in the 1960s in sociology and is responsible for close analyses of the structure of human conversation. The founding work is in *Lectures on Conversation,* by Harvey Sacks (1992). Some of the observations about the function of pause fillers and repairs in conversation come from this field.

Many thorough, readable books link democracy, eloquence, American social history, and attitudes about language. The classic history of American eloquence, with a focus on individual speakers, is *The History of Public Speaking in America* (1965), by Robert Oliver. Another stylish, detailed history is *The People's Voice* (1979), by Barnet Baskerville. Gavin Jones's *Strange Talk: The Politics of Dialect Literature in Gilded Age America* (1999) is a more linguistically and literarily informed study of language in the nineteenth century; an earlier work along the same lines is *Democratic Eloquence: The Fight Over Popular Speech in Nineteenth-Century America* (1990), by Kenneth Cmiel. Kathleen Hall Jamieson's *Eloquence in an Electronic Age* (1988) is the standard work on the impact of mass media on politics.

So much that Kermit Schafer did stands on its own. His 1979 book, *Blooper Tube*, presents biographical information, and other works are still fun to read or listen to. Erving Goffman's essay "Radio Talk," which contains his discussion of "knows better" and "doesn't know better" errors, draws on Schafer's blooper collections. In turn, my book owes Goffman's essay a significant intellectual debt.

Many other insights and answers came from the following academic experts: M.S. Anwar, Jennifer Arnold, Jeffrey Aronson, Bernard Baars, John Baugh, Ned Block, Heather Bortfeld, Deborah Burke, Ron Butters, Brian Butterworth, Wallace Chafe, Nicholas Christenfeld, Eve Clark, Herbert Clark, Kenneth Cmiel, Nikolinka Collier, Daniel Collins, Carl W. Conrad, Fred Conrad, Madalena Cruz-Ferreira, Susie Curtiss, Anne Cutler, Kathleen Doty, Wolfgang U. Dressler, Judith Duchan, Patrick Ehlen, Robert Eklund, Jerry Fodor, Paul Foulkes, Barbara Fox, Jean E. Fox Tree, Merrill Garrett, Craig Gibson, Phillip Glenn, Peter Green, Marc Hauser, Santosh Helekar, Robert Helmreich, Bernhard Hurch, Nina Hyams, Jeri Jaeger, Sheri Wells Jensen, Andreas Jucker, Carla Hudson Kam, Saul Kassin, John Kasson, Barbara Kryk-Kastovsky, Susan Kemper, Don Kroodsma, Peter Ladefoged, Robert Leonard, Mark Liberman, Heidi Lyn, Don MacKay, George Mahl, Samuel McCormick, Matthias Mehl, Ronald Merrell, Matthew McGlone, Martin Medhurst, Daniel O'Connell, Ynez V. O'Neill, Peter Patrick, James Pennebaker, Bruno Repp, Michael Schober, Carson Schutze, Bennett Schwartz, Jeffrey Searl, Elizabeth Shriberg, Roger Shuy, Felicia Jean Steele, Joseph Stemberger, Anne Graffam Walker, Jeffrey Walker, Walter Weintraub, Michael Weiss, Walter Wilczynski, Kristine Williams, J. Scott Yaruss, Michael D. Young, and Arnold Zwicky.

# Appendix B:
# A Field Guide to Verbal Blunders

**Anticipation:** A type of slip of the tongue in which a consonant, vowel, consonant cluster, syllable, or a part of a word
occur earlier than it should, as in "it's a meal mystery"
instead of "it's a real mystery" (Fromkin).

**Aphasia:** A blanket term for various language problems stem-
ming from disease or brain trauma; usually involves numerous paragrammatisms and forgotten words. In the terms of
this book, aphasia does not count as a source of verbal blundering, which is a behavior of normal speakers.

**Blend:** When two words (or phrases) are chosen from memory
but are fused into one (Levelt). There are two kinds of
blends: one where the two words are semantically related
("stougher" as a product of "stiffer" and "tougher"), the
other where some other idea or distraction in the speaker's
environment intrudes.

**Blooper:** A slip of the tongue, usually made in a performance,
especially in the broadcast media but also onstage. Also
called a "fluff."

**Boner:** A type of "doesn't know better" error that serves as
"evidence of some failing in the intellectual grasp and
achievement within official or otherwise cultivated circles"
(Goffman).

**Classical malapropism:** Unlike the malapropism, the classical malapropism is spoken voluntarily though it is unintentionally wrong. Example: "Are you correlating those papers?" (Zwicky). Arnold Zwicky conjectures that these occur when a speaker tries to select a word from the mental lexicon but gets another one—and doesn't realize that the actual utterance isn't the target utterance. Because the speaker remembers only the actual utterance, it is the one he or she says.

**Disfluency:** An interruption in speech that can include filled pause/pause fillers, repairs, silent pauses, repeated words, prolonged vowels/syllables, and blocks. Are most often not perceived by listeners.

**"Doesn't know better" error:** Deviations in behavior from the norm because the individual doesn't know the norm. Includes boners and gaffes (Goffman).

**Eggcorn:** A type of classical malapropism. Unlike other word-related errors, the eggcorn often expresses the intended meaning in a more colorful way, even though it is not the correct word or phrase. For example, the term "eggcorn" is an eggcorn of "acorn," which makes a certain sort of sense, given that an acorn is a seed, as is an egg, and that the shape of an acorn resembles that of a kernel of corn.

**Filled pause:** a sound or word that fills a pause that would otherwise be silent. (In this book, I have substituted "pause filler" for this term.) Most common filled pauses are "uh" and "um," and they exist as such in a number of the world's languages (though each language has a unique configuration of vowels that makes the most neutral vowel—that is, the one that is easiest to pronounce—slightly different). Filled pauses tend to occur next to each other; they serve to start conversational turns; they can focus the listener's attention on an important subsequent item in the sentence; and they occur more frequently before lexical words than function words. Because they operate below the level of consciousness, they are unobtrusive and may facilitate interaction between speakers and listeners—and do not, as is most commonly thought, impede communication.

**Freudian slip:** According to the *OED*, first used in 1959 to refer to a slip of the tongue, usually with sexual or hostile connotations. In Freud's original usage it was any verbal lapse that represented the self's failure to successfully repress an unconscious intention or desire.

**Gaffe:** A "breach in conduct" that is "unintended or unknowing" (Goffman). Example: for some people, wearing white shoes after Labor Day.

**Heterophemy:** "Action of the brain which takes place without the volition of the individual" that leads to an error that "consists of thinking one thing and speaking or writing another. . . . The speaker or writer has perfect knowledge, thinks clearly, remembers exactly, and yet utters precisely what he does not mean" (Richard Grant White). The word, coined by White (*hetero* = other; *phemy* = speaking), never caught on but was an early attempt to characterize what is also known as a slip of the tongue/pen, lapse, Freudian slip, or parapraxis.

**"Knows better" error:** A momentary loss of control in a performance that an individual otherwise knows; these include both slips and disfluencies (Goffman).

**Malaphor:** two idiomatic expressions blended together, as in "that was a breath of relief." Coined by Lawrence Harrison in 1976. Also called an "idiom blend" or a "syntactic blend." Other examples (from Hofstadter and Moser): "You hit the nail right on the nose," "she really stuck her neck out on a limb," "we'll burn that bridge when we come to them."

**Malapropism:** An inadvertent substitution of one word for another, sometimes because they sound alike, also because they are related in meaning. According to Fay and Cutler, 54 percent of the malapropisms they studied were semantic substitutions, while 46 percent were sound-based ones. Named after the character Mrs. Malaprop in Richard Sheridan's play *The Rivals.*

**Marrowskying:** A mid-nineteenth-century British term for a language game involving deliberate transpositions of sounds, syllables, or words. Also called "hospital Greek" or "medical Greek." May have been named after a Polish midget, Joseph Boruwlaski.

**Metaphasis:** Greek term for the switching of two sounds between two words.

**Mondegreen:** A misheard song lyric or line of poetry. Coined in 1954 by Sylvia Wright to describe her childhood mishearing of the line of poetry "and laid him on the green" as "and Lady Mondegreen."

**Parapraxis:** The usual English translation of the German word *Fehlleistung,* literally "faulty performance," that Freud used; introduced to English by early Freud translator James Strachey; see also "Freudian slip." Parapraxes/*Fehlleistungen* also include forgotten names, forgetting childhood memories, and slips of the pen along with slips of the tongue.

**Perseveration:** A type of slip of the tongue in which a consonant, vowel, consonant cluster, syllable, or a part of a word persists after it has occurred. Example: "black bloxes" (example from Fromkin).

**Paragrammatism:** "Grammatically incorrect sentences" (Butterworth and Howard); "confused and erroneous syntax and morphology instead of an absence of grammatical structure, omission of grammatical particles and 'telegraphic' style in speech" (Butterworth and Howard).

**Repair:** The interruption in speech that a speaker initiates in order to correct a perceived error, modify the message's informational content, or be socially appropriate (Levelt). Example: "Tell me, uh what—d'you need hot sauce?" (Emanuel Schegloff).

**Repetition:** A repeated sound, syllable, word, or phrase, often (but not always) associated with a repair. A high frequency of word-initial repetitions of sounds or clusters of consonants is often a diagnostic sign of chronic stuttering.

**Self-repair:** When speakers backtrack to correct or avoid a speech error, alter an unintended meaning, or alter the presentation of information. Called a "self-repair" because the speaker has no external feedback indicating that something needs to be fixed, such as a listener's question (Postma et al.)

**Slip of the ear:** Inadvertent misperceptions. When "a listener reports hearing, as clearly and distinctly as any correctly perceived stretch of speech, something that does not correspond to the speaker's actual utterance" (Bond). See "Mondegreen."

**Slip of the hand:** A slip made by speakers of sign languages.

**Slip of the tongue (also speech error or speech slip):** "An involuntary deviation in performance from the speaker's current phonological, grammatical, or lexical intention" (Donald Boomer and John Laver). Jaeger codes fifty types of speech errors; Fromkin's appendix contains twenty-seven different kinds of errors, all of which are taken from her collection. Some of her categories are subtypes that she has pulled out for their linguistic interest. I use her labels.

**anticipation of initial consonants:**

"a leading list" for "a reading list"

**perseveration of initial consonants:**

"she can she it" for "she can see it"

**consonant reversals:**

"I have caked a bake"

**final consonants (perseverations, anticipations, and reversals):**

"cuff of coffee" for "cup of coffee"

**consonant deletion, addition, movement:**

"in order for the stell to form" for "in order for the cell to form"

**consonant clusters:**

"coat thrutting" for "throat cutting"

**division of consonant clusters:**

"sprive for perfection" for "strive for perfection"

**affricates (a type of consonant):**

"chee cane" for "key chain"

**velar nasal (a type of consonant):**

"the rand orker of the subjects" instead of "the rank order of the subjects"

**vowels (reversals, additions, deletions, substitutions):**

"annototed bibliography" instead of "annotated bibliography"

**vowel + r:**

"cords sorted" instead of "cards sorted"

**single phonological features:**

"smell bother" instead of "spell mother"

# A Field Guide to Verbal Blunders

**within word errors:**
"plotoprasm" for "protoplasm"
**sh-clusters:**
"short shlady" for "short lady"
**stress:**
"he lives in the big WHITE house" instead of "the BIG white house"
**word reversals:**
"threw the window through the clock"
**haplologies and other telescopic errors:**
"I have a spart for him" instead of "I have a spot in my heart for him"
**derivation affixes:**
"groupment" for "grouping," "oftenly" for "often"
**independence of grammatical morphemes and morphophonemic rules:**
"a hole full of floors" instead of "a floor full of holes"
**a/an:**
"don't take this as an erection on my part" instead of "don't take this as a rejection on my part"
**blends:**
hangling (a blend of "dangling" and "hanging")
**word substitution (*see* malapropism):**
"the native vowels" instead of "the native values"
**pronoun, preposition, article:**
"bring sketches with him when you go" instead of "bring sketches with you when you go"
**multiword errors:**
"I have to smoke my coffee with a cigarette"
**ungrammatical utterances:**
"You're in a more better position"

**negation:**
> "I disregard this as precise" instead of "I regard this as imprecise"

**miscellaneous:**
> "bood and rorm" for "room and board"; "hurt the team on" for "turn the heat on"; "She'll be here on March firth."

**Spoonerism:** Colloquially refers to any exchange of sounds between words to produce new words. Example: "heft lemisphere"; "jawfully loined." Sticklers reserve the term "Spoonerism" specifically for exchanges that result in actual words, as in "with this wing I thee red." The phenomenon was named after Reverend William Archibald Spooner, an Oxford professor; the *OED* dates its first use to 1885. The spoonerism can also involve a reversal of words, as in "Seymour sliced the knife with the salami" (examples from Fromkin).

**Tip-of-the-tongue phenomenon:** The experience of being unable to remember a word, though one is certain one is close to saying it. Technically called a problem with "lexical retrieval"—that is, getting words. Because words are stored in the brain as matrices of meaning and sound, people who are experiencing the tip of the tongue phenomenon are often able to reconstruct parts of the desired word, such as its first sound or related meanings (Schwartz).

**Uh/um:** The most common type of pause filler and the most frequent disfluency in speech; also called an "editing expression." Universal in many of the world's languages (though may be phonetic variants of the same sound) because it represents the most neutral (i.e., takes the least effort to pronounce) vowel.

## Sources:

Bond, Zinny. 1999. *Slips of the Ear: Errors in the Perception of Casual Conversation.* San Diego: Academic Press.

Butterworth, Brian, and David Howard. 1987. "Paragrammatisms." *Cognition* 26: 1–37.

Goffmann, Erving. 1981. "Radio Talk." In *Forms of Talk.* Philadelphia: University of Pennsylvania Press.

Fay, David, and Anne Cutler. 1997. "Malapropisms and the Structure of the Mental Lexicon." *Linguistic Inquiry:* 505–20.

Hofstadter, Douglas, and David Moser. 2002. "To Err Is Human; To Study Error-Making Is Cognitive Science." *Michigan Quarterly Review* 28(2): 185–215.

Fromkin, Victoria, ed. 1973. *Speech Errors as Linguistic Evidence.* Mouton: The Hague.

Kellmer, Göran. 2003. "Hesitation, in Defense of Er and Erm." *English Studies* 2: 170–93.

Levelt, Willem. 1989. *Speaking: From Intention to Articulation.* Boston: MIT Press.

Postma, Albert, Herman Kolk, and Dirk-Jan Povel. 1990. "On the Relation Among Speech Errors, Disfluencies, and Self-Repairs." *Language and Speech* 33(1): 19–29.

Schwartz, Bennett. 2002. *Tip-of-the-Tongue States: Phenomenology, Mechanism, and Lexical Retrieval.* Mahwah, NJ: Lawrence Erlbaum.

Zwicky, Arnold. 1982. "Classical Malapropisms and the Creation of a Mental Lexicon." In *Exceptional Language and Linguistics.* Ed. Loraine K. Obler and Lise Menn. New York: Academic Press.

# Appendix C: Slips Versus Disfluencies

Some people might point out that slips of the tongue and speech disfluencies have separate and distinct causes. Isn't it confusing to put them into the same category as "verbal blunders"? It's true that the two are different: slips result from a mental plan gone awry, while disfluencies represent a delay or interruption in planning itself. However, I grouped them together because they share a number of properties: both present undesired if inevitable instances of failing to "get things in order in time," and they both can damage social performances. Both are subject to the same vicissitudes of human perception, and both have been objects of fascination by different people in different periods. Perhaps most important, both slips and disfluencies appear to be superficial manifestations of disorder which, on closer inspection, both reflect an underlying order and regularity that is worth trying to understand.

I had fewer qualms about putting slips and disfluencies in the same category than giving them the label of "blunders," a word with a distinct negative flavor. But I could not find another term that was light-hearted, easy to understand, and widely applicable. If anything, "blunder" successfully reflects how deviating from the ideals that we wish to follow is still embarrassing and anxiety provoking, even if we know full well why the deviations happen.

My goal has been to tell the natural and social history of verbal blunders as provocatively as possible, which required jettisoning discussions that are interesting but whose inclusion would slow down the narrative. One such discussion is about how our models of spoken communication, as well as much of the way we study spoken language, is based on assumptions that come from written language. This is part of a larger, ongoing academic debate about the relationship between spoken and written language and how societies change when they move from an oral culture to a literate and now digital one. Two particularly good books are *A Story as Sharp as a Knife* (1999), by Robert Bringhurst, and *Spoken and Written Discourse* (1999), by Khosrow Jahandarie.

# Acknowledgments

No one knows who the first verbal blunderer was. But many
people know a surprisingly large amount about verbal blunders,
and I am deeply indebted to those folks for engaging my
curiosity. A huge thanks goes to those who shared how verbal
blunders touch their working lives: David Broder, Barbara
Browning, Lauren Eiler, Isabel Framer, Jerry Giorgio, Lee
Glickstein, Barry Grant, Cate Hagman, Doreen Hamilton,
Anthony Lewis, Carrie Mitchell, Wiebke Rückert, Katharine Q.
Seelye, Alice Tate, Cathy Williams, and David Zulawski. I am
especially beholden to the dozens of academic experts who
replied to my e-mails and phone calls and answered my questions. I am also grateful to world-champion public speakers Ed
Tate, Jim Key, Darren LaCroix, and Randy Harvey; David
Brooks was a superb guide to the culture of Toastmasters. For
insights into the life of Kermit Schafer and blooper humor, I'm
indebted to Bob Booker, Meredith Conover, Peter Funt, Barry
Hansen, Raymond Kives, Al Schwartz, and especially Laurie
Hannan Anton. For talking candidly about growing up with linguists, I thank Anna van Valin and Elizabeth Zwicky. I am also
grateful to the subscribers of the Conlang listserv, the Association for Recorded Sound Discussion List, and the Linguist List.

# Acknowledgments

Thanks also to Gerald Fabris, the curator of the Edison National Historic Site, composer David Hahn, and Robert Eklund, for sending materials that would have been impossible for me to get otherwise. The UCLA Center for Oral History Research graciously permitted me to quote from their interview with Victoria Fromkin, and the Federal News Service allowed me to interview their transcribers, visit their office, and quote from their "duh" files. Donovan Deschner relinquished umthe book.com. Sadly, George Mahl passed away in 2006, but I'd like to thank him for speaking to me about the early days of his research, and for the signed copy of his book. I thank his daughter, Barbara Mahl, for reaching out.

Thanks to all my friends and family who provided critical infusions of encouragement; without you, yes you, this book would not have been written. Heather Bortfeld, Stephanie Bush, Jennifer Chenoweth, Herb Clark, Stephen Krashen, Jean Fox Tree, Robert Jackall, Jeri Jaeger, Leslie Kronz, Deborah Snoonian, and Arnold Zwicky were all kind enough to read and critique versions of the manuscript. For clearing out the blunders that haunted my text, I will always appreciate Roger Gathman's profoundly insightful editorial advice and translation work and Mimi Bardagjy's invaluable fact-checking. The responsibility for any remaining errors belongs to me, not to my repressed unconscious desires.

I'm very grateful for the wise counsel of my agents, Dan Green and Simon Green. Simon deserves credit for the title, *Um . . .* , which he suggested very early on but whose brilliance revealed itself more slowly to me than to everyone else. Every first-time book writer, if he or she is lucky, should have an editor like Alice van Straalen, who was patient and firm in shaping this book into something fun, smart, and cool. I also thank Dan

# Acknowledgments

Frank, Fran Bigman, and all the people at Pantheon who helped make my publishing experience so pleasurable.

All my love and admiration go to my wife, Misty, who has noticed a verbal blunder or two with me (both mine and hers) and who, among her many gifts of love, doesn't mind when I say "um."

# Index

# Index

Bell Laboratories, 53
Bellugi, Ursula, 191
Berle, Milton, 177
Bernstein, Basil, 99–100
Bettelheim, Bruno, 29
*Better Sort, The* (Brown), 206–7
*Blade* (movie), 186
Blaine, James G., 126*n*
blends, Wells's rules for, 50–51
*Blockheads, The* (Warren), 206–7
bloopers, 51, 167–80
   dialect humor and, 173–74
   sexual innuendo and, 168, 171,
      173, 178
Bock, Kay, 20*n*
Bombaugh, C. C., 17
boners, 72
*Book of Blunders, The* (Bombaugh), 17
Bortfeld, Heather, 91–93, 133
Boruwlaski, Joseph, 24–25
brain, 61–63, 92–93, 116, 139, 181,
      182*n*, 192, 197, 200, 204
Bremen, Ellen Beth Levine, 145–46,
      158
Breuer, Joseph, 29
Broder, David, 238–39
Brooks, David, 147–48, 158–64
Brown, James Cooke, 56
Bryant, Michael, 146
Burke, Deborah, 58
Burwell, Rebecca, 233
Bush, Barbara, 229
Bush, George H. W., 4, 224, 227
Bush, George W., 223–32, 234,
      239–42
   "counterism" used by, 4–5, 7
   dyslexia attributed to, 227, 229–30
   in election of 2000, 11–12, 224–25,
      229, 230, 231, 239
   Meringer vs. Freud in interpretation
      of slip of, 49–50

vérité quoting and, 236, 239
Bush, Neil, 229
Bushisms, 224–32
business, 53, 150, 152, 153, 155
Butterworth, Brian, 59–60, 95

*Candid Camera* (TV show),
     169, 179
*Candid Microphone* (radio show), 169,
     170, 179
Cantonese, 56, 58*n*
Carnegie, Dale, 152, 153, 155, 159
Carroll, Lewis, 204
Carson, Johnny, 171, 177
Carter, Jimmy, 59, 188
chambers of commerce, 154–55
Chandler, Daniel Ross, 234
Chapple, Eliot, 95–96
chappleograph, 96
Charles, Prince, 211
children:
   deaf, 56
   language learning of, 181, 216–17
   natural eloquence of, 159
   pause fillers used by, 93, 99–100
   verbal blunders of, 57, 58, 79,
      213–22
Chinese, 56, 58*n*, 241, 247–48
Chomsky, Noam, 181–84, 186, 188
Christenfeld, Nicholas, 141, 142,
     244–45
Churchill, Winston, 85
Ciceri, Rita, 71
Cicero, 59, 114–15, 150
Civil War, U.S., 151–52, 235*n*
Clark, Dick, 167–68, 179, 180
Clark, Herb, 136–40, 148, 248
Clark, John, 193
Clifton, Noel, 57
Clinton, Bill, 241
Cmiel, Kenneth, 207

# Index

# Index

# Index

# Index

# Index

# Index

# Index

# Index

# Index

# Index

# Index

word stress, 19
World Championship of Public
    Speaking, 147–48, 159–66
World War I, 152*n*
World War II, 81, 94
*Wörter und Sachen,* 46, 47
Wright, Sylvia, 194
Wynn, Ed, 129

Yairi, Ehud, 57
YMCA, 152–54

Ziglar, Zig, 161
Zulawski, David, 69–71
Zwicky, Arnold, 202–4, 209–11, 213,
    222, 232
Zwicky, Elizabeth, 252